Data Visualization for People of All Ages

Data visualization is the art and science of making information visible. On paper and in our imaginations, it's a language of shapes and colors that holds our best ideas and most important questions. As we find ourselves swimming in data of all kinds, visualization can help us to understand, express, and explore the richness of the world around us. No matter your age or background, this book opens the door to new ways of thinking and sharing through the power of data visualization.

Data Visualization for People of All Ages is a field guide to visual literacy, born from the author's personal experience working with world-class scholars, engineers, and scientists. By walking through the different ways of showing data—including color, angle, position, and length—you'll learn how charts and graphs truly work so that no visualization is ever a mystery or out of reach. It doesn't stop at what fits on a page, either. You'll journey into cutting-edge topics like data sonification and data physicalization, using sound and touch to share data across the different senses. Packed with practical examples and exercises to help you connect the dots, this book will teach you how to create and understand data visualizations on your own—all without writing a single line of code or getting tangled up in software.

Written with accessibility in mind, this book invites everyone to the table to share the joy of one of today's most necessary skills. Perfect for home or classroom use, this friendly companion gives people of all ages everything they need to start visualizing with confidence.

AK Peters Visualization Series

Visualization plays an ever-more prominent role in the world, as we communicate about and analyze data. This series aims to capture what visualization is today in all its variety and diversity, giving voice to researchers, practitioners, designers, and enthusiasts. It encompasses books from all subfields of visualization, including visual analytics, information visualization, scientific visualization, data journalism, infographics, and their connection to adjacent areas such as text analysis, digital humanities, data art, or augmented and virtual reality.

Series Editors:
Tamara Munzner, *University of British Columbia, Vancouver, Canada*
Alberto Cairo, *University of Miami, USA*

Recent titles:

Data Visualization in Excel
Jonathan Schwabish

Building Science Graphics
Jen Christiansen

Joyful Infographics
Nigel Holmes

For more information about this series, please visit: https://www.routledge.com/AK-Peters-Visualization-Series/book-series/CRCVIS

Data Visualization for People of All Ages

Nancy Organ

CRC Press
Taylor & Francis Group
Boca Raton London New York

CRC Press is an imprint of the
Taylor & Francis Group, an **informa** business

AN A K PETERS BOOK

Designed cover image: Miguel Porlan

First edition published 2024
by CRC Press
2385 NW Executive Center Drive, Suite 320, Boca Raton, FL 33431

and by CRC Press
4 Park Square, Milton Park, Abingdon, Oxon, OX14 4RN

CRC Press is an imprint of Taylor & Francis Group, LLC

© 2024 Nancy Organ

ISBN: 978-1-032-31360-3 (hbk)
ISBN: 978-1-032-30100-6 (pbk)
ISBN: 978-1-003-30937-6 (ebk)
ISBN: 978-1-032-72101-9 (eBook+)

DOI: 10.1201/9781003309376

Typeset in Avenir
by codeMantra

Access the Instructor and Student Resources: https://www.routledge.com/9781032301006

Contents

Series editor foreword   vii

About the author   ix

Welcome!   1

1   **What is data?**   9

2   **What is data visualization?**   19

3   **Length and height**   29

4   **Size and area**   53

5   **Position**   67

6   **Color for categorical data**   85

7   **Color for numerical data**   99

8   **Color for ordinal data**   113

9   **Shapes and patterns**   133

10 **Making colorblind-friendly visualizations**   147

11 **Angle**   165

12 **Connections and networks**   181

Contents

13 Visualization whoopsies   199

14 Sound and touch   223

15 Wrapping up   241

Appendix 1 – Glossary of words   259
Appendix 2 – Glossary of graphs   265
Appendix 3 – Solutions guide   283
Bibliography   311
Acknowledgments   315
Index   317

Series editor foreword

In this highly approachable book, Nancy Organ blazes an easy-to-follow trail through a forest of complexity that can launch any learner, whether young or older, into the world of visualization. She has wrestled with a huge tangle of technical material and emerged victorious! Her deft choices for which principles of visualization to explain, in what order, guide readers all the way from the basics to a sophisticated understanding of the many ways to visually present data.

Deeply inclusive, this book features many concrete examples focused on 20 students, a diverse cast of characters who we meet early on through delightful sketches and biographies. Their lives and times are also at the heart of the exercises at the end of each chapter, in sections called 'It's Your Turn!', which provide a chance to practice creating and fine-tuning visualizations.

This book is the first of its kind, bringing the ideas of visualization to a much broader audience than ever before. It doesn't stop with the visual realm: it even covers data sonification and data physicalization, harnessing the power of hearing and touching to show the properties of data. Dive in, have fun, and expand your horizons!

Alberto Cairo and Tamara Munzner

About the author

Nancy Organ is a Seattle-based data visualization professional with experience in research, education, and tech, including contributions at Microsoft and the University of Washington. She holds a degree in Statistics from the University of California, Berkeley. Endeavoring to make visualization accessible, fun, and empowering for young people and adults alike, she packs nearly a decade of visualization design experience into one light-hearted book.

Welcome!

A note to kids and young people

Let me tell you a secret: The things that I explain in this book are the same things that I teach to adults, and most adults don't ever learn them anyway. You're about to uncover new ways to understand and think about the world around you, and how to share what you learn with others.

If you can count, add, subtract, and know even a little bit about fractions, then you're ready for what we're about to do. All you need to begin are some pencils and paper. Some of what you learn might be completely new to you, and it might take some practice before you feel like a pro—and that's okay! Make mistakes, make a mess, change your mind, and start over. These are skills for the rest of your life, so you have *plenty* of time to work on them.

DOI: 10.1201/9781003309376-1

I'm so excited to share this book with you, whether you are 8, 18, or 78. I can't wait to see what you make!

A note to grown-ups

One of my clearest childhood memories is from the first grade. My beloved teacher, Mr. Buffet, crouched beside my desk near the back of the classroom. We were drawing shapes with rulers that day, and he had challenged me to draw a triangle where each side was the same length. I remember staring at my paper, pencil poised but unsure how to maneuver. I'd never thought about shapes this way!

I've taken a few classes since then, and worked a few jobs, too. I work at a healthcare startup now, but the common thread of my career is stronger than ever: Use visualization to help people share what is important to them. Someone might care about business, medicine, space travel, or fashion—as long as they have data, we can tell the world about it with data visualization. It's a special feeling to help someone see their own story more vividly.

Visualization isn't rocket science, but like any means of abstracted communication it can take some explaining. There are techniques and theories to learn, and the occasional pitfall to avoid. For some, there can be a good deal of *unlearning*, too, to debunk popularized edicts of visualization that constrain more than help. With a bit of practice though, feeling confident with visual expression is absolutely within reach.

The purpose of this book is thus twofold. Firstly, it's a primer in visual literacy—the ability to read and interpret information from images. Data visualization is sometimes relegated to an afterthought in math and science classes, considered a skill set that can be obliquely absorbed with exposure alone. That's insufficient. Understanding how to encode and read data from visual elements like shapes and colors is a *gigantic* asset for working with data. Fluency with visualization informs how we collect data, what we see in it, what we do with it, and how we share it. We really can't skip this part.

Secondly, this book is an ode to self-expression. Childhood and adolescence are whimsical times of discovery and ideas, but they're also fraught with an exasperating inability to fully communicate. If even the most articulate adults struggle to get a point across, imagine being 11! Data visualization, then, comes in handy as another means to express the thoughts that don't fit as well in prose. When words fail us, we still have pictures.

Though typically taught in a technical setting, data visualization doesn't need to be reserved for work or school, either; it's a full language for creatively expressing quantified thought on any subject. Categories, connections, comparisons, and quantities are all part of how we experience the world both in and out of the classroom.

I wish that I could crouch beside every student's desk to coax their most curious and imaginative thoughts onto paper. Short of that, however, I offer this book as a modest substitute. Designed to offer possibility in place of prescription, this text aims to give people of all ages the tools to express what's on their mind. Let's see what you have to say.

How to read this book

This book is divided into chapters based on the different ways that we can show data. Each chapter explains how we can use things like color, shape, or length, and gives examples of visualizations that use them. While each chapter should make sense on its own, it's best to start from the beginning instead of skipping around if you're new to visualization. You can find that chapter that you're looking for by looking at the icons in the top right corner of the page. Sound files for Chapter 14 and other materials can be found on the book's webpage, www.routledge.com/9781032301006. If you're reading the eBook+ version, you'll be able to listen to the audio examples directly from the text.

New words are introduced in **bold**. You can find the definitions of these words in the ***Glossary of Words***. The names of new visualizations are also in **bold**. You can find definitions and very simple examples of these visualizations in the ***Glossary of Graphs.***

Each chapter has practice questions in a section called ***It's Your Turn***! Solutions are in the ***Solutions Guide*** section at the end of the book. Most questions have more than one right answer, so your answer might be different from a friend's answer or the given solution. Try a few things before deciding on your final answer—that's the fun part!

Meet the class

Most of the examples in this book are about students from an imaginary classroom. Say hello!

Serena is a serious gymnast and spends a lot of weekends at competitions—but she loves ever second of it. Her favorite candy is a peanut butter cup, but she'll settle for something sour and fruity if necessary. She's currently growing her hair out so that she can donate it to a wig-maker.

Lorenzo is the youngest of three siblings. His mom teaches astronomy at the community college and his dad is a firefighter. He loves playing soccer and hanging out with his teammates, watching videos about collectible Lamborghinis, and pulling pranks on his older sisters.

Juanita has a lot of energy and likes to use it to practice her own choreography. Her dad is a master electrician and installed studio lighting in the room that she shares with her younger sister. When she grows up, she plans to be a talk show host.

Wei is tall like her aunts but a bit clumsy. She tripped going up the stairs a few days ago and is on crutches until her ankle heals. Fortunately, her apartment building has an elevator and she can still hang out at the basketball court to watch games.

There are lots of artists in Kwesi's family, and Kwesi is one of them! He likes to help his mom sell her paintings at art shows and craft festivals, and has his own small collection of paintings that inspire him. His favorite subject to paint is his cat Richard because he winds up in the strangest poses.

Alex loves movies—especially if they're animated—and would love to be a professional animator someday. When they're not watching a new movie or drawing, Alex loves going to the skate park with their brother and playing golf with Dad.

Quiana has always dreamed of being an engineer and is off to a great start! Her dad has been teaching her how to build computers, and she's almost done with the one that she designed. When she's not working on that, she likes baking and cake decorating.

Aarushi has been getting into pottery and is working on her first full set of dishes—if only she could get the teacups right. Some of her family from India is coming to visit soon, and she couldn't be more excited. Her cousin Shivani is the same age, and they have a lot to catch up on!

Sophia would play every sport if she could, but likes track and field the most. She placed second in the mile at the regional meet and wore the medal for a whole week as an "accessory". Still having braces isn't great, but her dentist makes them fun colors to get her through the final months

Charlie lives with his parents, grandparents, and twin sister. They all love to cook and often have family friends over to visit. On Saturdays Charlie and his sister get up early to help their grandparents in the garden before it gets hot out. He loves pizza, baseball, and taking apart old appliances.

Marina went to coding camp last summer and has been obsessed ever since. Her older cousin is studying Computer Science in college and sometimes comes over to help her write programs. She's into high fashion, too, and is saving up for a designer bag.

Ahmad's dad is a mechanic and has been teaching him how to work on cars. They've been spending a lot of time in the garage lately because one of their customers brought in a bright red Ferrari. Ahmad loves it so much that he's already started saving up for his own.

Rosie and her mom live with their British Shorthair cats in a little house with a creek in the back yard. They have a chicken coop, too, and it's hard to keep the cats away from it! Rosie is quick to make friends and always has something nice to say about everyone.

Jean-Luc plays tennis on Sundays with his parents in the summer. In the winter, however, he plays on the community youth hockey team. When he's not playing a sport, he's probably playing board games with his friends.

Rita loves animals more than anything, and spends two afternoons each week volunteering at the animal shelter. Her favorite job is feeding the kittens, even if it means getting the occasional scratch. She has her mind set on veterinary school and wants to get a parrot when she has her own house.

Ousmane loves superheroes and action-adventure, both in film and old-school comic books. He also loves nature, and joined a new scout troop last year. He got his fire-building badge on a camping trip this fall!

Veronica has a Golden Retriever named Sunflower that she got for her 7th birthday, and they're completely inseparable. She likes reading historical fiction, babysitting her cousin Angela who lives next door, and hanging out at her best friend Gabrielle's house.

Julio loves everything about airplanes—the big ones, the small ones, the old ones—he knows them all and is thinking of going to flight school like his cousin. He also likes playing basketball at the neighborhood court with one of his best friends, Wei. They live in the same apartment building and often meet there after school.

Martin moved from abroad during the fifth grade, and it was tough making friends and learning how school worked in his new home town. He's totally settled in now, though, and his family is planning to take him and a few friends camping for his birthday.

Gabrielle uses sign language at home because her mom and sister are both deaf. She spends most of her afternoons at the community center where she takes ballet lessons, and is excited about being in this year's Nutcracker performance.

1   What is data?

Before we can learn about **data visualization**, we must first understand what the words **data** and **visualization** mean by themselves. *Data* is a word that you might have heard in science class or on the news. It often comes up in movies, especially in mysteries and science fiction films. You might've even heard the word *data* from someone talking about their cell phone plan, or the files and pictures they have stored on their computer. What could possibly be so many things at once?

Data vocabulary. 10
Collecting data into a table 11
Data types 12
Chapter summary 15
It's your turn!. 16

DOI: 10.1201/9781003309376-2

Data vocabulary

Basically, **data** are pieces of information that we collect by observing, measuring, and recording the world around us. Data can be about anything: nature, the human body, weather, music, sports, money, voting, and even the words that people say. Data can also be in many formats like numbers, letters and words, images, or sounds. Data can be stored on paper, on hard drives, or on the clay tablets and knotted strings of ancient civilizations. If knowledge is stored, then it's data!

Many people don't know this, but the word *data* is actually a plural word, which means that it refers to more than one piece of information. For example, you'd say, "the data *are* written in my notebook" instead of "the data *is* written in my notebook." Some people find this confusing, though, and prefer to use data as a singular word like the words herd, family, or flock. In this book we'll say "data *are*", but you can use whichever feels more comfortable.

A bunch of data collected about the same subject—like counts, temperatures, weights, or prices—is called a **variable**. Several variables that are grouped together is called a **data set**. A single measurement in a variable is called a **value**. Taking one value from each variable makes a **data point** (Image 1.1).

Image 1.1
A data point is made up of all the values about one thing—one from each variable. Many data points make up a data set..

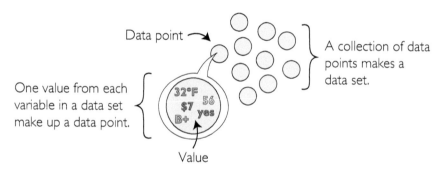

Data point

One value from each variable in a data set make up a data point.

32°F   56
$7   yes
B+

A collection of data points makes a data set.

Value

If you collect data about the number of pets each of your neighbors has, that makes a data set with two variables. The number of pets is one variable, and the name of each human neighbor is another. Each single name or number is a value. A name and number together are a data point (Image 1.2).

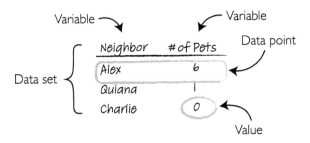

Image 1.2
*The Neighbor
and # of Pets
columns are
variables. Each
row is a data
point, and each
name or number
is a single value.*

When you talk about data, you might say things like "I noticed one data point that looked interesting" or "There are some missing values in this variable that we'll need to estimate." Let's do a few more examples to understand this better.

Collecting data into a table

Imagine that you look at the thermometer outside the kitchen window each morning when you are getting ready for school or work. Knowing the temperature outside helps you pick the right outfit for the day. One week, you decide to write the temperature down in a notebook each day to keep a record of the temperatures throughout the week. By Friday you have a data set like the one shown in Table 1.1.

Daily Temperatures This Week

Day	Temperature
Monday	74°F
Tuesday	73°F
Wednesday	73°F
Thursday	74°F
Friday	76°F

Data point

Value

The Day variable   The Temperature variable

Table 1.1
*The daily
temperatures
for each day in
a week, Monday
through Friday.
Each row is a
data point, and
each number or
day is a value in
the data set.*

This data set has two variables: Day and Temperature. Usually, variables in data sets are shown as columns from top to bottom. Each row—from left to right—is one data point because it shows all the information that happened on that day. Each number or day of the week is a single value. When data are arranged this way, it's called a **table**. Tables are a common way of keeping data organized.

You might also decide to measure the heights of each person sitting at your lunch table. While you're at it, you write down their hair color and ask them to give their lunch a star rating, too (Table 1.2).

Table 1.2
Data about people at the same lunch table, including name, height, hair color, and how much they liked their lunch

Data Collected at the Lunch Table			
Name	Height (inches)	Hair Color	Lunch Rating
Sophia	59	Blonde	3
Alex	65	Black	2
Veronica	63	Brown	4
Kwesi	61	Black	5
Serena	66	Red	5

This data set has four variables: Name, Height, Hair Color, and Lunch Rating. Since there are four variables, the data point about Sophia has four values. We can see that her name is Sophia, she is 59 inches tall, has blonde hair, and had an okay lunch that she gave three stars. Since the data are organized into a table, all of the information about her is in one row.

Data types

All three of these data sets show a mix of variables about different things like the number of pets, days of the week, temperatures, heights, names, colors, and star ratings. They also show examples of the four different data types. Knowing what a variable is about *and* its data type will give us clues on how to visualize it.

Numerical data, also called **quantitative**, or **ratio data**, count or measure the quantity of something using numbers. The weight of an elephant and your friends' heights are examples of numerical data because they measure the number of pounds or the number of inches. Percentages and prices are numerical data, too, because they measure the number of percentage points or money. With numerical data, a value of zero means that there's absolutely none of whatever you're measuring (Table 1.3).

Examples of Numerical Data	
Variable	Values
Numbers	0, 1, 2, 3, 4, 5
Dollars	$100.12, $3.99
Percentages	0%, 30%, 25%, 100%
Weight	6 lbs., 9 oz., 14 tons
Lengths	10 miles, 4 inches, 3 cm
Amounts of time	55 minutes, 24 hours, 3 seconds

Table 1.3
Numerical data count or measure the quantity of something using numbers.

Categorical data, also called **nominal data**, can be divided into different groups. Your friends' names are an example of categorical data because each person is separate from the next and their names don't measure amounts of anything. Types of animals are also categorical, because you could divide a room full of creatures into groups according to their type. ZIP codes and phone numbers are categorical data, too, even though they *look* like numbers. ZIP codes and phone numbers don't measure the amount of anything, but they do tell you who is who. Categorical data don't fall in any particular order, and one category isn't more or less than the others. The name Ahmad isn't *more* than the name Lorenzo (Table 1.4).

Examples of Categorical Data	
Variable	Values
Animals	Birds, Leopards, Sharks, Frogs
People	Ahmad, Rosie, Julio, Lorenzo
Countries	United States, Honduras, Japan

Table 1.4
Categorical data can be divided into different groups.

Ordinal data are like categorical data that *do* have an order to them but *don't* measure amounts. For example, A comes before B in the alphabet, but it doesn't make sense to say that the letter A is half of the letter B. Other examples of ordinal data are ratings and medals—bad is definitely worse than excellent, but we don't know *how much* worse. A gold medal is better than a silver medal, but not always by the same amount (Table 1.5).

Examples of Ordinal Data	
Variable	**Values**
Letters	A, B, C, D, F
Ratings	Bad, fair, good, great, excellent
Medals	Gold, silver, bronze
Stoplights	Stop, slow down, go

Lastly, **interval** data are a bit like ordinal data and numerical data put together. Interval values fall in a particular order like ordinal data, but they're also evenly spaced like numerical data. Monday is exactly as far away from Tuesday as Wednesday is from Thursday. However, interval data don't have a definite zero or starting point like numerical data do. For example, our calendars start about 2,000 years ago, but year 0 wasn't when time itself began. It might be 0°C outside, but that doesn't mean that there is absolutely no warmth—just not enough to make ice melt (Table 1.6).

Examples of Interval Data	
Variable	**Values**
Dates	June 5th, 11/24/95, 2025
Times	11:34 am, 16:19:30, 6 o'clock
Days of the week	Monday, Tuesday, Wednesday
Temperatures	76°F, 34°C, −14°F

Because interval data are similar to both numerical data and ordinal data, variables of interval data are mostly treated like one or the other in data visualization—it just depends on what the data are about and what the visualization is showing. For this reason, we'll stick to numerical, categorical, and ordinal data in this book to keep things simple. Still, it's good to know that interval data are special in their own way so that you can think about them accurately and make visualizations that show them in a way that makes sense.

For such a small word, then, *data* is no small thing! From huge data sets on a computer to tiny tables written in a notebook, data can be about anything. Values that are related to each other can be collected as variables, and each variable will have its own data type. Now that you know a little more about data, take a look around: where you do see data, and what does it tell you?

Chapter summary

Data are pieces of information that we collect through observation and measurement. A data set is made up of several variables, each about a specific topic and having its own data type. Often, a data set is written down in a table where each column of the table is a different variable, and each row contains values that make up a data point. There are four types of data: numerical data, categorical data, ordinal data, and interval data.

It's your turn!

Look around your environment, and get ready to collect some data of your own. Fill in the following variables with values for each data type.

Ex. Categorical data

    a. Variable: Names
    b. Value #1: Ahmad
    c. Value #2: Aarushi
    d. Value #3: Marina

1. What is an example of numerical data? Can you give three examples?

    a. Variable: _____
    b. Value #1: _____
    c. Value #2: _____
    d. Value #3: _____

2. What is an example of categorical data? Can you give three examples?

    a. Variable: _____
    b. Value #1: _____
    c. Value #2: _____
    d. Value #3: _____

3. What is an example of ordinal data? Can you give three examples?

    a. Variable: _____
    b. Value #1: _____
    c. Value #2: _____
    d. Value #3: _____

4. Pretend that you are putting together a shopping list that will include several items and their prices.

   a. Write the items and their prices into this table to create a small data set with three variables.

   b. Then, include data about a third variable of your choice!

My Shopping List		
Item	**Price**	_____

2   What is data visualization?

The word **visualize** means to imagine something in your mind or to draw a picture of it. You might be able to *visualize* in your mind's eye what your home or your best friend looks like, or draw a picture of them from memory. To give someone directions from your classroom to the auditorium, you might *visualize* the steps in your head and then draw a map for them on a piece of paper.

It makes sense then that **data visualization** is the process of showing data in ways that we can see. You can use shapes, colors, or pictures to *visualize* data—both in your mind and on a page—instead of simply reading values as numbers and words in a table.

In this book, we'll sometimes just say *visualization* instead of *data visualization*. The shorter versions *data vis* or *data viz* mean the same thing. Depending on the type of data visualization that you might come across, it might be called a *plot, chart, diagram, graph, graphic, infographic,* or *visual.* Each of these types refers to slightly different specialties, but they're data visualizations all the same.

DOI: 10.1201/9781003309376-3

Data visualization in your world *20*
Why is data visualization important? *22*
Chapter summary *26*
It's your turn! *27*

Data visualization in your world

If you take a look around, you'll notice plenty of data visualizations that are already in your everyday life. The flags at the beach, for example, use different colors and shapes to tell us about the surf conditions and which activities are safe. Purple? Watch out for marine life. Double red? Don't even think about swimming! Solid yellow? Keep an eye out for strong currents. These are visualizations of categorical data (Image 2.1).

Image 2.1
The flags at the beach show the categorical data of safety status.

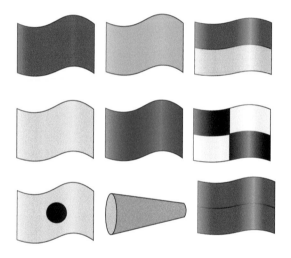

The signs on restrooms are also visualizations of categorical data. Instead of colors, restroom signs often use shapes to say who a bathroom is designed for. Depending on the shape, you'll have a good idea what to expect inside and if it has large stalls or an accessible layout (Image 2.2).

Image 2.2
Bathroom signs use simple shapes to tell us the types of facilities to expect.

Gold, silver, and bronze medals are another visualization that uses color—or type of medal, really—to show the ordinal data of the first, second, and third places. Gold is *always* first, and bronze is *always* after silver, but the competition can be down to the wire or miles apart (Image 2.3).

Image 2.3
Medals show the ordinal data of competition placing.

Finally, you may have a data visualization on your own finger! Mood rings use color to visualize emotions based on the temperature of your hand. Since mood rings show temperature without any numbers like 98.6°F or 37°C, we can think of them as visualizations of numerical data (Image 2.4).

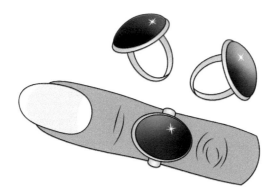

Image 2.4
Mood rings use color to visualize the temperature of your hand.

Data visualizations are everywhere you look, which is why it is so important to understand how they work and how they are made. Some of the visualizations we see day-to-day, like the ones mentioned above, are easy to understand because we see them so frequently. But not all visualizations are so common or so simple!

If you come across a data visualization that you haven't seen before, you'll need to understand how the shapes and colors show the data so that you can figure it out on your own. Or, if you have data that you want to show for yourself, you'll need to know how to make visualizations that other people can understand. This skill of knowing how to read and create visualizations is called **visual literacy**, which is exactly what we'll learn in this book. Data visualization and visual literacy are important for everyone—no matter your age—because they give us the ability to use data to think for ourselves.

Why is data visualization important?

Even if you're practically swimming in data, it can be difficult to see patterns or learn new things from it when it's only written down. To see for yourself, take a look at this data set from Chapter 1 about the people sitting at the same lunch table (Table 2.1). Try to answer the questions without peeking ahead to the next pages.

a. Of the people with black hair, who is the tallest?
b. Who is the tallest overall?
c. How many people had blonde hair?
d. Who liked their lunch the most?

Table 2.1
Data collected during lunch including each person's name, height, hair color, and a star rating of their meal

Data Collected at the Lunch Table			
Person	**Height (inches)**	**Hair Color**	**Star Rating**
Sophia	59	Blonde	3
Alex	65	Black	2
Veronica	63	Brown	4
Kwesi	61	Black	5
Serena	66	Red	5

Flip the page upside-down to see the answers. Did you get them right?

a. Alex is the tallest person with black hair.
b. Serena is the tallest overall.
c. Only one person has blonde hair: Sophia.
d. Kwesi and Serena both gave their lunches five stars.

Hopefully you were able to get some of the correct answers, but it might have taken a few minutes. Even in a small data set like this, it can be hard to find what you're looking for. Imagine how difficult it would have been if there were five *hundred* or five *million* rows of data instead of five!

Now look at the two data visualizations in Image 2.5 and try to answer a few more questions. It's okay if you're not sure—we haven't learned any of this yet! Just see what you can discover from the visualizations without knowing much about how they work.

a. Who is the shortest person overall?
b. Who has black hair and had a great lunch?
c. Who is taller than only two people?
d. Who is the second tallest?

Image 2.5
Two data visualizations showing the data about the lunch-table crew. On the left, each person is shown as a rectangle that is colored in to match their hair color. Taller people have taller rectangles. On the right, the stars show how each person felt about their lunches.

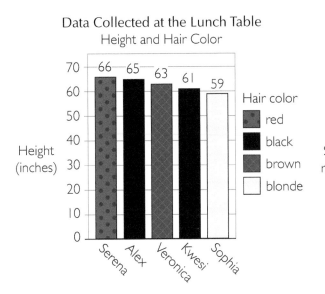

Data Collected at the Lunch Table
Height and Hair Color

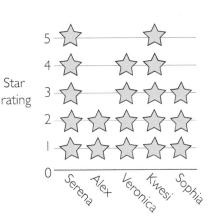

Data Collected at the Lunch Table
Lunch Rating

In the visualization on the left called "Height and Hair Color", each person is shown as a rectangle with their name listed below. The color and pattern of each rectangle tell us the person's hair color. The heights of the rectangles give us each person's height. The rectangles are sorted from the tallest to the shortest.

In the visualization on the right called "Lunch Rating", each person's lunch rating is shown above their name. You can either count the stars above each person, or look at the numbers on the left to see how many stars they gave.

The correct answers to the questions above are below. How did you do? Did you have an easier time looking at the visualizations or at the table?

d. Alex is the second tallest.
c. Veronica is taller than two people.
b. Kwesi has black hair and a five-star lunch.
a. Sophia is the shortest.

These visualizations aren't the only way to visualize these data, either. Perhaps we want to know how many people gave each star rating *and* the hair colors of those people. Looking at the table could take a while, but a data visualization like Image 2.6 would do the trick much more quickly.

Image 2.6
How many people gave two, three, four, or five stars, and what were their hair colors?

Data Collected at the Lunch Table
Lunch Ratings by Hair Color

This visualization shows the hair colors of each person giving each star rating. For example, two people rated their lunch at five stars. We know this because there are two dots above the 5—one for a person with red hair, and one for a person with black hair. Only one person gave their lunch three stars, though, and that person had blonde hair. No one gave their lunch one star, because there aren't any dots above the 1.

You might also be curious to see if lunch ratings, height, and hair color are related in any way. It's hard to say by looking at the table, but visualizing the data like in Image 2.7 could help you do some detective work:

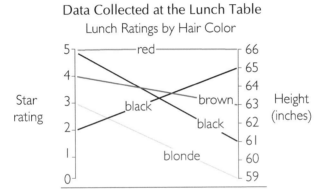

Image 2.7
Each person's data point is connected together by a line that shows their hair color.

This visualization connects the star rating and height for each person with a line that is colored and labeled with their hair color. Do you notice anything here that you didn't notice in the other visualizations? Or, does this visualization make you think that someone's hair color, height, and how much they like lunch are totally unrelated?

Creating data visualizations like these lets us see things in the data that we might not notice otherwise. Visualization can show us surprising differences or similarities, as well as the ways that things are related to each other—or not. Tables are still important for collecting data and keeping it organized, but they aren't as good at helping us to see patterns or make comparisons. For that, data visualizations are the way to go—and the possibilities are endless!

Scientists, bankers, analysts, engineers, and people from all careers and walks of life use data visualization in their work and studies. They use visualization to explain things to their communities, to keep records of their discoveries, and to solve problems. Knowing how to create and understand data visualizations on your own will be useful no matter what interests you or what you do in your own life. Now that we know the basics, let the fun begin!

Chapter summary

Data visualization is the process of showing data with shapes, colors, and things that we can see. Visualizing data allows us to see things that we might not notice otherwise like patterns, similarities, and relationships. Data visualization is a great way to share data we care about with other people, and to learn about data that other people collect. Data visualizations are all around us, and it's important to know how to understand and create them—no matter our age or our interests.

It's your turn!

Look closely at your environment or think about the places that you often go. Take a look in a magazine or a newspaper. Can you find two things that might be data visualizations?

It's okay if you aren't sure yet. We'll spend the rest of this book learning more! Do your best to start thinking about where you see data visualizations in the world around you.

1. What is the first thing you think might be a data visualization?

   a. Draw a picture of it and say where you found it or what it is.
   b. Use arrows on your drawing to point to the variables being shown in the visualization and the data type for each. Remember, the types are numerical, categorical, and ordinal.

2. What is the second thing you think might be a data visualization?

   a. Draw a picture of it and say where you found it or what it is.
   b. Use arrows on your drawing to point to the variables being shown in the visualization and the data type for each.

3   Length and height

Now that we know what *data visualization* means, we can finally start doing exactly that! This chapter is about the different types of data visualization that use **length** or **height** to show how much of something there is. We'll learn what it usually means for a shape to be taller or shorter and the ways that you can use length to make your own data visualizations.

Examples from everyday life. 30
The building blocks of length and height 31
Making a bar chart 33
Bar charts the right way 34
Stacked bar charts 35
Introducing legends. 37
Introducing axes 38
Titles and captions. 42
Using length to show distance, change, and time 44
Chapter summary 47
It's your turn!. 48

DOI: 10.1201/9781003309376-4

Examples from everyday life

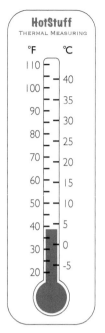

Without even realizing it, you might already be used to understanding that shapes of different lengths and heights can show different amounts. Thermometers, for example, show us temperatures by the length of the red line. The longer the line, the more heat the thermometer measures. The shorter the line, the less heat it measures (Image 3.1).

If you play video games, you might have seen energy or health bars that keep track of how well your character's health is doing. Some of these bars are solid like thermometers, while others are made of little blocks that disappear as your character gets damaged. The longer the bar or row of blocks, the healthier the character is (Image 3.2).

Image 3.1
A thermometer uses the length of the red line to show temperature.

Image 3.2
The health or energy bars in many video games use length to show how strong or healthy your character is.

Finally, phones and computers often show how much charge is left with a battery icon that is partly filled with a longer or shorter rectangle. When you have a decent charge on your device, the rectangle is long and the battery icon looks full. The rectangle is short and the battery icon looks empty when your charge is low (Image 3.3).

Image 3.3
Icons that show the charge on your phone or computer use the length of the bar in the battery to show the amount of charge remaining.

Examples of where length and height are used to show data are all around us. Let's learn how this all works and use length to make a few visualizations of our own.

The building blocks of length and height

Imagine that you've been given a very simple data set like the one shown in Table 3.1. It has two variables: a Pattern variable that lists three different patterns, and a Number variable that counts the number of squares with each pattern.

Counts of Different Pattern Squares	
Pattern	Number
Striped	9
Solid	8
Spotted	5

Table 3.1
Twenty-two
squares of three
different patterns

Now imagine that you've been asked to draw these data so that you can explain them to someone who can't see the table. Which of the next two options in Image 3.4 do you think does a better job?

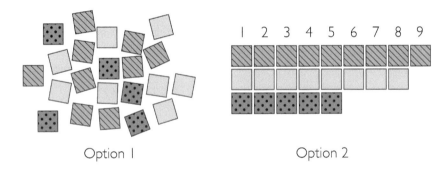

Option 1   Option 2

Image 3.4
Sorting the
squares into
color groups and
putting them in
rows makes it
easier to count
how many
squares of each
color there are.

Option 1 might *technically* show the data, but it doesn't help us to understand very much about what's happening. Without checking off the squares one by one, it's hard to tell how many squares of each pattern there are. Can you say at a glance if there are more striped squares or solid squares? Are you sure?

Option 2, on the other hand, makes it much simpler to understand what's going on in the data. Thanks to the numbers above the tidy rows, we can see that there are nine striped squares. From there, we can see eight solid squares, and five spotted squares. It's no problem to say that there are more striped squares than solid—and this time, we're sure!

Image 3.5
A pictograph
chart of the
patterned
squares data.

Counts of Different Pattern Squares

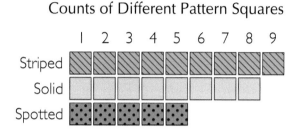

And with that, we've arrived at our very first official data visualization—a **pictograph chart**! Pictograph charts like in Image 3.5 use tidy rows or stacks of symbols or pictures to show amounts. In this example, the pictures are different kinds of patterned squares, but if we were counting cats or planets the pictures could be of something else. Each picture represents the same amount; so longer rows or higher stacks of pictures or symbols mean more things.

In the last chapter we saw a visualization about how a few people rated their lunches. This was a pictograph chart, too, that used stars as symbols instead of squares. We could have shown the stars in little clusters, but stacking them on top of each other makes it much easier to compare the lunch ratings between people (Image 3.6).

Image 3.6
A pictograph
chart of lunch
ratings. More
stars mean
higher ratings,
while fewer stars
mean lower
ratings.

Data Collected at the Lunch Table

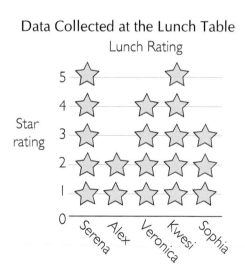

Making a bar chart

It's easy enough to draw five stars or nine squares, but what if your data visualization is about something more complicated to draw, like thousands of cities, or tiny molecules of oxygen in the atmosphere? In these cases, it's more sensible to combine rows or stacks of pictures into rectangles. Instead of looking at the lengths of rows or stacks of pictures, rectangles of different lengths can show amounts, too (Image 3.7).

Visualizations that use different lengths of rectangles to show quantities are called **bar charts**. The rectangles in bar charts are called **bars**, and each bar represents a single category from a categorical variable. In the example about the squares, the Pattern variable has three categories: striped, solid, and spotted.

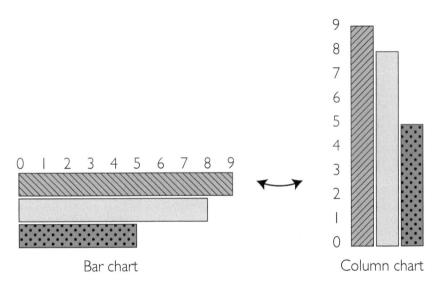

Image 3.7
Bar charts and column charts use rectangles of different lengths to show quantities.

Bar chart   Column chart

When the bars in a bar chart are standing up, these visualizations are sometimes called **column charts**. Column charts and bar charts work in exactly the same way, but you might choose one over the other to fit better on a page or because it suits the data better. That's up to you!

The lunch rating pictograph makes a great column chart as well. In both graphs below, the Person variable has five categories: Serena, Alex, Veronica, Kwesi, and Sophia. The heights of the stacks of stars and the heights of the bars also mean exactly the same thing (Image 3.8).

Image 3.8
Combining the shapes in a pictograph chart into rectangles creates a bar chart or column chart.

Bar charts are one of the most common types of data visualization. Now that you know about them, you'll likely see bar charts and column charts all over the place—in books, magazines, online, and in the news.

Bar charts the right way

There are a few things to keep in mind when you are using lengths to show amounts in a data visualization.

Firstly, it's best for each shape to start at the same place. In Image 3.9, it's easy to compare the lengths of the bars on the left because they all begin at the black line. The bars on the right, on the other hand, start at random places on the page. It's hard to tell exactly how much longer or shorter one bar is compared to the next.

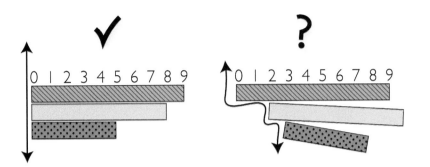

Secondly, each shape should always start at zero. Because the length of the shape is the important part of the visualization, it's confusing to make each shape shorter than the amount it represents. In Image 3.10, the bar chart on the right starts at four instead of zero. It might seem fine at first, but is the dotted category really *that* much smaller than the solid or striped categories? No! There were five dotted squares, not one, so the length of the rectangle should show that.

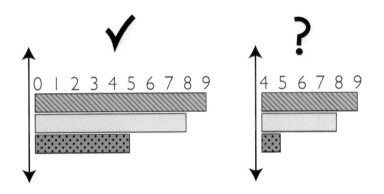

Image 3.10
Starting bar charts at zero means that the lengths of the bars represent the actual amounts. Always start at zero!

Stacked bar charts

Now imagine that three friends go to get ice cream and decide to make a data visualization about the flavors and number of scoops that each person had on their cone. They put together a data set that looks like this:

The data set has three variables: Person, Flavor, and Scoops. Each row in Table 3.2 is a complete data point that tells how many scoops of a certain flavor someone had. For example, the highlighted row shows that Rita had two scoops of pumpkin pie ice cream.

Table 3.2
Ice cream scoops and flavors for three people. Each row is a single data point made up of values for the Person, Flavor, and Scoops variables.

Number of Scoops and Flavors on Three People's Ice Cream Cones		
Person	Flavor	Scoops
Rita	Red velvet	1
Rita	Horchata	1
Rita	Mint chip	1
Rita	Pumpkin pie	2
Quiana	Red velvet	1
Quiana	Horchata	3
Charlie	Horchata	1
Charlie	Mint chip	1
Charlie	Pumpkin pie	1

Data point →

Using the data, the three friends draw stacks of squares to show the number of scoops of every flavor on each person's cone. Depending on the Flavor variable, they color the squares in maroon, cream, speckled green, or orange. The values in the Scoops variable tell them how many squares to draw (Image 3.11).

Image 3.11
Showing stacked squares instead of stacked ice cream scoops is half way to a data visualization!

Number of Scoops and Flavors on Three People's Ice Cream Cones

Rita   Quiana   Charlie   Rita   Quiana   Charlie

Most of the hard work for making this data visualization is already done! By counting the stacked squares, it's easy to see how many scoops of each flavor everyone had, as well as how many scoops they had over all. Connecting the squares of each flavor and adding a few easy-to-use numbers completes the job (Image 3.12).

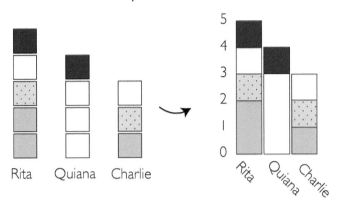

Number of Scoops and Flavors
on Three People's Ice Cream Cones

Image 3.12
Gluing the squares together into rectangles turns the visualization into a stacked bar chart. The numbers let us see how tall each stack is.

Visualizations like this are called **stacked bar charts**, because each bar has several smaller bars *stacked* on top of one another. Unlike our first example that only counted squares of different patterns, or the bar chart that showed the star rating for everyone's lunches, stacked bar charts are perfect for showing quantities of things that are split over two categorical variables. In this case, the two variables are Person and Flavor. The bar chart shows the number of Scoops each Person had as well as the number of scoops in each Flavor on their cone.

We'll learn more about stacked bar charts in Chapter 6 when we learn how to pick colors for categorical data like flavors of ice cream.

Introducing legends

At this point, you might be wondering how someone who hadn't seen the data set would know that green represents the mint chip flavor and maroon represents red velvet. Who's to say that the colors don't stand for beetroot sorbet, cheesecake, matcha, and carrot?

To solve this problem, we need something called a **legend** or **key**. Legends explain what the colors, patterns, and shapes on a visualization actually mean. A legend for the colors in our ice cream example would look like this (Image 3.13).

Number of Scoops and Flavors
on Three People's Ice Cream Cones

With the legend, there's no question about what each color represents. It tells us that the that each color means a different flavor, *and* what each of those flavors is. Notice that the squares in the legend are stacked in the same order as the bars, too. In visualizations with many categories or colors that are similar to each other, sorting the legend and the bars in the same order makes it easier to see what each stack in the stacked bars is showing.

Introducing axes

In the examples above, every square, star, or scoop represented one item. Because there were only a few of each thing it was easy to count them by hand or guess the length of the bars.

What if, however, we needed to show very large numbers like 10,000, or very small numbers like 0.08? In these situations, it wouldn't make sense to draw squares first and then connect them into rectangles… or to write out every number from 0 to 10,000.

The answer to this pickle is to draw an **axis**. An axis, or **axes** if you have more than one, is the part of a data visualization that tells you the exact length or placement of something on a graph.

The axis that goes from bottom-to-top is called the **y-axis**. The axis that goes from left to right is called the **x-axis** (Image 3.14).

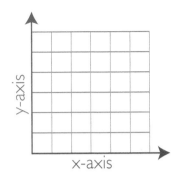

Image 3.14
The x-axis (in purple) of a visualization goes from left to right. The y-axis (in red) goes up and down. Axes can show any of the data types: numerical, categorical, or ordinal data.

On bar charts and column charts, the axes show us the length of the bars on one side, and the categories of bars on the other. Depending on how the graph is drawn, the categories could be on the x-axis or the y-axis (Image 3.15).

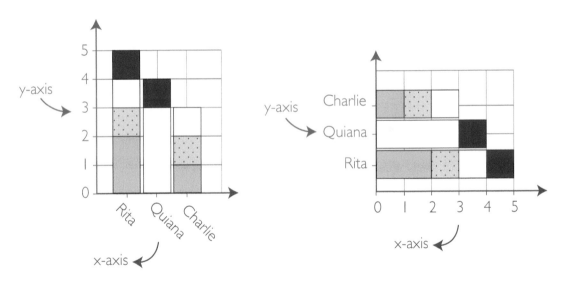

Axis titles tell us the variable that the axis is showing—like the Number of Scoops of ice cream or a Person's name. The **axis labels** tell us the possible values that the variable could have. Since you *could* have as few as 0 scoops and as many as 5 scoops, the axis showing the Number of Scoops is sure to show those options. All the same, the axes could go up to 6 or 7 to leave room for even more ice cream (Image 3.16).

Image 3.15
The same bar chart shows the same data even if it's flipped on its side.

39

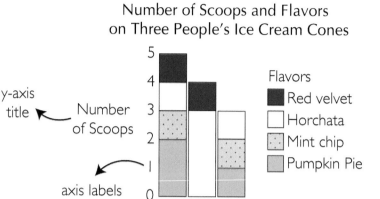

Image 3.16
Axis titles and axis labels tell us the variables that the axes show and the possible values for each variable.

However, it's not required to label every single value on a number axis if there are too many numbers to show. The axis labels could only show the even or odd numbers to make it less crowded, and the empty space between the tick marks would still have meaning. In Image 3.17, Charlie still had one scoop of pumpkin pie ice cream even if the 1 isn't labeled on the y-axis. And, if Alex tagged along and decided to only get a half scoop of red velvet ice cream, their bar would be half as tall as a single scoop. It's okay that the ½ isn't labeled on the axis, because we know that ½ is half way between 0 and 1.

Image 3.17
The space between tick marks on a number axis still has meaning, even if some of the possible values aren't labeled.

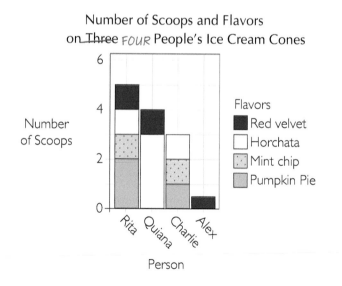

Sometimes, axis labels are at the end of **tick marks**, or little dashes that stick out of the axes to show us exactly where the values fall. These tick marks are often connected to **gridlines**, thin lines that run back-and-forth or up-and-down across the whole graph to make it easier to see where the pieces of the visualization are compared to the axes (Image 3.18).

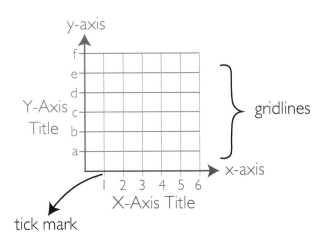

Image 3.18
Axis titles, axis labels, tick marks, and gridlines tell us what each axis is about and how to find the different values in a visualization.

Changing the axis labels or axis titles can change the whole meaning of a visualization. In Image 3.19, the same ice cream graph is shown three times. Each of the graphs has a Number of Scoops y-axis on the left side with different axis labels. Depending on which graph you use, the three people would have had *very* different amounts of ice cream.

Image 3.19
Changing the axes changes the meaning of the visualization.

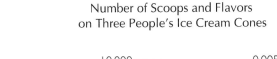

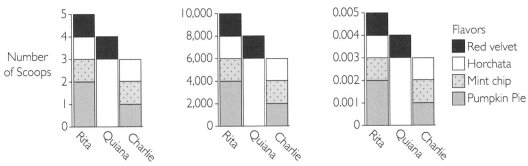

In the first graph, Rita had two scoops of pumpkin pie cream. In the second, she had 4,000 scoops of it. In the third, she barely even smelled it—she only had 0.002 scoops of the pumpkin pie flavor. That's part of the magic of data visualization: the same simple shapes and colors can tell totally different stories with just a few small changes.

Titles and captions

Finally, don't forget to give your visualization a title that says what it is about or the question it should answer. That might be something like "Number of Different Cats Spotted on My Street Since January 2020" or "Top Speeds of Different Aircraft". In our case, "Number of Scoops and Flavors on Three People's Ice Cream Cones" leaves nothing to the imagination: we know *exactly* what the graph is about.

If you think a graph needs a bit more explaining, you can add a **caption**, too. A caption is a few sentences that explain the point of the visualization or why the visualization is important. A caption can also share what the visualization *isn't* able to tell us, like that you couldn't collect as much data as you wanted, or that some of the values are guesses. Captions can also help people understand how to read a new kind of visualization that they haven't seen before (Image 3.20).

If we put *all* the pieces together, our finished ice cream graph looks like Image 3.20.

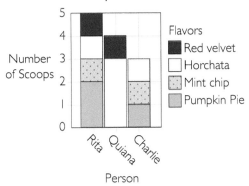

Number of Scoops and Flavors
on Three People's Ice Cream Cones

Flavors
■ Red velvet
□ Horchata
▦ Mint chip
▨ Pumpkin Pie

Person

Image 3.20
The ice cream stacked bar chart with a title, axis titles, axis labels, tick marks, gridlines, a caption, and a legend.

The data for this stacked bar chart were collected on Friday, August 28th at 4:30pm. Rita did get five scoops, but she did not finish all of the pumpkin pie.

It has a title to tell us what it's about. It has bars of different lengths that show amounts of two categorical variables—Person and Flavor. It has an x-axis that shows the categories in the Person variable and a y-axis that shows the values in the Scoops variable. The axes have titles and labels to explain what they mean. It even has a legend to explain what each color represents, and a caption to tell us more information. This visualization gives us everything we need to understand who had what and how much.

A quick note, though: As you come across more and more visualizations, you'll notice that some of them don't always use every single one of these pieces. Gridlines and tick marks, for example, aren't really needed on the x- or y-axis in Image 3.20. Even the axis title that says "Person" might be obvious enough to skip because the main title on the graph is already clear. Captions are nice, but sometimes the graph says what it needs to say by itself. The ice cream visualization, then, could also look like Image 3.21.

The important thing is that someone looking at your visualization can easily understand what each piece means... so when in doubt, spell it out! It's always safer to use good axis titles, axis labels, tick marks, and gridlines.

Image 3.21
*Some
visualizations
might skip a
few pieces—like
gridlines or an
axis title—if
there is enough
information in
the rest of graph
to make it easy
to understand.*

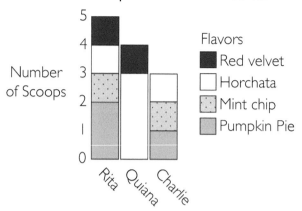

Image 3.21
*Some
visualizations
might skip a
few pieces—like
gridlines or an
axis title—if
there is enough
information in
the rest of graph
to make it easy
to understand.*

Using length to show distance, change, and time

We just saw how length and height can be used to show quantities, but that's not the only thing length and height are good for. Depending on the kind of visualization you create, length, and height can also show distances between places, amounts of change, or even durations of time!

Dumbbell charts, for example, use the distance between two dots to show before-and-after data or comparisons between two things. In the dumbbell chart in Image 3.22, we can see Marina's report card grades from this quarter and last quarter. The red dots show her grades from this quarter, and the blue dots show her grades from the last quarter.

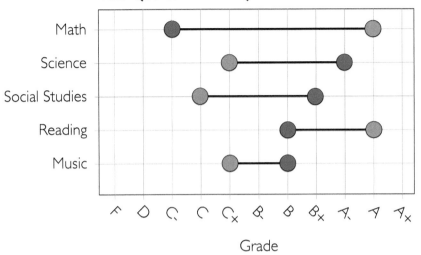

Marina's Report Card Grades
This Quarter vs Last Quarter

Math — Science — Social Studies — Reading — Music

This Quarter
Last Quarter

Grade

According to the visualization, she made a *huge* improvement in Math! Last quarter she brought home a C-, but she managed to get an A this time around. She wasn't so fortunate in Science though—her grade went from an A- to a C+. Better luck next time! The data for this chart would look like Table 3.3, with a Subject variable, a Quarter variable, and a Grade variable:

Marina's Report Card Grades
This Quarter vs Last Quarter

Subject	Quarter	Grade
Math	Last	C−
Science	Last	A−
Social studies	Last	B+
Reading	Last	B
Music	Last	B
Math	This	A
Science	This	C+
Social studies	This	C
Reading	This	A
Music	This	C+

Length can also show durations of time. Take the **Gantt chart** in Image 3.23 that shows how long each activity in Sophia's daily schedule lasts.

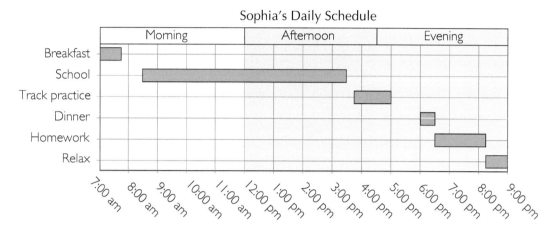

The lengths of the green bars represent the amount of time spent doing each activity. Each bar starts at the beginning of the activity, and runs along the x-axis from left to right until it reaches the time that the activity ends. For example, Sophia spends a little less than an hour at breakfast—starting at 7:00 am and ending a bit before 8:00 am—but a full seven hours at school. You can see the exact values in Table 3.4.

Table 3.4
*The start, stop,
and duration of
Sophia's daily
activities*

Sophia's Daily Schedule			
Activity	Start	End	Duration
Breakfast	7:00 am	7:45 am	0.75 hours
School	8:30 am	3:30 pm	7 hours
Track practice	3:45 pm	5:00 pm	1.25 hours
Dinner	6:00 pm	6:30 pm	0.5 hours
Homework	6:30 pm	8:15 pm	1.75 hours
Relax	8:15 pm	9:00 pm	0.75 hours

The bars in Gantt charts obviously don't begin at the same place, and it's true that that does make it harder to compare the lengths. In this case that's okay, however, because the purpose of the visualization is to also show when something starts and ends and the distance between those two times. If you wanted to compare *amounts* of time for each activity, making a bar chart to go along with the Gantt chart would help.

In the bar chart in Image 3.24, the bars from the Gantt chart are simply scooted over to the y-axis, and the x-axis shows number of hours instead of times. The lengths are the same!

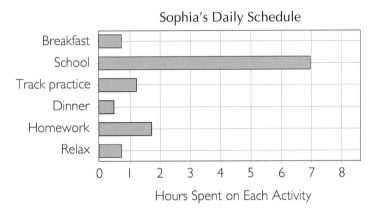

Image 3.24
The bars from the Gantt chart can be lined up against the y-axis to make a bar chart that compares the length of time for each activity.

Having just learned about five data visualizations that all use length or height to show amounts, it won't surprise you that length and height are some of the most important and useful ways to make visualizations. Keep the visualizations in this chapter in your pocket, because we'll see them again and again throughout the book and in the world around you. We've only just begun, though, so in the next chapters we'll learn about more ways that we can show data with things we can see.

Chapter summary

Pictograph charts use rows of pictures or symbols to show amounts. Bar charts and column charts are common types of data visualization that use rectangles of different lengths or heights to show amounts. Stacked bar charts are made up of several smaller bars stacked on top of one another; this type of visualization shows how many things there are in several different groups. Dumbbell charts and Gantt charts use length to show amounts of time or change.

The axes on a data visualization allow us to measure the length or height of something on a visualization so that we can show amounts that are very large or very small.

It's your turn!

1. Count up each shape below and create a stacked bar chart that represents the number of each shape and their colors.

   a. Fill in the data table to help you keep count.

Number and Color of Shapes		
Color	Shape	Count
White	△	
White	✕	
White	○	
Blue	△	
Blue	✕	
Blue	○	

Black	Δ	
Black	✕	
Black	○	

b. Fill in the empty graph with a stacked bar chart that shows the data from part a.

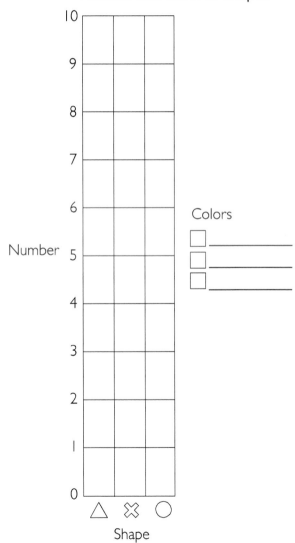

Number and Color of Shapes

2. Using the data set below, draw a bar chart to show each person's 1-mile run time.

Mile Times By Person	
Name	**Minutes**
Lorenzo	8
Sophia	6.5
Serena	10
Jean-Luc	8

Be sure to include:
a. Numbers on x-axis to show time (0–10)
b. Each person's name on the y-axis
c. One bar for each person showing their time

Mile Run times

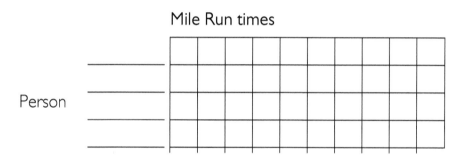

Person

Minutes

3. Create a Gantt chart of your daily schedule.

    a. Use the table below to help you organize your data. You don't need to include every activity—just pick a few of them!

    b. Fill in the empty Gantt chart with your data.

My Daily Schedule		
Activity	Start Time	End Time

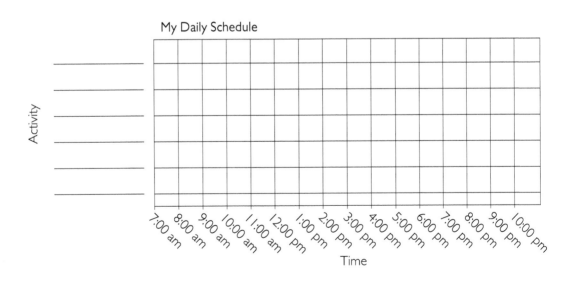

My Daily Schedule

Activity

Time

4 Size and area

The more of something there is, the more space it usually takes up. Five people take up more space than one person. A thousand books take up more space in the library than four books. "More" usually makes us think "bigger"!

In visualization, we can use the size of a shape to show how much of something there is—or how much more there is of one thing than another. Let's see how we can change the size of shapes to make data visualizations.

Shapes of different areas. 54
Making legends for size. 56
Using size for words. 58
The problem with area 60
Chapter summary 62
It's your turn!. 62

DOI: 10.1201/9781003309376-5

Shapes of different areas

The last chapter showed us how pictograph charts, bar charts, dumbbell charts, and Gantt charts use length to show amounts. Just like length, the **area** of a shape—the amount of space a shape takes up if it's flat on a page—can show how much of something there is, too.

Take the visualization in Image 4.1 that uses circles of different sizes to give a rough idea of how much Charlie and Rosie like video games:

Image 4.1
Using different sizes of the same shape can show if there is more or less of something.

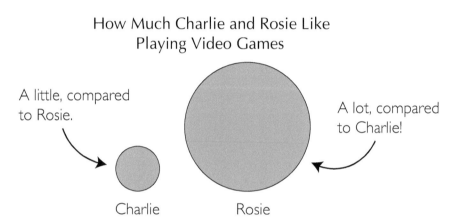

This is called a **proportional area chart**, which is any type of visualization that uses different areas of a shape to show differences in amount. There aren't any axes here, but it's quick to understand that Rosie seems to enjoy video games more than Charlie because her circle is so much bigger. Even then, we would need to see the data or use labels to understand exactly *how much* more. This example illustrates what area does well *and* not so well in data visualization: showing who has more or less of something without saying exactly how much more or less.

As it turns out, we do have the data from the graph above—and then some (Table 4.1).

Table 4.1
*Data about
how much nine
people like video
games on a
scale from 0
to 10*

How Much Several Classmates Like Playing Video Games	
Person	**Amount**
Charlie	2
Rosie	10
Juanita	7
Ahmad	2
Serena	2
Gabrielle	10
Alex	1
Lorenzo	7
Marina	8

Adding a circle for each new data point to the graph above creates a **packed circle chart**. Packed circle charts like in Image 4.2 are a kind of proportional area chart that use circles of different sizes to show different quantities. The circles are bunched or *packed* together as closely as possible, but it doesn't matter where in the visualization they are. There aren't axes here, either.

How Much Several Classmates Like
Playing Video Games (1 - 10)

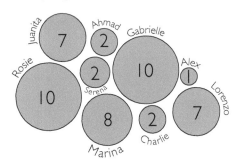

Image 4.2
*Packed circle
charts use circles
of different sizes
to show different
amounts.*

The visualization above still tells us that Rosie likes video games more than Charlie, and that on a scale from one to ten she gives them a ten! Charlie, on the other hand, gives his love of the games a tiny two. Packed circle charts often have the values written on the circles themselves.

In a few chapters we'll learn more about the best ways to use color in visualizations, but making each person a different color is a nice way to tell each circle apart and talk about the visualization. Image 4.3, for example, would let you say something like "The purple circle shows that Lorenzo rated his love of video games seven out of ten, unlike Serena whose light green circle shows that she rated them two out of ten."

Image 4.3
Making each circle in a packed circle chart a different color can make it easier to talk about the visualization or single out an interesting data point.

How Much Several Classmates Like
Playing Video Games (1 - 10)

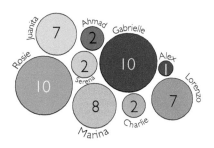

Making legends for size

By now, you might be wondering if there's a better way to understand the meaning behind the size of a shape in a data visualization than just guessing or looking at a label. Sure, we *can* write the amount on each shape, but is that the best we can do?

In the last chapter we learned about two other ways to show how much of something there is or what group it belongs to: axes and legends. The stacked bar chart showing ice cream data had both of these. It used a y-axis to show the number of ice cream scoops and an x-axis to show which bar belonged to whom. It also used a legend to explain what each color meant.

Axes don't make as much sense for explaining the size of a shape because shapes get wider *and* taller. A legend, on the other hand, can show by example what a certain size means. There are several ways to show size in a legend, but the important thing is that the legend has a few example shapes to show the meaning of different sizes. It's especially important to show the meanings of the smallest and largest shapes so that some-one looking at the visualization knows what they look like.

How Much Several Classmates Like
Playing Video Games (1 - 10)

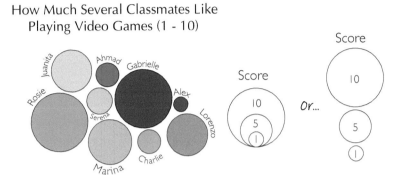

Image 4.4
Two ways
of making a
legend for size.
It's useful to
show what the
smallest and
largest sizes
mean, as well
as a few other
example shapes.

Image 4.4 shows two ways of making legends for different circle sizes. Someone looking at either visualization could guess that a score of six, for instance, would be shown with a circle that is a bit larger than the one in the middle of the legend labeled with a 5. If a circle in the visualization is as small as tiniest circle, they'd know it meant a value of one.

Take a minute, however, to compare the size legends to the legend we used to tell the ice cream flavors apart. Do you think they're as easy to use? Are you able to see *exactly* how much each person likes video games? Can you tell *exactly* which flavor of ice cream the color means?

You're not alone if you think it's hard to say exactly how big one circle or shape is compared to another. Even more, it can be hard to know what the sizes mean, especially if they're not exactly the same size as a shape in the legend. Using size in a visualization is a good way to give someone an *idea* of how much more or less of something there is, but even if there is a legend it can be hard to know the true amounts.

If we turn the packed area chart from above into a bar chart, however, we can see how much easier it is to use length to compare each person's data—no legend required (Image 4.5).

How Much Several Classmates Like Playing Video Games (1 - 10)

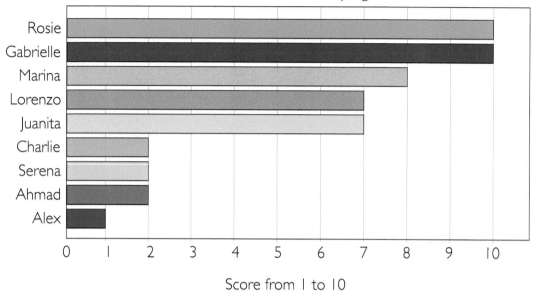

Score from 1 to 10

Image 4.5
Shapes of different lengths, like the bars in bar charts, are better at showing exact amounts than shapes of different sizes or areas.

Using size for words

Shapes aren't the only things that can be made smaller or larger in a visualization. You can use differently-sized words to show different amounts, too. **Word clouds** are a type of visualization that show how often certain words are written or said in a story or a piece of writing. The words that appear most often are written in large letters, and uncommon words are written in smaller letters.

The word cloud in Image 4.6 describes an imaginary book about woodland animals that happen to wear fancy clothes. According to the word cloud, the book uses the words *fabulous, fresh, button,* and *moose* very often. Only a little bit of the animals' clothes must sparkle—the word *sparkle* is quite small. We can tell that a good amount of it is classy—the word *classy* is medium-sized. If only there were pictures!

Common Words in the Best-Selling Book
Woodland Creatures in Fashion

Image 4.6
The larger words appeared more often in the story than the smaller words.

The data for this word cloud might look something like this, where each word is shown along with the number of times it appears in the story (Table 4.2).

Table 4.2
Word counts for Woodland Creatures in Fashion

Common Words in *Woodland Creatures in Fashion*	
Word	**Number of Times**
Fabulous	73
Moose	65
Fresh	54
Button	49
Yes	48
Classy	42
Frog	40
Bird	39
Exciting	39
Corduroy	32
Casual	30
Bold	30
Soft	30
Elegant	30
Velvety	30
Sparkle	21

Word clouds are a fun way to see the mood or theme of a story, but they do have one issue: words are already different lengths! Even if a long word has small letters, it can still look bigger than a short word with large letters. When you read or make a word cloud, make sure you're looking at the size of the *letters* instead of the lengths of the words (Image 4.7).

Image 4.7
In word clouds, words that are already long can look big even if they are written in small letters.

The problem with area

Now that we've seen a few ways to use size and area to show data, you might expect that area comes with a few warnings—it surely isn't as clear as using height to make a bar chart, for example. Bigger shapes mean more of something, but it seems harder to tell just *how much* more, right? Unfortunately, it's true—using area in visualizations isn't always as useful as you might think.

For one thing, we're not as good at comparing sizes of things as we are lengths. There's nothing wrong with your eyes or brain, it's just more difficult! Take a look at the illustration in Image 4.8 as an example.

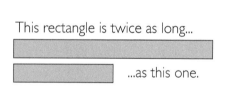

Image 4.8
It's much easier to compare lengths than areas, so using area in visualizations probably isn't the best choice for showing exact amounts.

It's fairly easy to tell that top rectangle is twice as long as the bottom rectangle. The first square, on the other hand, doesn't *really* look twice as big as the second one… and it certainly doesn't look four times as large as the third one. Some simple cuts and folds, however, show us what our eyes have a hard time seeing for themselves (Image 4.9).

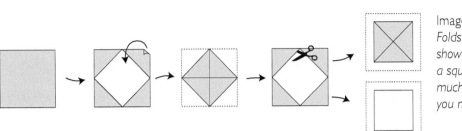

Image 4.9
Folds and cuts show how half of a square looks much larger than you might think!

Start with a square, like the first one in dark yellow. Fold the corners to the center, and then cut them off along the folds. A smaller square will be left in the middle. Tape the cut-off corners together to make a new square so that you can compare the two. They're the same size as each other, aren't they? Even weirder, each smaller square is half of the original one.

As confusing as size is for squares, it's even more difficult for circles. Take a look at these circles in the next illustration. On the top left, the larger circle is twice as wide as the smaller circles, but four times the area. On the top right, the larger circle is as wide as three small circles, yet it's nine times the area. To make matters worse, only two circles fit neatly inside the circle that is four times the area, while seven fit in a circle that is nine times the area (Image 4.10).

Image 4.10
How much bigger is one circle than another? It's hard to tell by looking, and our guesses are often off.

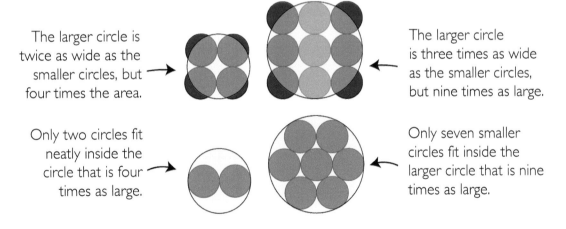

The larger circle is twice as wide as the smaller circles, but four times the area.

The larger circle is three times as wide as the smaller circles, but nine times as large.

Only two circles fit neatly inside the circle that is four times as large.

Only seven smaller circles fit inside the larger circle that is nine times as large.

So, what does it even mean for a shape to be twice as big as another? Does it mean that it's twice as wide? Double the area? Big enough to fit two smaller shapes inside? Just *looks* twice as big? This is the problem with using area in data visualization—it's just too messy to show amounts in an exact way.

Is all this to say that you shouldn't ever use size to show data? No, certainly not. It only means that you should remember that size is good at showing *roughly* how much of something there is, and that it's useful to use labels or and legends to help the visualization make sense. As we'll see later in this book, size can be used along with other types of visualization for types of data that don't need to be exact.

Chapter summary

Changing the size or area of shapes or words is a useful way to show amounts, like in proportional area charts, packed circle charts, and word clouds. Usually, bigger shapes mean more of something, and smaller shapes mean less of something. Using a legend to show what each size means or adding labels to the shapes can help people understand what the visualization means. Changing the size of a shape isn't a perfect way of showing an amount, but it is a good way to show roughly how much of something there is in one category compared to another.

It's your turn!

1. Use the data set below to make and compare two different types of visualizations.

Rolls of Wrapping Paper Sold for the Holiday Fundraiser	
Person	Rolls Sold
Ousmane	5
Marina	6
Sophia	2
Jean-Luc	3

a. Use a shape of your choice to show how many rolls of wrapping paper each person sold for the holiday fundraiser. Use the same shape in different sizes for every person.

Rolls of Wrapping Paper Sold
for the Holiday Fundraiser

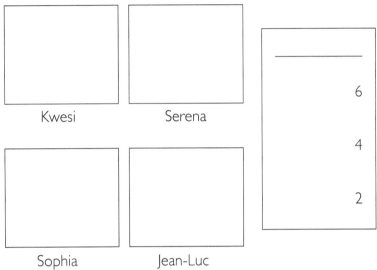

Kwesi

Serena

Sophia

Jean-Luc

6

4

2

b. Fill in the legend to show what each size means.
c. Use the same data to make a bar chart.

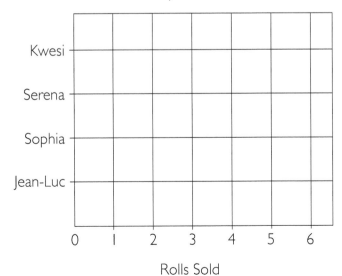

Rolls of Wrapping Paper Sold
for the Holiday Fundraiser

Kwesi

Serena

Sophia

Jean-Luc

0   1   2   3   4   5   6

Rolls Sold

d. Which visualization do you like better? Which do you think would be easier for someone else to understand?

2. Imagine that you've counted up the words in one of your favorite stories and made a data set. Use the data set and the measuring tools below to make a word cloud of the data.

Word	Count
Dark	10
Creaky	9
Doors	8
Quiet	7
Squeak	6
Jump	5
Fog	4
Giggle	4
Crumple	3

a. The rectangles below are different heights, and there is a small number in the top corner of each one. Trace the rectangles onto your own piece of paper, and then fill them in with the words in the table so that the number on the rectangle matches the number in the table. Like this:

b. Cut out the words, and arrange them into a word cloud. You can either take a picture of what you make, or glue the words onto another sheet of paper.

c. What do you think the story is about by looking at the word cloud?

	10

	9

	8

	7

	6

	5

	4

	4

	3

5 Position

In the last few chapters, we learned how height, width, length, and size can show a quantity of something. This included learning about axes that show us how tall, wide, or long something is, as well as names of categories or groups that might be in the data. In this chapter, we talk about what it means when pictures or symbols are in different *places* or *positions* on a data visualization, and how those places show quantities, categories, and relationships.

Remembering axes 68
Scatterplots. 69
Bubble charts 72
Connecting the dots 74
Scatterplots with categories. 77
Fixing crowded and overlapping points 79
Chapter summary 81
It's your turn!. 82

DOI: 10.1201/9781003309376-6

Remembering axes

Let's start by reminding ourselves how axes work. We already know that axes are useful for showing different amounts or groups. For example, a visualization with only a category axis could look something like this (Image 5.1):

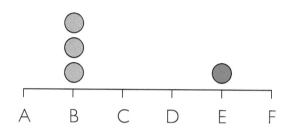

Image 5.1
This category axis shows that the pink dots are part of Group B and the teal dot is part of Group E.

Without knowing anything else about it, we might guess that this visualization means that there are three things in Group B and one thing in Group E. The **position** of each circle on the axis tells us the group that it belongs to.

Another way to show this same visualization would be with a number axis. In Image 5.2, the *position* on the axis tells us the amount, not the group. Groups B and E are now shown as letters. We could also read this visualization as saying that Group E had one of something and Group B had three of something.

Image 5.2
This number axis by itself shows that there is one of something in Group E and three of something in Group B.

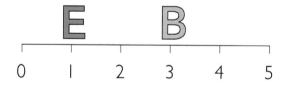

Similarly, you could show that there were 3½ things—or any other fraction! As long as the number makes sense for the things you are counting, the spaces between each number still mean something. For example, you might not be able to measure 3½ people, but counting 3½ pieces of toast is perfectly reasonable (Image 5.3).

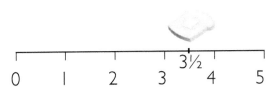

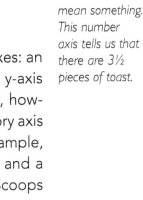

Like we saw in Chapter 3, most visualizations use two axes: an x-axis that goes from left to right on the bottom, and a y-axis that goes up and down on the left or right. Until now, however, all of the visualizations we've seen have one category axis and one number axis. The ice cream visualization, for example, has an x-axis that shows the category variable People and a y-axis that shows the numerical variable Number of Scoops (Image 5.4).

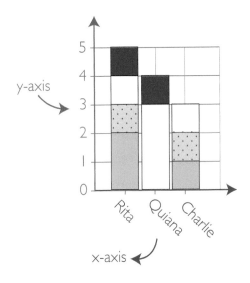

Image 5.4
The x-axis on the ice cream visualization is categorical; it shows people. The y-axis is numerical; it shows numbers of scoops.

Scatterplots

What if we had data for *two* numerical variables, though, and were curious to see if their values were related? The data set below, for example, shows data from Lorenzo's lemonade stand. In addition to the Weekday variable which is ordinal, the data set has an interval variable for the temperature outside as well as a numerical variable for his daily sales (Table 5.1).

Table 5.1
*Profits from
lemonade sales
by temperature*

Lorenzo's Lemonade Sales by Temperature		
Weekday	**Sales**	**Temperature (°F)**
Monday	$3.75	86
Tuesday	$5.00	93
Wednesday	$3.75	95
Thursday	$1.25	72
Friday	$2.50	88

For data like these, a bar chart wouldn't be able to tell us how the temperature affected Lorenzo's lemonade business, but a **scatterplot** would. Scatterplots are a common type of visualization that use two numerical axes to show how two variables are related. The dots or shapes on a scatterplot are called **points**.

Take a look at the scatterplot in Image 5.5 of a single data point from the data set—Monday, to be exact. The x-axis on the bottom shows the temperature in degrees Fahrenheit for that day. The y-axis on the left side shows the sales in dollars.

Image 5.5
*This graph's axes
help us figure
out that Lorenzo
made $3.75
selling lemonade
on a day that
was 86°F.*

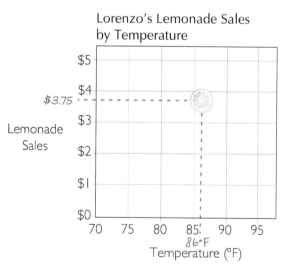

The lemon slice point tells us that on Monday when it was about 86°F outside, the lemonade stand earned about 3¾ dollars, or $3.75.

If we added a few more days' worth of data to this scatterplot, we could see that the hotter days tended to sell more lemonade than the cooler days. We know this because the points that are further to the right—meaning that the day was hotter—are also closer to the top. Thanks to both axes working together, the position of lemon slices lets us know both the temperature *and* the sales at the same time (Image 5.6).

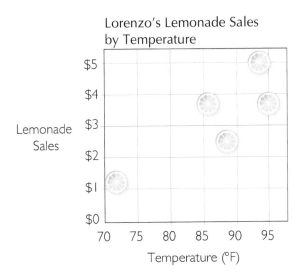

Image 5.6
As the temperature goes up, Lorenzo's lemonade sales go up, too. Lemons that are further to the right are also usually further up on the graph.

Let's do one more example using the data collected at the lunch table. Recall the bar chart and pictograph chart of these friends' heights, hair colors, and how much they liked their lunches that day (Image 5.7).

Image 5.7
This visualization shows a lot of data, but it's not very easy to see if someone's height has anything to do with how highly they rate their lunch.

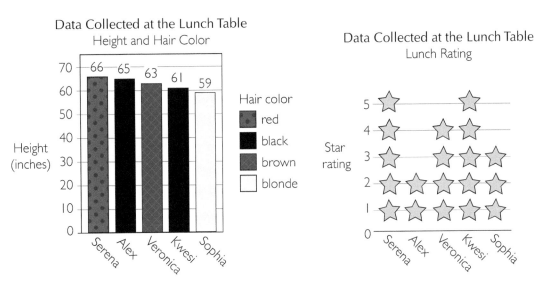

It's useful, but a scatterplot would be interesting, too. Visualizing heights *compared* to lunch ratings in a scatterplot would help us better understand if our taller friends liked lunch more—or if being tall had nothing to do with liking lunch at all!

Take a look at the scatterplot in Image 5.8. Did the taller people like lunch more or less than the shorter people?

Image 5.8
As it turns out, someone's height doesn't seem to have anything to do with how much they like their lunch.

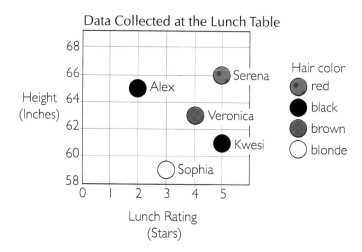

Looking at the graph, it's hard to say! Serena is the tallest—we know this because her point is the closest to the top—and she *did* rate her lunch with five stars. Alex, on the other hand, is also quite tall—their point is in line with number 65—but they only rated their lunch with two stars. The points on the scatterplot are all over the place, and there isn't a clear pattern like the points in the visualization about Lorenzo's lemonade sale.

So, what's the answer? All we can say is that among these particular people, being tall or short doesn't make you like lunch more or less. The two variables appear to be unrelated. And that's okay! Sometimes there *is* a pattern or a relationship between two variables (like temperature and lemonade sales), but sometimes there *isn't*. A scatterplot can show you what's really happening.

Bubble charts

Now let's imagine that after the fifth day of running his lemonade stand, Lorenzo switches to using larger cups. In that case, the data set would get a new variable, Size. The new Day variable helps us tell the weekdays apart (Table 5.2).

Table 5.2
*Lorenzo's profits
from lemonade
sales by
temperature and
serving size*

Day #	Weekday	Sales	Temperature (°F)	Size
Lorenzo's Profits from Lemonade Sales by Temperature and Serving Size				
1	Monday	$3.75	86	Small
2	Tuesday	$5.00	93	Small
3	Wednesday	$3.75	95	Small
4	Thursday	$1.25	72	Small
5	Friday	$2.50	88	Small
6	Monday	$4.00	91	Large
7	Tuesday	$5.50	96	Large
8	Wednesday	$4.50	82	Large
9	Thursday	$6.00	88	Large
10	Friday	$5.50	89	Large

Using points of different sizes would help us to see if the larger cups made any difference in Lorenzo's lemonade sales. Scatterplots that use size to show a third variable from the data are called **bubble charts**, because the points look like bubbles floating off the page.

Using two sizes of points—large and small—lets us see that the lemonade stand made the most money on hot days while selling larger servings of lemonade. The larger points are both higher up *and* further to the right. Even on days that were similar temperatures, like when it was around 95°F outside, the larger servings made more money (Image 5.9).

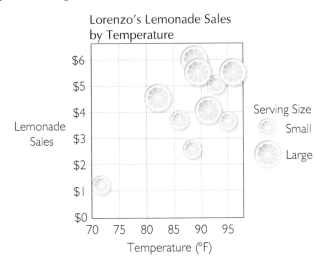

Lorenzo's Lemonade Sales by Temperature

Image 5.9
*Points (or
lemons) of
different sizes let
us see how hot
weather changes
lemonade sales
for small and
large cups.*

Like we learned in Chapter 4, the legend in this graph explains what the different sizes mean. In this case, Size is an ordinal variable with Small and Large categories, but if it were a numerical variable shown in ounces or cups, then the legend could show that too (Image 5.10).

Image 5.10
The size legend of a bubble chart explains what the sizes mean and if the size variable is a categorical, ordinal, or numerical variable.

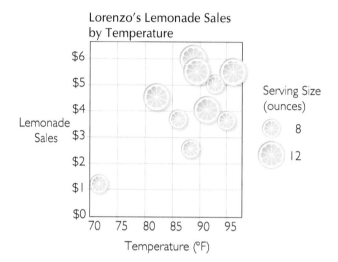

Connecting the dots

Scatterplots and bubble charts are useful for showing the relationship between variables, but they aren't very useful for showing the *ordering* of data points. If you want to understand the change from point-to-point in a certain order, you'll need to use a different type of visualization, like a **line graph**.

A line graph looks similar to a scatterplot, but each point is connected to form a wiggly line that runs from left to right. The values on the x-axis are either ordinal or numerical data that tell us the order of each data point. The connections between each point make it easier to see how much the values on the y-axis change from one point to the next. Because line charts show data in a particular order, a line in a line chart can only have one point for each value on the x-axis.

We could, for instance, create a line chart showing how Lorenzo's lemonade sales went up and down over time, since the days are in a certain order and there's only one of each day. The x-axis could show the numbered days that he opened his stand, and the y-axis could show his sales (Image 5.11).

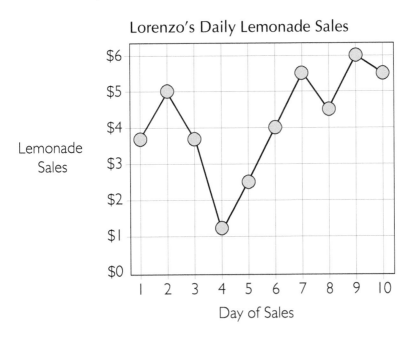

Lorenzo's Daily Lemonade Sales

Lemonade Sales

Day of Sales

Image 5.11 Line charts connect the dots in a scatterplot, making the change from point-to-point easier to see.

We can see that his fourth day of business sold the least lemonade, but after the rough patch he did much better as the days went on.

Line graphs also give us a way to guess values that might happen *between* points. If he had forgotten to write down his sales on day 7, for example, he could connect the dots between days 6 and 8 to make a pretty good guess. It might not be exactly right, but it would likely be closer than picking a number from a hat (Image 5.12).

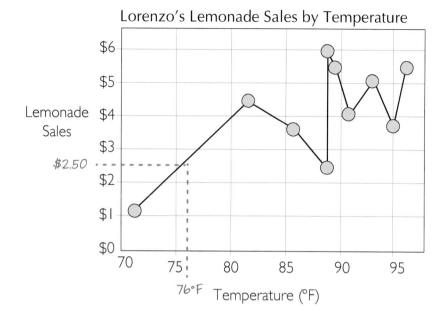

Image 5.12
*Line graphs let
us make better
guesses about
what might
happen between
points.*

Lorenzo's Lemonade Sales by Temperature

Image 5.13
*Connected
scatterplots
connect the dots
between points
on a scatterplot,
but instead of
going from left
to right, they
connect in an
order from a
third variable.*

If we wanted to see the temperature, sales, *and* the order of the days, we could make something called a **connected scatterplot**. These visualizations connect each point in a scatterplot in the order of a third variable—one that isn't on the x-axis or the y-axis. For us, that would be the Day variable (Image 5.13).

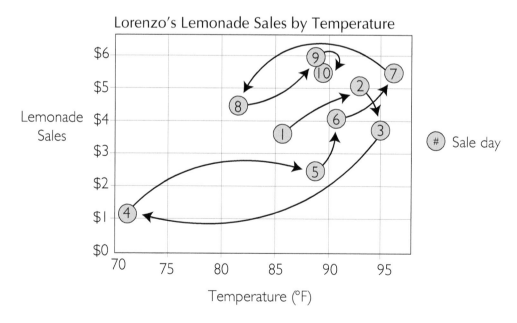

Lorenzo's Lemonade Sales by Temperature

By following the arrows from one point to the next, the visualization above shows us how the temperature outside and the amount of money Lorenzo made are related, as well as the order of each day. If the arrow points up and to the right, that means that both values are increasing at the same time. Down and to the left means that they both are going down. Going up and to left or down and to the right means that one value is increasing, while the other is decreasing.

You can see on the first day of selling lemonade that Lorenzo made $3.75 and that it was 86°F. On the second day the temperature went up to 93°F and he made $5.00. Follow the arrows to his last day to see that he made $5.50 when it was 89°F outside.

Scatterplots with categories

So far, most of the visualizations in this chapter have helped us understand how two numerical variables are related. However, you might also be interested in how the values from a numerical and categorical variable are related when there are too many values in each category to make a bar chart. Let's do an example with a data set showing the late arrivals for three bus lines (Table 5.3).

Table 5.3
*Bus delays for
three bus lines*

Monday's Bus Delays (in Minutes)					
Bus Number	Bus Line	Delay	Bus Number	Bus Line	Delay
1	Red	4	6	Blue	7.2
2	Red	10.3	7	Blue	9.4
3	Red	7.4	8	Blue	8
4	Red	8	9	Blue	12.5
5	Red	5.6	1	Orange	2.6
6	Red	11.5	2	Orange	4.8
7	Red	0.9	3	Orange	0.8
8	Red	–	4	Orange	7.3
9	Red	–	5	Orange	2
1	Blue	4.3	6	Orange	1.6
2	Blue	10.9	7	Orange	1
3	Blue	6.5	8	Orange	3.3
4	Blue	9	9	Orange	–
5	Blue	5			

The table has three variables: Bus Number, an ordinal variable (because there are no busses between 1 and 2), Bus Line,
a categorical variable, and Delay, a numerical variable. As
usual, it's hard to say what's happening from the table alone.
A visualization like in Image 5.14 would help us see if one bus
line was late more often than another, or how late the busses
could be.

Image 5.14
*The position of
each point on
the x-axis tells
us which bus,
and the position
on the y-axis
tells us how late
it was.*

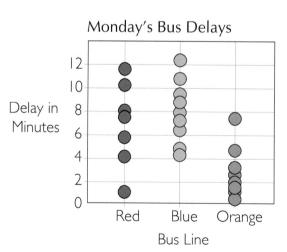

This visualization is called a **strip plot**, because the points are organized in strips by category. Just like the scatterplots about lemonade sales and peoples' heights, strip plots are a kind of scatterplot where one of the axes shows categories instead of numbers.

We can see from the strip plot that some bus lines had longer delays than others; the Blue line in particular was sometimes more than twelve minutes late! We can also see that the Orange line had fewer *super* late busses than the Red or Blue lines, and that its latest bus was still less than eight minutes late.

You might have noticed that there's a small problem with this strip plot, however. The overlapping points make it hard to see if there are any points hiding behind other points. Let's fix that.

Fixing crowded and overlapping points

Being able to see all the points in a scatterplot, bubble chart, or strip plot is important, and there are two good ways to make sure that happens. Keep these in mind for graphs that have a lot of data, or for when you want to make sure that every point on your visualization has enough space to be seen.

The first way to make every point visible is called **jittering**, which means moving the points side-to-side enough that they no longer overlap (Image 5.15).

No jittering   Jittering

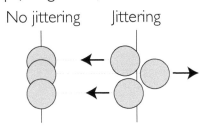

Image 5.15
Moving points from side-to-side so that they don't overlap is called jittering.

Jittering the points in the Bus Delays visualization doesn't change their meaning at all because the points aren't moving up and down along the y-axis. The points are *only* moving left and right while staying above the correct bus line on the x-axis.

Jittering the points from left to right creates a **bee swarm plot**—called this because the points look like bees swarming together. Bee swarm plots are a special kind of strip plots... which means that they're cousins of scatterplots, too (Image 5.16).

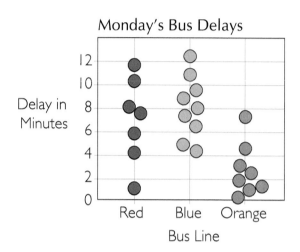

Image 5.16
Jittering makes the points easier to see because they don't overlap. The points only moved left or right because moving them up and down would change their meaning on the y-axis.

Another way to make points visible on a crowded visualization is to change the **opacity** of the points. This makes it easier to see where the points overlap. Opacity is a way of describing how hard it is to see though something. If it's hard to see through, then it's **opaque** or has a high **opacity**. **Transparency** is the opposite: if something is *easy* to see through, you can say that it is **transparent**.

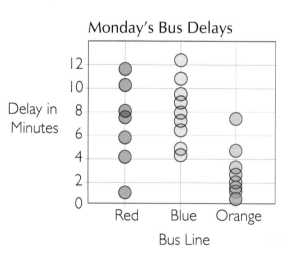

Image 5.17
Making the points more transparent (or a less opaque) lets us see where they overlap.

In this version of the visualization (Image 5.17), we can see darker groups of dots where the delays were more frequent. For example, the points for the Orange line's delays are bunched up around two minutes and the overlapping points look darker. We can't necessarily see every point exactly, but we have a better idea of where there are the most points.

Position, then, is another useful way of sharing data that shows up in all kinds of visualizations. You can use position with all three data types and mix it with size, order, color, and opacity— to name a few! With the help of axes, position makes it possible to visualize an endless variety of values and observe interesting relationships in your data.

Chapter summary

Scatterplots, bubble charts, line charts, connected scatterplots, strip plots, and bee swarm plots are types of visualizations that use the position of points along two axes to show how two variables are related to each other. All of these charts have one variable on the x-axis and another on the y-axis. Bubble charts use size to show a third variable, and connected scatterplots use arrows to show ordering. Visualizations with many points might need some help to make all points visible by using jittering or making the points less opaque.

It's your turn!

1. Using the data set below, draw a line chart to show how many flowers Serena's rose bush grew over time.

Flowers on Serena's Rose Bush	
Week	Number of Roses
Week 1	0
Week 2	1
Week 3	3
Week 4	5
Week 5	6

   a. Don't forget to add titles for the graph, the x-axis, and the y-axis.
   b. Make sure that you draw a point for each data point, and connect the points with a line.
   c. How is Serena's rose bush doing? Is it easier to understand by looking at the table or the visualization?
   d. How many roses do you think she had after 3½ weeks? Why?

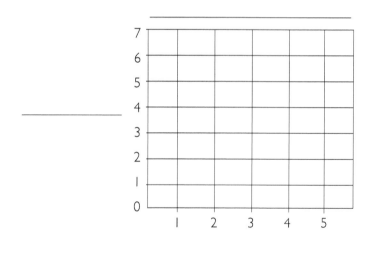

2. The local rescue shelter has a data set of the heights, weights, and age groups of their dogs.

Heights and Weights of Rescue Dogs

Name	Weight (lbs.)	Height (inches)	Age
Otis	11	8	Adult
Sunny	12	10	Puppy
Gertie	31	14	Adult
Lorraine	40	21	Puppy
Paws	52	25	Adult
Rex	60	20	Adult
Moose	80	30	Puppy

a. Use the data set to draw a bubble chart of the heights and weights of each dog. The size of the bubble should show if the dog is a puppy or an adult.

b. Be sure to include a main title as well as titles for the axes and legend.

c. Are adults or puppies usually bigger? Do any of the dogs stand out?

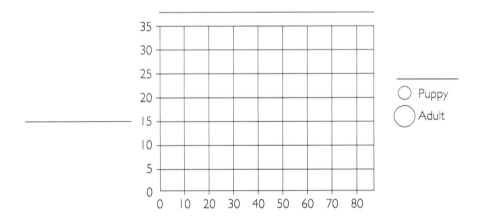

3. Two classrooms each take the same math test, and then create a data set with the scores by classroom.

Test Scores by Class	
Mrs. Henderson	Mr. Chen
98	85
92	79
83	81
90	98
92	86
97	97
84	82
97	88
89	99

a. Draw a strip plot of test scores by class using a little bit of jittering if necessary to make sure that each point is clear.

Note: You might notice the zig-zag line at the bottom of the y-axis below. This is called an **axis break**, and is a way to show that an axis isn't starting at zero, or that there's a gap in the numbers.

b. Did one class do better on the test than the other? Which one? What makes you think that?

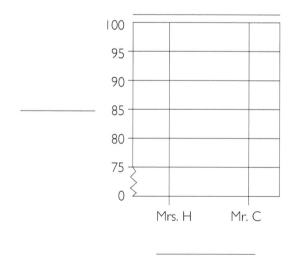

6 Color for categorical data

Color is often one of the first things we notice in a data visualization, and it certainly makes charts more fun. However, there are lots of things to keep in mind when using color to show data—including many ways that it can go wrong! In the next few chapters, we'll learn how to be smart about using color so that your visualizations are pretty and useful.

Before we even think about color though, we should remember that there are three types of data: numerical data, categorical data, and ordinal data. Each of these data uses color in a different way. In this chapter, we'll start our adventure through the rainbow by learning how to visualize different categories or groups with color.

Using colors to show categories 86
Creating a categorical color palette 86
Categorical colors in scatterplots and line charts. 88
Stacked and grouped bar charts. 91
Using colors to draw attention 93

DOI: 10.1201/9781003309376-7

Chapter summary *95*
It's your turn!. *96*

Using colors to show categories

Remember the ice cream example that helped us learn how visualizations use length to show amounts? In that visualization, we used a different color for each of the four flavors: red velvet, horchata, mint chip, and pumpkin pie. Since each flavor is totally is separate from the other two and they don't follow any order, we know that the flavors are categorical data (Image 6.1).

Image 6.1
Using different colors is a good way to show category data as long as the colors are as different as the categories.

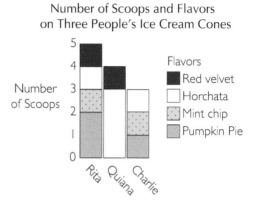

Why these colors, though, and how do you go about picking colors to show categories?

Creating a categorical color palette

There are two main things to think about when you're making a categorical **color palette**—or a collection of colors to use for a certain purpose or in a project. The most important thing for categorical colors is whether or not they're easy to tell apart.

Take a look at the color palettes in Image 6.2. The colors in the palettes on the left look quite different from each other. It wouldn't take long to realize that they meant different groups or categories if you saw these colors in a data visualization. The palettes on the right side are more confusing; it would be hard to know which data belonged to each group because the colors look so much alike.

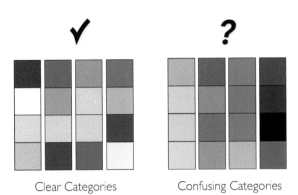

Clear Categories   Confusing Categories

Image 6.2
It's important to pick colors that look different from each other when you are choosing colors to show category data.

As long as the colors are very different from each other and there's a legend to explain what each color means, all kinds of colors can show categories. The bar chart in Image 6.3 may look a little weird, but it still does a good job at showing how many scoops of each flavor the three people had. Each color is as different as the flavor it stands for!

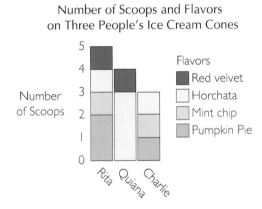

Number of Scoops and Flavors on Three People's Ice Cream Cones

Image 6.3
While it might be better to use colors that look like what they are showing, the most important thing is that the colors are different enough to tell apart.

The second thing to think about when you're making a categorical color palette is whether or not certain colors make sense for each category. In the visualization above, *none* of the colors are related to the flavors, so they're fairly easy to understand. However, it would be even better to use colors that already come to mind when someone thinks of each category. The red, cream, green, and orange in the original version did exactly that.

But beware! Mixing up colors that remind people of a *different* category is a recipe for disaster. Take a look at the version of the ice cream visualization shown in Image 6.4.

Image 6.4
Using colors that remind people of a different group is confusing and can cause someone to misunderstand the data in a visualization.

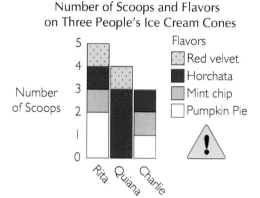

Number of Scoops and Flavors
on Three People's Ice Cream Cones

As hard as you might try, it's tricky to see the green color showing red velvet and the cream color showing pumpkin pie. It's too tempting to see them as the other flavors! With a mixed-up color palette like this, it would be easy for someone to misunderstand the visualization or remember the data incorrectly. Try to use the colors that make sense with each group, and don't scramble colors in ways that are confusing.

Categorical colors in scatterplots and line charts

Now that we know a bit about making categorical color palettes, think back to the visualization below about Lorenzo's success selling lemonade in small and large cups. We know that the serving sizes are ordinal data because Small and Large can be arranged in an order. It made sense, then, to show the different serving sizes with differently-sized points (Image 6.5).

Image 6.5
Small and large lemons show the ordinal data of small and large serving sizes.

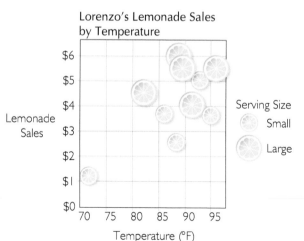

Lorenzo's Lemonade Sales
by Temperature

But what if, instead of two serving sizes, we wanted to visualize what happened when two *people* had lemonade stands? For this situation, we can imagine that Wei also sets up shop in her neighborhood and records the temperature outside and the sales that she makes. After a few days of peddling the tasty refreshments, the two friends have a nice data set for a visualization (Table 6.1).

Profits from Lemonade Sales by Temperature and Person			
Person	Day	Sales	Temperature (°F)
Lorenzo	Monday	$3.75	86
Lorenzo	Tuesday	$5.00	93
Lorenzo	Wednesday	$3.75	95
Lorenzo	Thursday	$1.25	72
Lorenzo	Friday	$2.50	88
Wei	Monday	$0.50	73
Wei	Tuesday	$2.25	77
Wei	Wednesday	$2.25	84
Wei	Thursday	$4.75	89
Wei	Friday	$5.00	96

Table 6.1
Sales and daily temperatures from two peoples' lemonade stands for five days

People can't be arranged in an order like large and small cups can, so it wouldn't make sense to use the large and small lemon slices to visualize this data set. We could, however, use color. In the next visualization, Lorenzo's lemonade sales are shown in yellow, and Wei's lemonade sales are shown in blue. As usual, a legend reminds us what the colors mean (Image 6.6).

Image 6.6
Since people are categorical data, it makes more sense to use colors than sizes to show each person's lemonade sales.

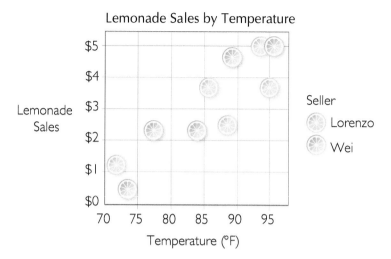

Lemonade Sales by Temperature

From this visualization we can see that Wei and Lorenzo both sold the most lemonade when it was the hottest outside. We can also see that they sold the least on the coolest day. The colors are easy to tell apart, the yellow lemons make sense for a lemonade stand, and there's nothing confusing about them like there was in the switched-around ice cream example.

We can make a line chart from this data set, too, by connecting the points for each person with matching colors. Line charts like this that have more than one category are sometimes called **multiple line charts**. The legend explains the meaning of each color in this type of graph, too. As we learned in the last chapter, a line chart makes sense here because the days of the week are in order and there are never two Mondays or Wednesdays in the same week (Image 6.7).

Image 6.7
Connecting the dots in a scatterplot with different categories makes a multiple line chart.

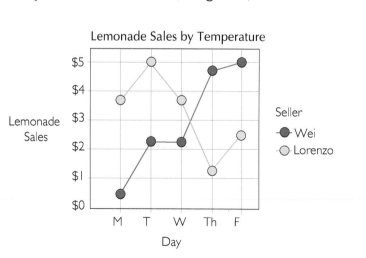

Lemonade Sales by Temperature

Now we can see how both people's sales changed from day to day through the week, and who made more or less each day.

Stacked and grouped bar charts

Earlier in this chapter, we learned that the most important thing in picking a categorical palette is that each color looks different from the rest. But wait, there's a catch! Using similar-looking colors can come in handy for showing categories that are related.

The blob of squares in Image 6.8, for example, shows four different categories that could be split into two separate groups. Depending on the data, the groups might be blues and reds or darks and lights

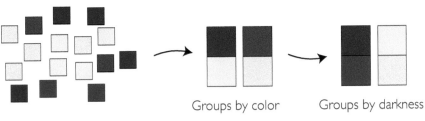

Groups by color   Groups by darkness

Image 6.8
Using groups of similar-looking colors can be useful for showing things that are related. Here, the colors could show a blue and red group, or a light and dark group.

Let's see a color palette like this in action. The data set below shows the number of in-game tokens Rosie and Martin traded for supplies the last time they played their favorite time-travel game, *On the Frontier of Time*. There are two categories of supplies: Food and Gear. The Food category contains bread and fruit, and the Gear category contains clothes and tools (Table 6.2).

On the Frontier of Time In-Game Supply Purchases			
Person	**Category**	**Item**	**Tokens**
Martin	Food	Fruit	56
Martin	Food	Bread	200
Martin	Gear	Clothes	65
Martin	Gear	Tools	40
Rosie	Food	Fruit	40
Rosie	Food	Bread	150
Rosie	Gear	Clothes	60
Rosie	Gear	Tools	75

Since we're interested in showing amounts for different categories, a visualization that uses length and color is a good place to start. The stacked bar chart in Image 6.9 has two bars: one for Martin and another for Rosie. Each bar is made up of four different layers—instead of ice cream; this time each layer shows a different kind of supply. The height of each bar overall shows how many tokens were traded in total. Each color shows many tokens were traded for a different category of thing—food or gear. Each layer on its own shows how many tokens were traded for the type of each thing in that category—fruit, bread, clothes, or tools.

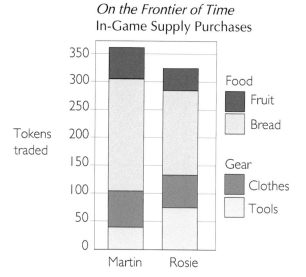

On the Frontier of Time
In-Game Supply Purchases

The stacked bar chart shows us that Martin traded more tokens for food and gear combined because his total bar is taller. Rosie traded fewer tokens overall, but she traded more tokens for gear because her blue section is taller. Both people traded more tokens on food than gear. Both people also bought more bread than fruit.

Another way of showing the same data set would be with a **grouped bar chart**, like the one shown in Image 6.10. In this version, each person has a group of side-by-side bars instead of one tall stacked bar. This version makes it more difficult to tell who traded more tokens overall, but it does make it easier to compare the smaller bars to each other.

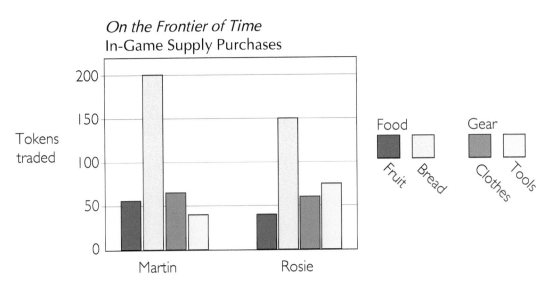

In both versions, the color palette works in two ways: to show how things are different and similar from each other. The same visualization with four completely different colors would be fine, but it would miss out on a good chance to show how some of the values are connected.

Using colors to draw attention

So far, we've learned about how to use colors to tell different categories apart—and to make them look related—but sometimes it's important to make one particular category stand out.

Image 6.10 Grouped bar charts are like stacked bar charts that have been knocked down. The colors in this grouped bar chart still show the Food and Gear categories.

Say, for example, that Veronica has a few friends over for a barbeque and yard games. The long jump competition is first, and Veronica is curious to know how far she can jump compared to the others. She writes down the distances alongside each athlete's name in Table 6.3, and colors in her row:

Veronica's Long Jump vs Other Friends	
Person	Distance (feet)
Gabrielle	10
Rita	9¼
Veronica	6¾
Charlie	6

The bar chart she makes from the data set is in Image 6.11. Even though Person is a categorical variable, she didn't have to make every bar a different color; each person already has their own bar and position on the y-axis. To satisfy Veronica's curiosity the most easily, however, she can choose to fill in her bar with a different color than the others. This makes it quick to see that she jumped almost seven feet! Rita and Gabrielle jumped a bit further, but Charlie was behind Veronica by almost a foot.

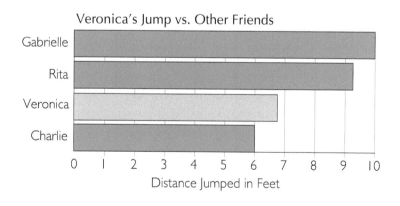

Image 6.11
Making one bar in a bar chart a different color than the rest makes it easier to see how it compares to the others.

Using color to bring attention to a particular part of a visualization works in almost any graph, too. As you can see in the next scatterplot, a little bit of color can make the day that Wei sold the most lemonade pop out from the rest. A little note to explain why that point is a different color makes sure that no one is confused (Image 6.12).

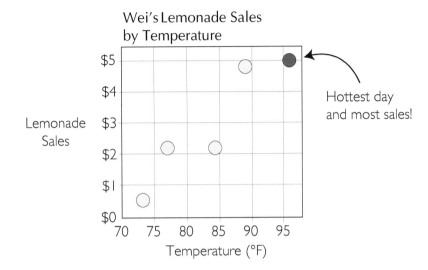

Wei's Lemonade Sales by Temperature

Image 6.12
Making a single point a separate color from the rest makes it easier for to pick it out from the crowd.

In data visualization, color is so much more than simple decoration or icing on the cake. It's one of the first things people notice, and something that often has a lot of meaning by itself. For categorical data, smartly-chosen colors can help us to see how categories are different or related, or make a special value shine. A good color palette can even remind us what the visualization is about. Used wisely, color can be one of the most interesting and exciting parts of creating a data visualization.

Chapter summary

When choosing colors for categorical data, it's important to use a color palette with colors that look different from each other. If possible, try to make categorical colors look like the categories they represent. Colors that are too similar to each other may appear to be in groups—which can be a good thing, if they actually are! Colors can also be useful to draw attention to one thing in particular, like a point on a scatterplot or a certain bar in a bar chart.

It's your turn!

You'll need colored pencils or crayons to do these activities.

Note: If you have a hard time seeing some colors or you know that you are colorblind, please let your teacher or a friend know so that they can help you. We'll learn more about making colorblind-friendly visualizations in Chapters 9 and 10.

1. Color in this bar chart two ways:

   a. First, use colors that make sense with the fruit.

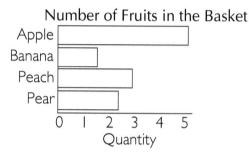

   b. Now, color in the same graph with different category colors of your choice. Make sure that you don't choose colors that look similar to each other.

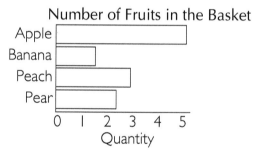

   c. Which graph is easier to use? What is clear or confusing about both?

2. Examine this stacked bar chart and answer the following
   questions:

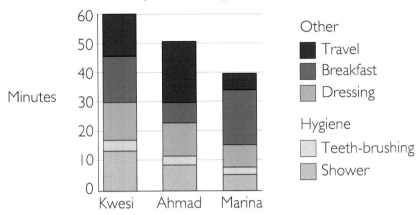

a. Who spends the most time in the shower?
b. Who spends the least time traveling to school?
c. Whose morning routine is the longest?
d. What activity usually takes the longest? Is it the same for
   each person?

3. Think about the number of cousins you have, and ask a few people about their own families.

    a. Fill in the following table with data about yourself and a few people that you know. You can make the data up or use real information.

    b. Plot the data as a bar chart.

    c. Highlight the bar about yourself with a special color.

How many cousins do people have?	
Person	Number of Cousins
Me	

How many cousins do people have?

Name

Me

Number

7 Color for numerical data

In the last chapter, we learned how to create color palettes for categorical data, and that each color in a categorical palette should look as different as possible from every other color. This chapter takes us in the opposite direction to the data type whose values aren't split up at all: numerical data.

Before we go any further though, it's important to know that colors *can* show numerical data, just not as precisely as they do for categorical data. Colorful visualizations of numerical data are beautiful, but it can be hard to tell the exact numerical value that a color represents. In this chapter we'll learn how to use colors to show numerical data in ways that make sense for the values.

What are gradients?. 100
Low-to-high gradients. 100
Low-middle-high diverging gradients. 104
Multi-color and rainbow gradients. 107
Chapter summary 111
It's your turn!. 111

DOI: 10.1201/9781003309376-8

What are gradients?

Numerical data like counts, temperatures, prices, and percentages all have something special in common: they're **continuous**. This means that between each whole number like one and two, or 84 and 85, are fractions like 1½ or 84.0002. The distances between each value are also the same—one is as far away from two as 84 is from 85. It makes sense, then, to show these data with colors that are also continuous, moving from one color to the next without skipping anything in between (Image 7.1).

Image 7.1
Sets of colors that blend smoothly together are called gradients. This is a rainbow gradient.

We can do this by creating **gradients**, which are sets of colors that blend smoothly together without any sudden changes or gaps. Depending on the values in your data, there are several types of gradients to choose from. Let's start with the simplest and most common: a low-to-high gradient.

Low-to-high gradients

If your visualization needs to use color to show numbers that go from low to high, a gradient between two colors—one light and one dark—will often do the trick. There are two ways to make this type of gradient.

Light-to-dark and bright-to-dark gradients
The first way to make a low-to-high gradient is to use a light or bright color on one end, and black or a dark color on the other. The colors in between get darker and darker as you move along the gradient. In visualizations, the lighter or brighter parts of a gradient usually mean lower values, and the colors on the darker end of the gradient mean higher values. This makes the most interesting values stand out on a white page. Examples of light-to-dark and bright-to-dark gradients are in Image 7.2.

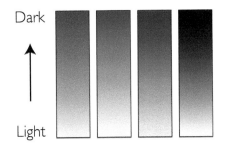

Dark

Light

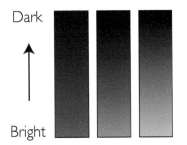

Dark

Bright

Notice how in each of the gradients above, the light and dark colors blend together without any patches or chunks standing out. They smoothly go from light to dark, and never change their minds half-way through—just like numerical data.

A gradient like the one in Image 7.3, on the other hand, is all over the place—light to dark to light all over again. It would be *terrible* for showing numerical data because it isn't smooth and continuous like the values are themselves.

?!

Image 7.3
*Chaos! This
gradient is a
terrible choice for
numerical data.*

Visualizations that use color gradients and position to show numerical data are called **heat maps** because the colors can make you feel like you're looking through heat vision goggles. The simple heat map in Image 7.4 uses a light-to-dark gradient to show the number of pages that Juanita read in one week. The values in the Day of the Week variable are shown at different positions on the axis. According to the legend, the lighter shades of green mean fewer pages—the lowest number is zero. The highest possible number of pages is 100, shown as black.

Number of Pages Juanita Read This Week

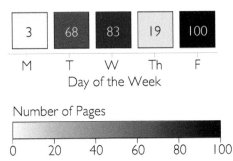

Image 7.4
*The darker
the green, the
more pages
Juanita read. The
gradient legend
tells us what
each color in
the visualization
means.*

Looking at the colors alone gives us a good idea if Juanita read a lot or a little. We know she read the most pages on Friday because the color is the darkest, and the fewest on Monday and Thursday where the colors are light. However, it's hard to tell the exact number of pages by looking at the colors alone. Only by looking at the numbers on each square can we say for certain that she read *exactly* 100 pages on Friday and *exactly* three pages on Monday.

The data set for this visualization looks like this (Table 7.1):

Table 7.1
*The number of
pages Juanita
read on each
day this week*

Number of Pages Juanita Read This Week	
Day of the Week	**Number of Pages**
Monday	3
Tuesday	68
Wednesday	83
Thursday	19
Friday	100

Two-color gradients

Gradients that blend between two colors can show low-to-high values in numerical data, too, as long as they still start at a light color and end at a darker one. It's also better if the mix between the two colors is a nice color itself—not gray or brown where most of the values in your data will probably be. The gradients in Image 7.5 do both of these things.

Image 7.5
*Gradients for
numerical data
can run from one
color to another.*

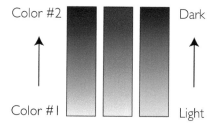

Two-color gradients like these are good for heat maps, as well. Image 7.6 is a heat map that shows the number of pages that Juanita and four other people read during the week. Now, the values for the categorical Person variable are shown in different positions on the y-axis. The ordinal Day of the Week variable is still visualized with position on the x-axis.

Number of Pages Juanita & Her Friends Read This Week

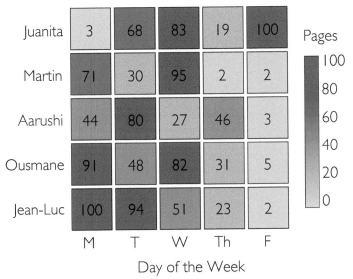

	M	T	W	Th	F
Juanita	3	68	83	19	100
Martin	71	30	95	2	2
Aarushi	44	80	27	46	3
Ousmane	91	48	82	31	5
Jean-Luc	100	94	51	23	2

Day of the Week

Pages
100
80
60
40
20
0

Image 7.6
The two-color gradient legend tells us how many pages each person read on each day. The darkest red means 100 pages, so Juanita and Jean-Luc both had a big reading day this week.

If we look at it quickly without reading the numbers, we can see the bright red square for Juanita's busy Friday where she read 100 pages. We can also see that Jean-Luc had a very productive Monday. The lighter yellow squares show us that most people read the fewest pages on Friday.

The data set now has three variables: Day of the Week, Number of pages, and a Person variable. Juanita's values are colored in to make them easier to find (Table 7.2).

Table 7.2
The number of pages that Juanita and four other friends read each day this week

Number of Pages Juanita and Her Friends Read This Week		
Person	Day of the Week	Number of Pages
Juanita	Monday	3
Martin	Monday	71
Aarushi	Monday	44
Ousmane	Monday	91
Jean-Luc	Monday	100
Juanita	Tuesday	68
Martin	Tuesday	30
Aarushi	Tuesday	80
Ousmane	Tuesday	48
Jean-Luc	Tuesday	94
Juanita	Wednesday	83
Martin	Wednesday	95
Aarushi	Wednesday	27
Ousmane	Wednesday	82
Jean-Luc	Wednesday	51
Juanita	Thursday	19
Martin	Thursday	2
Aarushi	Thursday	46
Ousmane	Thursday	31
Jean-Luc	Thursday	23
Juanita	Friday	100
Martin	Friday	2
Aarushi	Friday	3
Ousmane	Friday	5
Jean-Luc	Friday	2

Low-middle-high diverging gradients

Sometimes, numerical data may have values that go from low to high through an important middle point. For this kind of data, the values above the middle are different than the values below it—so they should look different from each other, too. You'll need a special kind of gradient to visualize these data: a **diverging** gradient with colors that go in opposite directions.

There are two ways to create diverging gradients for numerical data. One way is to use two low-to-high gradients and smush them together at the lower ends. The middle sometimes looks a little muddy, but if it's easy to tell each side apart then diverging gradients like these are just fine (Image 7.7).

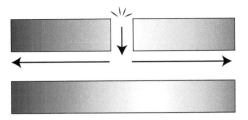

Another way to create a diverging color gradient is to stick two low-to-high gradients together with a special color in the middle, like white. Diverging gradients like these make it even clearer to see where the middle values are in the visualization, and don't have strange colors at the center where the two gradients overlap. It's easier to say, "The middle values are shown in white," than it is to say, "The middle values are shown in orangey-purplish-gray" (Image 7.8).

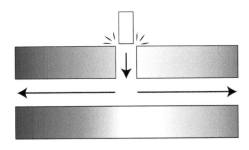

The heat map in Image 7.9 uses a red, white, and blue diverging gradient to show swimming pool temperatures at several different pools. The cold temperatures are different tints of blue and the warm temperatures are different tints of red. The ideal pool temperature—86°F—is white.

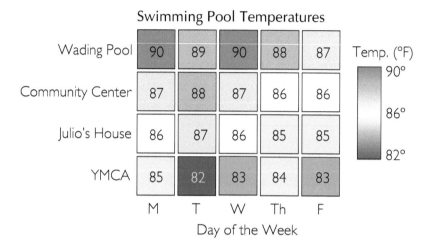

From the visualization we can see that the wading pool is often quite warm, whereas the pool at the YMCA is quite cool. The pool at the Community Center and Julio's house are often close to perfect.

The data from this visualization are similar to the data about the number of pages that the five people read. The Pool variable on the y-axis is categorical, the Day of the Week variable on the x-axis is ordinal, and the Temperature variable is numerical (Table 7.3).

Swimming Pool Temperatures		
Pool	Day of the Week	Temperature (°F)
Wading Pool	Monday	90
Community Center	Monday	87
Julio's House	Monday	86
YMCA	Monday	85
Wading Pool	Tuesday	89
Community Center	Tuesday	88
Julio's House	Tuesday	87
YMCA	Tuesday	82
Wading Pool	Wednesday	90
Community Center	Wednesday	87
Julio's House	Wednesday	86
YMCA	Wednesday	83
Wading Pool	Thursday	88
Community Center	Thursday	86
Julio's House	Thursday	85
YMCA	Thursday	84
Wading Pool	Friday	87
Community Center	Friday	86
Julio's House	Friday	85
YMCA	Friday	83

Table 7.3
Swimming pool temperatures for four pools this week

Multi-color and rainbow gradients

Instead of using light-to-dark or diverging gradients, you might have noticed that weather forecast maps often use rainbow gradients to show temperatures or the types and amounts of precipitation that are on the way. Weather maps like these sometimes look like Image 7.10.

Image 7.10
*Rainbow
gradients are
often used in
weather maps
like this one.
Unfortunately,
the yellow
regions that
stand out the
most have the
most boring
weather!*

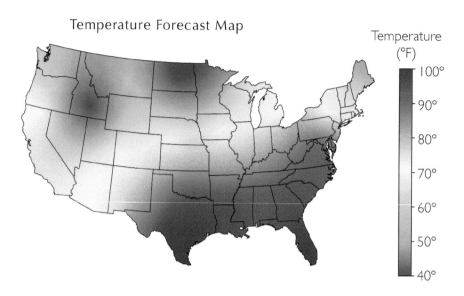

Usually, the reddish colors on one end of the gradient mean hotter or more severe weather, and the blueish colors on the other end mean cooler or wetter weather. Just like we're used to seeing stoplight colors for sequences, many people know how to understand maps with rainbow gradients because they've seen them on TV or in a weather app.

However, rainbow gradients and gradients with more than a few colors aren't the best choice for data visualizations. As we saw in the very first example about Juanita, it's hard enough to say exactly what a color means in gradients with only *two* colors. Rainbow gradients that have *many* colors make that even more challenging!

One of the biggest problems with rainbow gradients is that some colors stand out more than others. Yellow, for example, is very bright and can make values look important or extreme when they really aren't—especially when it's close to darker colors. Dark blue, on the other hand, is less flashy and can make values seem unimportant or uninteresting when they're anything but that.

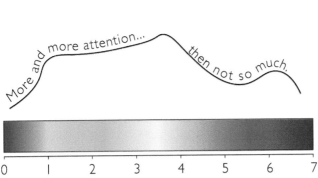

Image 7.11
Color gradients that blend across several colors can draw attention to some values and away from others.

Take a look at the rainbow gradient in Image 7.11. Do you see how the yellow and turquoise bits stand out from the rest? Imagine how distracting that could be in a visualization where values like 1 and 3½ weren't anything special. Looking back at the weather map, too, you might notice that the yellow areas pop out the most even though they have the mildest temperatures—the dark red should be stealing the show instead!

Fortunately, gradients with fewer colors—like the low-to-high gradients we saw before—aren't confusing in the same way. These gradients show changes in the data more evenly and accurately. The ends of each gradient are the most interesting, and the middle parts blend together without any funny business (Image 7.12).

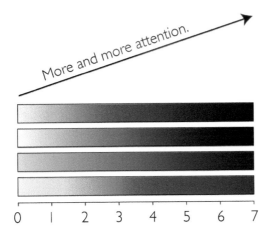

Image 7.12
Color gradients that blend from dark to light show changes in the data most accurately.

Diverging gradients made out of two low-to-high gradients are no different. They should feel smooth and even as the colors change from the outside to the middle. The little dip in the middle is exactly how it should be—you know it's there, but it isn't distracting or confusing (Image 7.13).

Image 7.13
*Diverging
gradients
made from
two low-to-high
gradients should
blend together
smoothly from
end to end, with
the darkest
colors on the
outside and the
lightest colors at
the middle.*

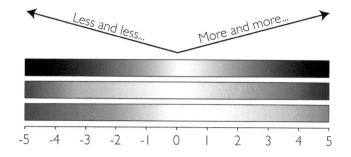

Replacing the rainbow colors on the weather map with a diverging gradient shows us just how big of a difference the colors in a visualization can make (Image 7.14).

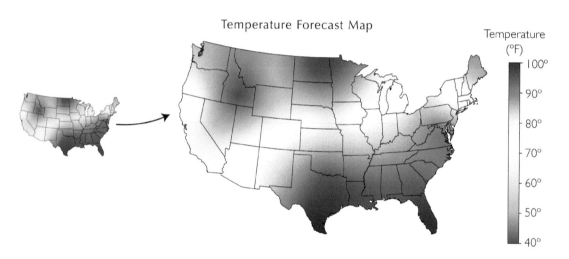

Image 7.14
*Using a light-to-
dark diverging
gradient instead
of the rainbow
gradient from
before makes
it easier to see
which regions
are cold, which
are hot, and
which have mild
weather.*

Before, the yellow parts of the map stood out the most, even though they had the mildest weather. The darker reds and blues were visible, but it wasn't clear if they meant the *most* or *least*. With a diverging gradient, on the other hand, it's still easy to tell who had balmy weather, but even more obvious where it was very cold or very hot.

Now that you've learned how to make categorical color palettes *and* gradients, you can hopefully see why it's so important to be smart about the way we use color for data visualization. Color is powerful, which means that it can change the way we understand a visualization for better or for worse. Knowing how to pick useful colors to visualize groups and numbers will always come in handy, and making them look good is something you'll get better at with practice.

Chapter summary

Numerical data can be shown using gradients, or sets of colors that blend smoothly from one to the next. If you can label the values in your visualization, too, so that people looking at your visualization will know exactly what each color means. Some data will need a gradient that blends between a light and dark color to show low-to-high data. Data that have a middle point will need a gradient that blends between three colors, stopping half-way at the middle color—usually white. Multi-color gradients are often used in maps but can be confusing to read.

It's your turn!

Several different gradient legends are given provided below. First, identify the type of gradient: low-to-high, low-middle-high, or multi-color. Then, complete the legends with numbers that would make sense for the topic and the gradient.

1. Take a look at this gradient:

Car Speed vs the Speed Limit

   a. What is this type of gradient?
   b. Add numbers to this legend that make sense for the topic and the type of gradient, or list them out in order.

2. Take a look at this gradient:

Seconds in the Microwave

   a. What is this type of gradient?
   b. Add numbers to this legend that make sense for the topic and the type of gradient, or list them out in order.

3. Take a look at this gradient:

Forecasted Feet of Snow

a. What is this type of gradient?
b. Add numbers to this legend that make sense for the topic and the type of gradient, or list them out in order.
c. Do you think this is the best gradient to show different amounts of snow? Why or why not?
d. What kind of gradient might show these data better?

8 Color for ordinal data

Earlier in this book we learned that ordinal data are similar to both numerical and categorical data. On the one hand, ordinal data can be sorted into an order. Setting a fan to low will be less breezy than setting it to medium or high, and J comes before K in the alphabet. On the other hand, the values in ordinal data are totally separate groups that don't have in-between amounts like *low-and-two-thirds* or *most of the way* from J to K.

Visualizing ordinal data with color is no different—the colors must show an order *and* be separate from each other. In this chapter, we'll combine what we know about gradients and color palettes to learn how color can show ordinal data.

Stoplight colors: the original ordinal palette 114
Low-to-high ordinal palettes 114
Accidental ordinal colors can cause confusion 119
Low-middle-high diverging palettes 120
Introducing small multiples 123
Multi-color and rainbow ordinal palettes 124

DOI: 10.1201/9781003309376-9

Chapter summary *128*

It's your turn!. *128*

Stoplight colors: the original ordinal palette

Before we go any further, think for a minute about a data visualization that you see all the time—a stoplight. Stoplights use an ordinal color palette to show different speeds. Green means moving, yellow means slowing down, and red means stopped. We know that this is an ordinal color palette because there aren't any in-between colors that mean *slow to a crawl* or *speed up most of the way*, and the three colors are always in the same order. Since most people know what they mean, stoplight colors are often used for other data, like to show that something is good, okay, or bad (Image 8.1).

Image 8.1
Stoplight colors are handy for ordinal colors because we're used to seeing them in a certain order. Red, yellow, and green often appear in the same order.

However, stoplight colors aren't the only way to show values that fall in a certain order. As with categorical palettes and gradients, though, there are a few things to keep in mind when you're making an ordinal color palette of your own. Let's look at some examples.

Low-to-high ordinal palettes

You might remember the colors in Image 6.2 from Chapter 6 about categorical color palettes. Each stack of colors would be good for showing categorical data because the colors are easy to tell apart and they *don't* look like they're in a certain order.

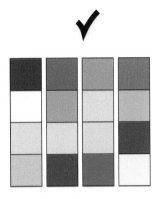

Clear Categories

Low-to-high gradients are quite the opposite. They show an order through and through. Gradients like the ones in Image 8.3 are good at showing numerical data because they blend smoothly from a light color to a dark color—just like how numbers run from low to high without any jumps or gaps.

Low-to-high gradients

Image 8.3
Low-to-high gradients blend smoothly from a light color to a dark color to show numerical data that is continuous.

The colors in an ordinal palette do a little of each. They should be different enough to easily tell apart, but step from one color to the next in a clear order. There are two ways to make palettes like these.

Light-to-dark and bright-to-dark palettes
One way to choose low-to-high ordinal colors is to start with a very light or dark color and make it darker and darker or lighter and lighter. For example, you could pick very light green, light green, medium green, and dark green—or different shades of blue, pink, or gray (Image 8.4).

Color for ordinal data

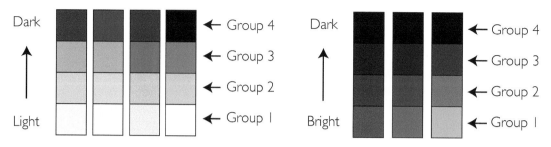

Image 8.4
Ordinal colors step from light to dark or bright to dark just like low-to-high gradients.

Just like the light-to-dark and bright-to-dark gradients we made in the last chapter, notice that the colors above step neatly from one color to the next without taking any big jumps. Compare them to the colors in Image 8.5 that step between darker and darker blues, suddenly jump to lighter red, get darker again, and then pop back to blue. A palette like this would be terribly confusing for visualizing the order in ordinal data.

Image 8.5
Ordinal palettes don't jump from dark to light or from one color to the next.

The visualization in Image 8.6 is a combination of a table and a heat map that uses an ordinal color palette made from different shades of pink. Instead of using colors from a gradient to show different numbers, this heat map uses colors from an ordinal color palette to show Beginner, Intermediate, and Advanced levels.

Image 8.6
The captains of each team attending the local chess competition. The ordinal colors in the last column make it easy to pick out the level of each team.

Chess Competition Captains		
Team Name	Leader	Level
Dancing Queens	Gabrielle	Advanced
Check Yo Self	Wei	Intermediate
The Squares	Ousamane	Beginner
Left Jab, Right Rook	Quiana	Beginner
Dark Knights	Juanita	Intermediate

Each row of the table lists the Team Name, Leader, and Level for an upcoming chess competition. The Level column is filled in to make a heat map—the more advanced the team, the darker the color. If you were interested in joining the competition, the heatmap would make it easy to find the level you're looking for.

Two-color ordinal palettes

Using a single color that steps from light to dark, or bright to dark, is great for showing ordinal data, but it's not the only way. Like with gradients, you can create ordinal color palettes that step between two colors, too. Also like with gradients, you should still pick a lighter color for on one end and a darker color for the other (Image 8.7).

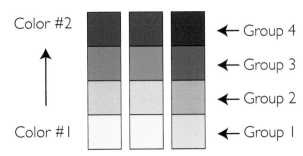

Color #2 ← Group 4 / Group 3 / Group 2 / Color #1 ← Group 1

Image 8.7
Ordinal colors can step from one color to another as long as they also step from light to dark.

Palettes like the ones above are pretty and fun to use, but it can be tricky to pick colors that look good *and* show an order. To make palettes like these, it's easiest to start with the first and last color. Once you know where the palette starts and ends, you can choose middle colors that fit between them.

It helps to pick starting and ending colors that are already close together in the rainbow, like pink and purple, or green and blue. Choosing colors that are too far apart—like red and green, or purple and yellow—can leave you with muddy colors in the middle or step through too many different colors on the way from one end to the other (Image 8.8).

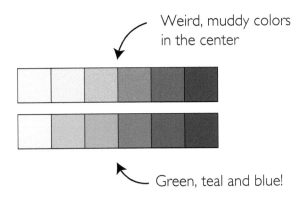

Weird, muddy colors in the center

Green, teal and blue!

Image 8.8
To pick ordinal colors, start with the first and last colors, and then pick a few colors that fall between. Try to use colors that are close together, though, so that the middle colors aren't murky or different colors entirely.

How do these two-color ordinal palettes look on a real data visualization? Let's see for ourselves by adding ordinal colors to the graph about the long jump competition in Veronica's back yard. In the original version from the chapter about categorical colors, we used a special color to highlight Veronica's jump in particular (Image 8.9).

Image 8.9
This version of the visualization uses yellow to highlight Veronica's long jump compared to everyone else.

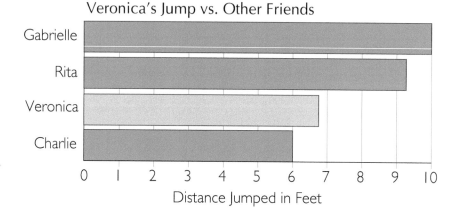

If we were more interested in the overall placings, though, we could use ordinal colors instead to color each bar with the placing of each athlete. This would let us see how far each person jumped *and* how they placed. As usual, the legend in the visualization tells the meaning of each color (Image 8.10).

Image 8.10
Ordinal colors help us know how each person placed in the competition.

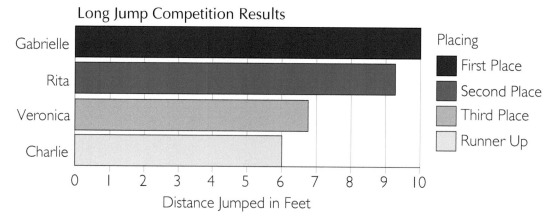

The placing of each person is now a variable in the data set, and we know it's ordinal because first, second, third, and runner up fall in an order (Table 8.1).

Veronica's Long Jump vs Other Friends		
Person	**Distance (feet)**	**Placing**
Gabrielle	10	First
Rita	9¼	Second
Veronica	6¾	Third
Charlie	6	Runner up

Table 8.1
The Placing variable is ordinal because the values can be sorted into a specific order, but the distance between each placing could change

Accidental ordinal colors can cause confusion

The long jump example we just made gives us a good chance to see why it's so important for ordinal colors to step from one end of the palette to the other in a way that *looks* like an order, and why they should only be used for values that actually have an order. Confusing things happen when the values in your data don't line up with the order of the colors.

Take the example in Image 8.11. In this version of the long jump visualization, the ordinal colors from above are scrambled up into a different order. First Place is still dark purple, but now Second Place is shown in the lightest shade of blue. The colors in this order are basically just categorical colors, and only make the bar chart more complicated, not more useful.

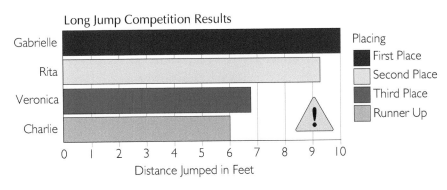

Image 8.11
Caution! If the colors in a palette look like they go in a certain order, make sure that order goes along with the data.

Even worse, rearranging the bars to match the out-of-order colors could cause someone to think that Veronica came in second place and that Rita was the runner up. Even though the bars are the correct length and the legend isn't *technically* wrong, the ordinal colors give the wrong message (Image 8.12).

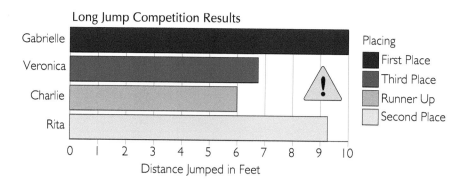

Image 8.12
*Oh, no! Using
ordinal colors
to show data
out of order can
give someone
the wrong idea
about what a
visualization
means.*

So, what's the moral of the story? Make sure that the ordinal colors you choose stay in order, and that they go along with the order of the values you are visualizing. And, don't use ordinal colors for categorical data—someone might think that those categories are ordinal when they aren't at all.

Low-middle-high diverging palettes

So far, the ordinal color palettes we've created have gone from low to high. Sometimes though, it makes sense to use ordinal colors that go in opposite directions. If the data you have collected have both good, medium, and bad qualities or if it's important to see which values are above or below a special point, a diverging color palette will fit the bill. Just like with diverging gradients, there are two ways to create diverging color palettes for ordinal data.

Image 8.13
*A diverging
ordinal color
palette is made
out of two
ordinal palettes
stuck together.*

The first way is to stick two low-to-high ordinal palettes together at the ends. This works well when your data go in opposite directions and the middle values are the least interesting (Image 8.13).

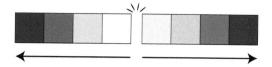

Some data, however, *do* have interesting middle values or a middle point that doesn't fall on either side. For data like these you'll need a diverging palette to show everything accurately. The second way to create a diverging color palette, then, is to stick two low-to-high ordinal color palettes together with a special color in the middle. Usually, the middle color is white (Image 8.14).

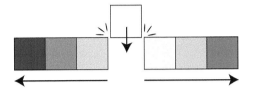

Image 8.14
Some diverging color palettes have a middle color to show when the data aren't strongly in either direction.

Let's see how big of a difference a diverging ordinal palette can make. Imagine that you are a part of the production team for the community Theatre club. It's finally show time, and you're curious about how well the audience liked the play. On the way out the door you ask the people leaving the theater what they thought. They could say that they found the show to be Awful, Poor, Fair, Fine, Good, or Great. You tally the number of people who gave each rating in this Table 8.2:

What did you think of the play?		
Show Time	**Rating**	**Count**
Saturday evening	Awful	3
Saturday evening	Poor	4
Saturday evening	Fair	2
Saturday evening	Fine	10
Saturday evening	Good	10
Saturday evening	Great	5
Sunday afternoon	Awful	2
Sunday afternoon	Poor	2
Sunday afternoon	Fair	10
Sunday afternoon	Fine	10
Sunday afternoon	Good	5
Sunday afternoon	Great	5
Sunday evening	Awful	4
Sunday evening	Poor	4
Sunday evening	Fair	1
Sunday evening	Fine	5
Sunday evening	Good	10
Sunday evening	Great	10

Table 8.2
How did everyone like the play? This table shows the number of people who thought the play was awful, poor, fair, fine, good, or great after three different shows.ç

The table has three variables: Show Time which is ordinal, Rating which is also ordinal, and Count which is numerical. A stacked bar chart like the one in Image 8.15 can show all three.

Image 8.15
*The data
collected
about the play,
visualized with
a low-to-high
ordinal color
palette.*

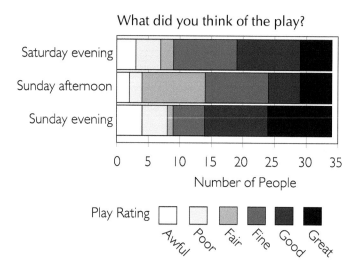

Each bar in the visualization shows a different performance, and the length of each bar shows the number of people who attended that show—which was 34 people each night. Each stack in the bars shows the number of people who gave a certain rating. The stacks are colored in using an ordinal color palette where white is the Awful rating and dark blue is Great.

The results are in, and this visualization is off to a great start. The ordinal colors make it easy to tell each category apart, and it's clear that the categories are in order. There is a problem though, or at least something that we could improve: the colors make it hard to see how many people liked the play at all—even a little bit— compared to the people who didn't like it very much. Whether or not someone loved it or really disliked it, the colors are still blue.

A diverging ordinal palette will fix this. By swapping the blue low-to-high ordinal palette for a red and green diverging palette, it becomes much easier to see how people felt overall.

The color shows if they liked it—green if they did, red if they didn't. The darkness of each color shows and how strongly they felt. The lightest colors show that someone thought it was Fair or Fine, but the darkest colors show the people who felt that it was either Great or Awful. There was no option to say, "I'm not sure if I liked it or not" or "I have no opinion", so we don't need to have white in the middle (Image 8.16).

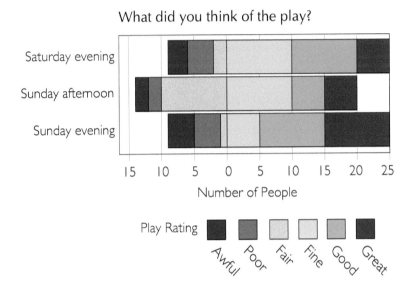

Image 8.16
The data collected about the play, visualized with a diverging ordinal color palette.

Scooting the bars around so that the good and bad ratings are on different sides of the chart helps even more. Now we can see *how* many people liked the play or not, and notice that Sunday afternoon was the least popular showing. The same number of people enjoyed it on Saturday afternoon and Sunday evening, though more people thought it was Great on Sunday evening. Funnily enough, the most people thought it was Awful on Sunday evening, too. What a picky crowd!

Introducing small multiples

We could use the same diverging ordinal color palette to make separate bar charts for each day, too, like in the visualization in Image 8.17.

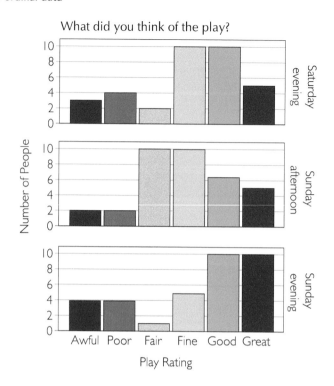

Facets, or small multiples, break a single visualization into several smaller visualizations. Here, each bar from the graph in Image 8.16 was made into its own facet.

These mini-graphs are called **facets** or **small multiples**. They let us make several versions of the same graph for each value of a categorical or ordinal variable. In this case, that means three bar charts showing the number of people who felt a certain way about the play—one facet for each showing. Visualized this way, it's easier to see how people felt about each show, and we can still compare the numbers of people who liked or disliked the play.

Multi-color and rainbow ordinal palettes

You've probably seen this coming, but there is one more type of ordinal color palette left to learn about: rainbow and multi-color palettes. It will be no surprise that palettes like these are popular but, like their rainbow gradient cousins are sometimes confusing to use.

One of the most common places to come across a rainbow ordinal color palette is on maps that show elevation. The **contour map** in Image 8.18 uses a rainbow ordinal color palette to show the elevation at different parts of a small park. Contour maps use stacks of curvy shapes to show the height and terrain of hills and mountains. Often, contour maps use ordinal colors to make each layer of the landscape appear higher or lower.

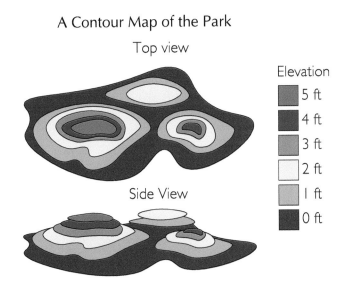

A Contour Map of the Park

Top view

Side View

Elevation

5 ft
4 ft
3 ft
2 ft
1 ft
0 ft

Image 8.18
Contour maps use ordinal colors to show how high or low the land is.

In this contour map, the lowest parts of the park are around the edges—they're dark green. The highest hill on the park is five feet above that, shown in dark blue. Two smaller hills—or bumps, really—get up to a whopping four feet and two feet high, shown in purple and yellow.

This might look fine, but there's a problem. When many colors are together in one palette, the brightest colors call more attention to themselves compared to the darker colors. Even if they don't represent the lowest or the highest values in the data, the flashier colors will get more attention—like the yellow level in the contour map.

As the diagram in Image 8.19 shows, some colors in the rainbow stand out more than others even if they aren't more important. Do you notice your eyes being drawn to the yellow 4 in the middle and the turquoise 2 near the beginning? Did you even notice the orange at 5?

Image 8.19
Color palettes that step across several colors can draw attention to some values and away from others.

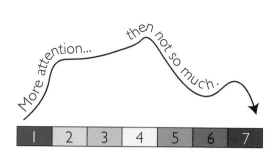

The low-to-high palettes from earlier in this chapter only use one or two colors so they don't have this issue. Each color gets in the palette more attention than the last because each color is brighter or flashier than the one before it. The lightest and darkest colors are the most noticeable—which they should be, because they're probably the most interesting values in your data (Image 8.20).

Image 8.20
Palettes that step smoothly from dark to light (or light to dark) show changes in data smoothly, too.

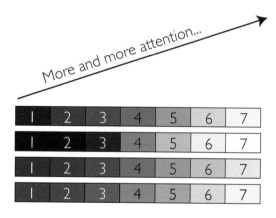

Diverging palettes made out of low-to-high ordinal color palettes also call the right amount of attention to the most interesting parts of the data. The ends of these palettes are the darkest and most colorful where the data are very low or very high. The light middle stands out from the darker colors and shows us where the values change direction (Image 8.21).

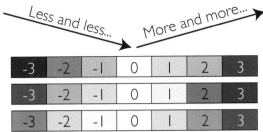

Image 8.21
Diverging color palettes made from two low-to-high palettes draw the most attention where the data are the most interesting—at the ends and the very middle.

Replacing the rainbow colors in the contour map above with a low-to-high ordinal color palette, then, makes more sense for the data. The visualization in Image 8.22 still pretty and colorful, but now it's easier to understand where the hills were the highest and lowest. The middle colors aren't confusing because they aren't flashier than colors at the beginning or end of the palette.

A Contour Map of the Park

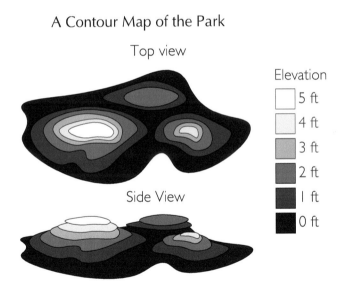

Image 8.22
This version of the contour map is easier to understand because it uses an ordinal palette that steps from dark to light.

There's no doubt about it, getting good at using color in visualizations might take some time—and that's okay! Think of the last three chapters as a solid first step toward becoming a color expert. Now that you know the kinds of color palettes that each data type needs, you can experiment with your own choices until you feel more confident. There's usually more than one way to do something, and making color palettes is no different. Use colors that you like, make sure they fit your data, and switch things up if something doesn't seem right. You'll be coloring like a pro in no time!

Chapter summary

Ordinal color palettes show how different groups are ordered or sorted. Stoplight colors are a familiar ordinal color palette that shows *Stop*, *Slow* down, and *Go* with red, yellow, and green. Ordinal data can be visualized with low-to-high color palettes that step from light-to-dark or bright-to-dark colors, or even by gradually changing from one color to another. Two ordinal color palettes can be stuck together to make a diverging color palette for ordinal data that go in opposite directions. Rainbow ordinal color palettes are common in maps, but it's often better to use a low-to-high or diverging ordinal color palette so that the colors are not confusing.

It's your turn!

You'll need colored pencils, markers, or crayons to do these activities.

Note: If you have a hard time seeing some colors or you know that you are colorblind, please let your teacher or a friend know so that they can help you!

1. Create a low-to-high ordinal color palette with light-to-dark or bright-to-dark colors. Then, use the data set to color in the visualization with your colors.

	Online Star Ratings of Local Restaurants		
Star Rating	Shirley's Diner	Plant Goddess	Sweet Cheeze Pizza and Pie
1	1	0	3
2	3	1	2
3	6	8	5
4	12	23	1
5	20	24	23

a. What color did you pick to go from light to dark or bright to dark?
b. Use the data set to color in the visualization with your colors. Make sure the bars you fill in are the correct height.

c. Which restaurant is the most popular? What makes you think that?

2. Pick seven colors to make a diverging ordinal color palette: three colors to go in one direction, three to the other, and a middle color that joins the two sides together.

   a. Use your palette to fill in the empty visualization below. The middle color in your palette should be at B+.

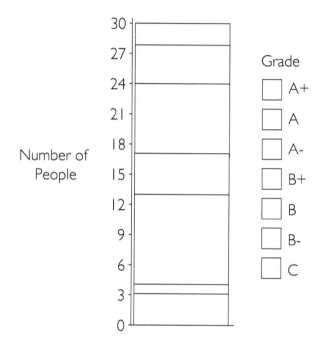

Grades on Last Week's Math Test

   b. Looking at the grades, do you think the Math test was hard? Why or why not?
   c. How are the colors for A+ and C similar to each other?
   d. How are the colors for A− and B similar to each other?

3. Fill in the middle colors of the palettes below to make ordinal color palettes. If you don't have the exact colored pencil or crayon colors that you need, try mixing a few colors together or lightly shading one color on top of another.

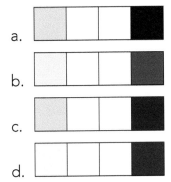

a.

b.

c.

d.

9   Shapes and patterns

In the past three chapters, we learned how to use color to visualize categorical, numerical, and ordinal data with different types of color palettes and gradients. That's all great to know, but what if you only have one pencil or pen on hand? A beautiful color palette won't shine, either, if you have to print or copy a visualization in black and white.

For the times when you can't use different colors, you'll need to show your data in another way. In this chapter, we'll learn how to use shapes and patterns instead of colors to tell things apart. We'll learn how to use shapes and patterns on their own, as well as how they can also be used *with* colors in the same visualization.

Shapes for categories. 134
Using shapes and colors together. 136
Using shapes and colors separately 137
Solid and dotted lines. 138

DOI: 10.1201/9781003309376-10

Filling areas with patterns and textures 142

Chapter summary 144

It's your turn! 144

Shapes for categories

Let's look back at the visualization about Lorenzo and Wei's lemonade stands. Originally, we used color to tell Lorenzo and Wei's sales apart—Lorenzo's points were yellow and Wei's points were blue. If we photocopied the visualization in black and white, though, it would be almost impossible to tell one person from the other (Image 9.1).

Image 9.1 Lorenzo and Wei's lemonade sales were shown in yellow and blue lemons in the original version. The same visualization in black and white makes it harder to see which points belong to whom.

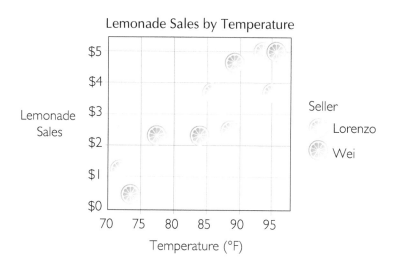

One way we could fix this is by making Wei's points a much darker shade of blue so that they appear darker than Lorenzo's when the visualization is printed. If we were drawing the graph with single pen or pencil, though, we'd need to try something else entirely. Making each person's points a different shape would do the trick.

In the next version of the graph, Lorenzo's points are shown as circles and Wei's points are shown as triangles. Just like in the blue and yellow visualization, the legend tells us who is who (Image 9.2).

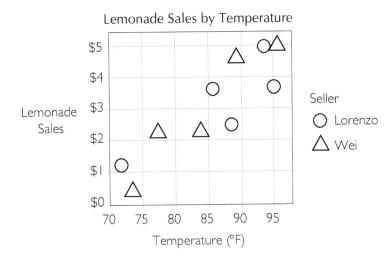

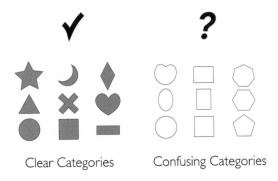

Image 9.2
Instead of using colors, different shapes can show Lorenzo and Wei's lemonade sales.

Printing this version in black and white or drawing it with a single pen or pencil would be no problem, and we can still tell Lorenzo and Wei's data apart. Circles and triangles are just a few of the shapes you could use to show category data, though, so how did we know that these were good shapes to use?

When we learned about using colors to show categorical data, we learned how important it is to pick categorical colors that look very different from each other. In many ways, picking shapes to show categorical data is the same. For example, take a look at the two sets of shapes in Image 9.3.

Image 9.3
It's important to choose shapes that look very different so that they aren't confused with each other.

The three sets of dark gray shapes on the left are all examples of shapes that look quite different from each other. The star, triangle, and circle would be hard to mix up, as would the moon, X, and square. There'd be no confusion about the diamond, heart, and rectangle, either. Any of these sets of shapes would be a good choice for showing different categories.

The shapes on the right, however, look more like each other. The shapes in the first column all look like circles and might be confused with each other. The different heights and widths of rectangles would be a disaster to tell apart on a scatterplot! The last set of shapes are almost the same except for the different number of sides. *None* of these sets of shapes would work very well in a scatterplot like the one we made above.

Using shapes and colors together

Of course, you can also use shapes and colors together, and you might do this for a few reasons. Firstly, the shapes might have a meaning on their own that you want to make even clearer with color—like red hearts, green check marks, or yellow lemons. Secondly, you might prefer to use color by itself but want to print your visualization in black and white. Using colorful shapes would make the best of both.

Colorful shapes in our lemonade example might look something like this (Image 9.4):

Image 9.4
Using different shapes and different colors makes it easy to tell Lorenzo and Wei's points apart, even if the page is printed in black and white. Lorenzo is always yellow or a circle, and Wei is always blue or a triangle.

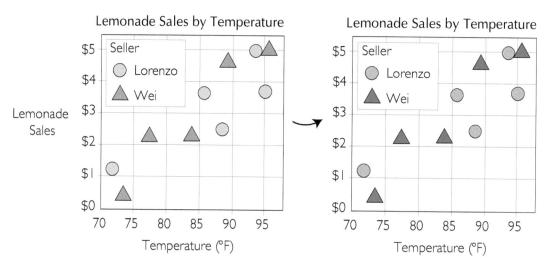

In the version on the left we can tell the difference between Lorenzo and Wei using the shape *or* the color. There's no chance of confusion since Lorenzo's points are yellow circles and Wei's points are blue triangles. The version on the right shows what it would like if we printed in black and white. Since the shapes don't change, the visualization is still easy to read.

Using shapes and colors separately

In the last visualization each color went with a specific shape— Wei's points were always blue *and* a triangle, and there were never any blue circles. However, you may find yourself with so many different variables that you'd like to use color and shape to show separate things altogether.

Imagine, for example, that on some of the days that Lorenzo and Wei were selling lemonade, they also offered iced tea. Their tea sales looked like this (Table 9.1):

Profits from Lemonade and Iced Tea Sales by Temperature and Person				
Person	Drink	Day	Profit	Temperature (°F)
Lorenzo	Lemonade	1	$3.75	86
Lorenzo	Lemonade	2	$5.00	93
Lorenzo	Lemonade	3	$3.75	95
Lorenzo	Tea	3	$1.75	95
Lorenzo	Lemonade	4	$1.25	78
Lorenzo	Lemonade	5	$2.50	88
Lorenzo	Tea	5	$1.50	88
Wei	Lemonade	1	$0.50	73
Wei	Lemonade	2	$2.25	77
Wei	Tea	2	$0.50	77
Wei	Lemonade	3	$2.25	84
Wei	Lemonade	4	$4.75	89
Wei	Tea	4	$3.50	89
Wei	lemonade	5	$5.00	96

Table 9.1
On some days, Lorenzo and Wei also sold iced tea

To make sure that the lemonade and iced tea points look different on the visualization, we could use different shapes for each drink. Lorenzo's points are still yellow and Wei's points are still blue—a bit darker than last time so that it will appear darker than the yellow if the visualization is printed in black and white (Image 9.5).

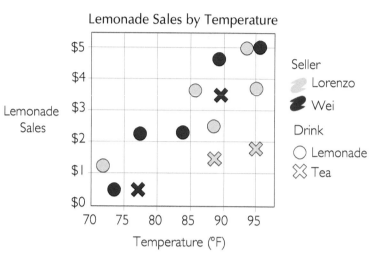

Image 9.5
Using different shapes and colors can help us show two variables on the scatterplot. Here, yellow shapes are for Lorenzo, and blue shapes are for Wei. Circles mean lemonade, and x's mean tea.

Now we can use color to tell Lorenzo from Wei, and shape to see the difference between the two drinks. It looks like Lorenzo sold the most iced tea on hot days, whereas Wei sold a little on a cooler day and quite a bit on a warm day.

Solid and dotted lines

Similar to using different shapes on scatterplots, different line patterns come in handy for making line charts that you might normally draw in different colors. Instead of using only solid lines, we can make some of the lines in a visualization dashed or dotted. This lets us tell the lines apart even if they're in black and white or drawn in the same color (Image 9.6).

Image 9.6
Just like with colors and shapes, picking dashed lines that look different from each other can make them easier to tell apart on a visualization.

It's important to make sure that you use lines that look different from each other if your visualization has more than one type of dotted or dashed line. In the example above, the black lines on the left are easy to tell apart—the long dashes are very different from the short dots or the solid line. The lines on the right, however, are trickier to tell apart because the dashes and the spaces are roughly the same lengths.

Let's look at an example where dashed and dotted lines make sense. When we learned about using colors for numeric data, we made a blue and red heat map about the water temperatures at different pools in the neighborhood. The original version had a blue and red diverging gradient to show which pools were cooler or warmer than ideal. That worked great when the visualization was in color, but if we had to print it in black and white then it would be much harder to read (Image 9.7).

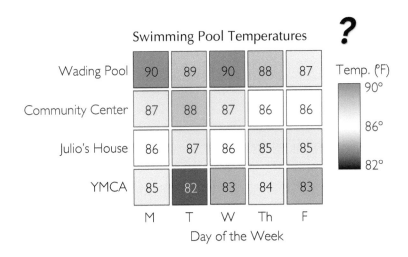

Image 9.7
Diverging gradients printed in black and white are harder—or impossible—to read. A different type of visualization would be better for showing these data in black and white.

A different type of visualization that lets us use shapes or line patterns would work better. The visualization in Image 9.8 shows the same data in a line chart instead. The x-axis still shows the Day of the Week variable, but the y-axis is now Temperature instead of Pool. Since Pool is a categorical variable, we can show each one with a different type of line.

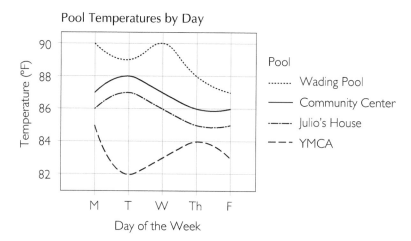

This visualization gives us a new way to see how the pool temperatures went up and down during the week. You might notice that most of the pools were warmer earlier in the week than later in the week, and that the YMCA was always the coldest. The wading pool was the warmest every day—probably because the shallow pool heats up more quickly in the sun.

We could make same visualization more colorful, too. The version in Image 9.9 is a little more fun but would still be fine to print out on paper or draw with a pencil.

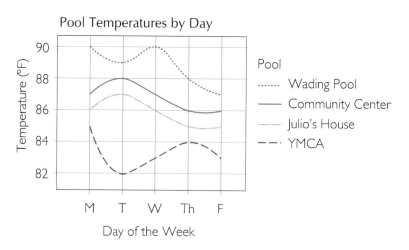

Image 9.9
*The dashed and
dotted lines on
this version of
the parallel line
chart are also in
different colors.*

Finally, we could use solid lines and shapes together to show each data point more clearly. In Image 9.10, each pool is shown in a different shape. It's easy to tell each category apart, and printing or drawing the visualization in one color would work just fine.

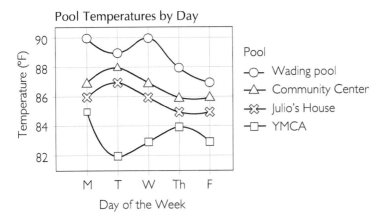

Pool
- ─O─ Wading pool
- ─△─ Community Center
- ─✖─ Julio's House
- ─□─ YMCA

Image 9.10
This version of the pool data visualization uses dotted and dashed lines as well as shapes for each data point.

Using the same shapes in several visualizations about the same data set can make it easier to understand a bigger story, too. Imagine, for example, that we had data set like the one in Table 9.2 that tells us how many adults and kids went to each pool during one week.

Number of Kid and Adult Swimmers This Week		
Pool	Kids	Adults
Wading Pool	120	30
Community Center	200	150
Julio's House	6	1
YMCA	40	300

Table 9.2
The total number of kid and adult swimmers at four pools for one week

Visualizing these data by themselves would tell us about the popularity of each pool for different ages of people (Image 9.11). Looking at the scatterplot below alongside the multiple line plot would tell us even more.

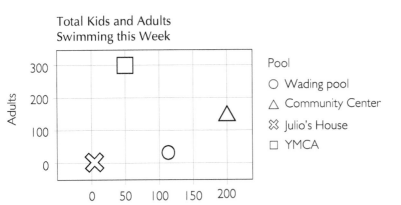

Pool
- O Wading pool
- △ Community Center
- ✖ Julio's House
- □ YMCA

Image 9.11
Using the same shapes in different visualizations makes it easier see different data about the same person or thing. The shapes in this visualization have the same meaning as they did in Image 9.10.

141

We already expect from the graph above that the wading pool will be shown as a circle and the pool at Julio's House will be marked as an X, so there's nothing new to figure out in this scatterplot. Looking back and forth between the two visualizations is much easier, too. We can see that the warm wading pool had many more kids than adults, and that Mostly adults swam in the chilly YMCA pool. Julio's pool had the fewest people swimming over all.

Filling areas with patterns and textures

Last but not least, we can use patterns and textures to fill in shapes or areas. Like with shapes and dashed lines, you can use different patterns instead of using different colors, or in addition to them. As usual, it's important that the patterns you pick look different from each other if they are meant to show different categories in categorical data, or similar to each other if they are showing groups that are related.

The visualization about Martin and Rosie's in-game supply purchases used color to do both of these things. The original version used different shades of blue to show gear purchases and shades of pink for food purchases. Each category was separate, but we could still tell the food or gear purchases apart. We could make the same visualization using only patterns, too (Image 9.12).

Image 9.12
If you need to print a visualization in black and white, or if you only have a pencil, you can fill in the bars in a bar chart with patterns instead of color.

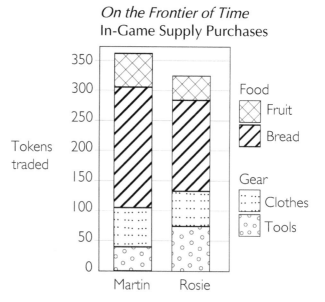

142

In the version above, food purchases are shown with patterns that use diagonal lines and gear purchases are shown with patterns that use dots. Each layer looks different from the others, but we can still pick out food from gear by looking at the type of pattern.

As with the scatterplots and line graphs we saw earlier in this chapter, we could use the original colors and our new patterns together, too. The version in Image 9.13 is colorful and fun, but would also print nicely in black and white.

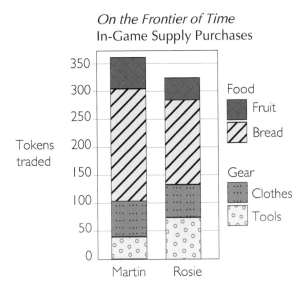

On the Frontier of Time
In-Game Supply Purchases

Image 9.13
Using colors and patterns makes it possible to understand this visualization if it's in color or in black and white.

Shapes and patterns—like every other way of visualizing that we've learned so far—are tools in your box that you can use when the time is right. They can give hints about what the visualization is about, make a visualization easier to photocopy or print, and can help you out in a pinch if you need to draw a visualization without any colors on hand. As you practice making different kinds of visualizations for different people, you may discover that you like using shapes for some things and not others. The important thing is that you keep trying new styles and ways of showing data, and that you're always on the lookout for what makes your visualization easier to understand *and* fun to see.

Chapter summary

Shapes, patterns, and textures can replace categorical colors to show different categories in visualizations. They can be used alone or with colors. It's useful to use shapes and patterns instead of colors so that you can print a visualization in black and white, or so that you can draw a visualization using only one pen or pencil.

It's your turn!

1. Using the data set below, draw a line chart with points to show how many flowers each plant makes over time. You can use color if you'd like, or make the visualization in black and white.

Flowers on Quiana and Ahmad's Rose Bushes		
Person	**Week**	**Roses**
Quiana	Week 1	0
Quiana	Week 2	1
Quiana	Week 3	1
Quiana	Week 4	2
Quiana	Week 5	3
Ahmad	Week 1	1
Ahmad	Week 2	3
Ahmad	Week 3	4
Ahmad	Week 4	3
Ahmad	Week 5	2

Be sure to:

a. Use different shapes for Quiana and Ahmad.
b. Use different types of dotted lines for Quiana and Ahmad.

c. Fill in the legend showing which shape and line belong to each person.

d. Write a title for the graph.

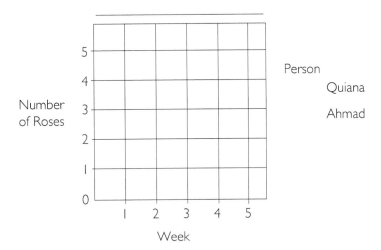

2. Fill in the stacked bar chart below with different patterns for each group in the data. Hint: The order of the stacks in the bars matches the order of the legend from top to bottom.
    Make sure to:

a. Make similar groups appear similar to each other.

b. Fill in the legend showing which pattern goes with each group.

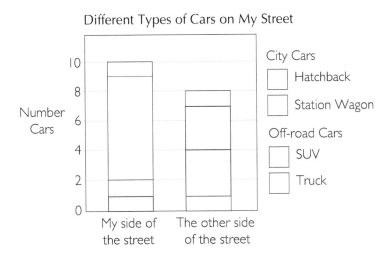

10 Making colorblind-friendly visualizations

The last chapter was all about what to do if you couldn't use colors in a visualization because you didn't have a way to show them—like only having a pencil or a black and white printer. So what if you *can* show colors, but you or someone else can't *see* them? Not everyone sees colors in the same way, and some people *can* see fewer colors than most. Colors that might look very different to you can appear to be very similar to someone else.

Having trouble telling colors apart is called **color blindness**, and around one in every twelve people are color blind. That means that you likely know several people who are color blind in some way—or that you are colorblind yourself!

It's important to know how other people see colors so that we can make visualizations that are useful to the most people.

DOI: 10.1201/9781003309376-11

In this chapter we'll learn about what it means to see in color and why some people see colors differently. This will help us in picking colors that everyone can tell apart.

How we see color at all. 148
Why colorblindness happens. 150
Different types of colorblindness. 151
How to be colorblind-friendly. 155
Colorblind-friendliness helps everyone 159
Chapter summary 160
It's your turn!. 161

How we see color at all

You've probably learned in science class that our bodies are made up of tiny structures called **cells** that act as the building blocks of all living things. The different parts of our body are made up of different types of cells, like muscle cells, skin cells, and bone cells. Our eyes alone are made up of several kinds of cells, including a few special ones that allow us to see light and color. These are called **rod cells** and **cone cells**.

Rod cells are best at seeing in dim lighting—these are the cells that help us out in dark environments. If you've ever tip-toed to the kitchen at night for a glass of water, your rod cells were hard at work! While they are great at seeing in low light, however, they do not help us to see color (Image 10.1).

Image 10.1
The rod cells in our eyes that help us see in dim lighting. There is only one kind of rod cell.

Rod cells detect dim light but do not help us to see color.

Cone cells, on the other hand, are great at seeing color—or rather, different colors of light. We have three types of cone cells in our eyes, each with their own specialty. One type detects the amount of blueish light coming from an object, another detects the amount of greenish light, and the third type detects the amount of reddish light (Image 10.2).

Cone cells detect color but work the best in bright conditions.

Interestingly, the colors that we see are not made from single colors of light, but combinations of different colors. The cone cells in our eyes add up the amounts of each different color that they see and send those tallies to our brains. Our brains then use that information to figure out what the final color will look like to us.

Some objects—like computer screens, lightbulbs, and phones—give off light on their own. Other objects—like people, plants, and paints—are only visible because there is light coming from somewhere else and bouncing off of them.

The diagram in Image 10.3 shows how someone who is *not* colorblind—like Wei—sees color. If Wei is standing in a room with a light on, the light coming from the light bulb will look white. Really though, the white light is a mix of every color. Depending on what the light hits, only some of the colors of light will bounce back into the room. Some of what bounces off a t-shirt, for example, will make it to Wei's eyes. Wei's cone cells will catch the colors that they're best at detecting and add up how much light they catch. They'll then send their tallies to her brain so that it can figure out the color of the t-shirt. In this case, the t-shirt is orange.

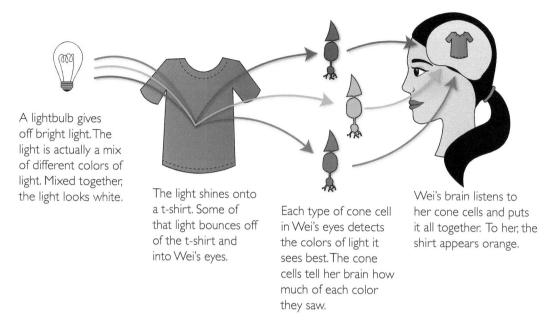

A lightbulb gives off bright light. The light is actually a mix of different colors of light. Mixed together, the light looks white.

The light shines onto a t-shirt. Some of that light bounces off of the t-shirt and into Wei's eyes.

Each type of cone cell in Wei's eyes detects the colors of light it sees best. The cone cells tell her brain how much of each color they saw.

Wei's brain listens to her cone cells and puts it all together. To her, the shirt appears orange.

Image 10.3
The colors we see are a combination of the colors of light that bouce off of the objects around us or shine from things like screens and bulbs.

Why colorblindness happens

While most people, like Wei, have three different types of cone cells, some people are born with only two types of cone cells that are fully working. This can happen if one or more of the different types is missing or isn't working properly.

The result of having missing or unusual cone cells is that fewer colors of light get tallied up in the brain. This means that colors that look very distinct to people who have three types of regular cone cells look very similar to people who only have two types of regular cone cells, or even two regular types and one unusual type (Image 10.4).

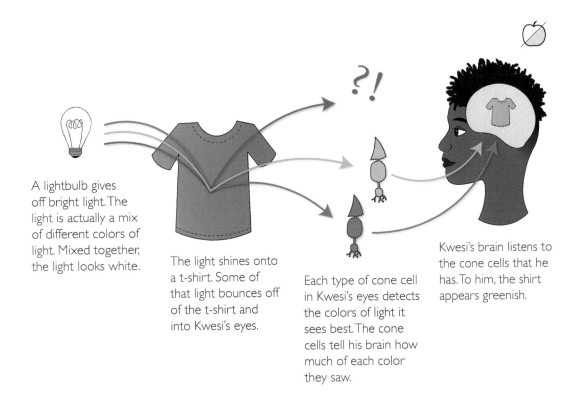

A lightbulb gives off bright light. The light is actually a mix of different colors of light. Mixed together, the light looks white.

The light shines onto a t-shirt. Some of that light bounces off of the t-shirt and into Kwesi's eyes.

Each type of cone cell in Kwesi's eyes detects the colors of light it sees best. The cone cells tell his brain how much of each color they saw.

Kwesi's brain listens to the cone cells that he has. To him, the shirt appears greenish.

Kwesi, for example, would see the same orange t-shirt differently than Wei. Because his eyes don't have working red cone cells, only the greenish and bluish colors of light can be added up and sent to his brain. His brain doesn't know that any reddish light bounced off of the t-shirt because his eyes can't tell him about it, so he sees it as greenish.

Image 10.4
People without the usual three cone cells see color as a combination of the colors that they can see, so some colors are hard to tell apart.

Different types of colorblindness

Colorblindness, then, doesn't mean that everything is in black and white—though that does happen very rarely for some people who only have one type of cone cell or no cone cells at all. Usually, people who are colorblind can still see some colors even if they have a hard time telling certain ones apart. For example, red and green, or blue and green, or yellow and pink might look the same to someone who is colorblind.

Because there are three types of cone cells, there are three ways that colorblindness normally happens, each because of a problem in any one of the three types of cells.

Red-green colorblindness

The most common type of colorblindness is red-green color-blindness—like what Kwesi has. This happens when some-body's red or green cone cells are missing or not working properly. To people with red-green colorblindness, green and red look the same or similar. Greenish colors like teal or reddish colors like orange might also look differently from what they would to someone who isn't colorblind.

Image 10.5 gives a peek at what the world looks like to someone with red-cone or green-cone colorblindness. The left side shows what people with normal vision see—the colors are bright, and the pink tulips look very different from the orange tulips. The right side shows the same field of flowers through the eyes of someone with missing green or red cones. In both cases, the colors are less vibrant and the pink and orange tulips look much more alike. Of course, if *you* are someone with red-green color-blindness, both sides of this picture might look the same.

Image 10.5
Green-cone colorblindness means that someone has missing or unusual green cone cells in their eyes. Red-cone colorblindness means that someone has missing or unusual red cone cells in their eyes.

Normal color vision

Red-cone colorblindness

Green-cone colorblindness

It's no big surprise, then, that certain color combinations could be confusing to someone who is red-green colorblind. Take a look at Image 10.6, for example, to see how the same graph looks through the eyes of someone with normal color vision, red-cone colorblindness, and green-cone colorblindness.

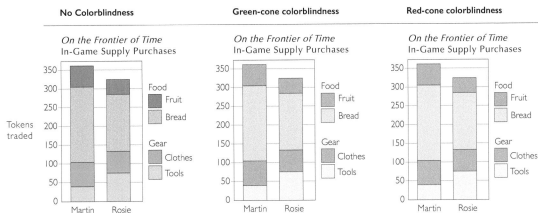

On the Frontier of Time
In-Game Supply Purchases

On the Frontier of Time
In-Game Supply Purchases

On the Frontier of Time
In-Game Supply Purchases

The first bar chart is filled in with shades of green and pink—and for many people, this looks great! Like we learned in the chapter about categorical colors, the pink and green are easy to tell apart, and the light and dark shades show that things like Fruit and Bread are different types of Food. However, people with unusual or missing red or green cone cells will see something very different. To them, the pinks and greens look more like grays and yellows. The colors aren't so useful anymore!

Image 10.6
The same graph looks quite different to someone who is not colorblind than to someone who has red-green colorblindness.

Blue-yellow colorblindness

It's less common, but it's also possible to have missing or unusual blue cone cells. People with this type of colorblindness have a hard time telling blue from green and yellow from red or pink. Notice in Image 10.7 how the tulips on the right side of the photo look similar to each other again, but this time they appear to be all pink instead of all yellow. Even the sky and the trees look like different shades of teal.

Image 10.7
Blue-cone colorblindness means that someone has missing or unusual blue cone cells in their eyes.

Normal
color vision

Blue-cone
colorblindness

Looking again at the bar charts, we can see how challenging it would be for someone with blue-cone colorblindness to read a visualization with certain colors. A pink and yellow bar chart, for example, would look all pink—and all the groupings would be gone (Image 10.8).

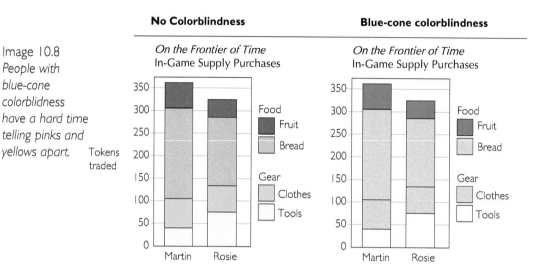

Image 10.8
*People with
blue-cone
colorblidness
have a hard time
telling pinks and
yellows apart.*

A blue and green version wouldn't be much better. To someone with blue-cone colorblindness, the whole visualization would look teal (Image 10.9).

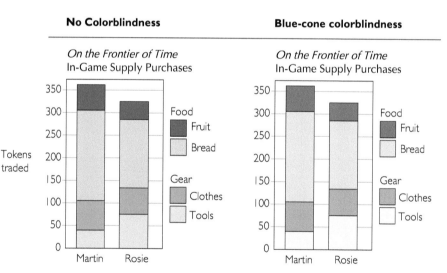

Image 10.9
*Greens and
blues look very
similar to people
with blue-cone
colorblindness.*

Black-and-white colorblindness

Even rarer than blue-cone colorblindness, some people have trouble seeing color at all. This can happen if all three kinds of cone cells are missing or not working, or if someone only has blue cone cells. Usually, people with this kind of colorblindness will have other vision problems, too.

Our tulip photo can once again show what the world might look like to someone who has difficulty seeing color in general. It becomes much harder to see the difference between the orange and pink tulips, for example—the only difference is that the pink tulips appear a tiny bit darker (Image 10.10).

Normal
color vision

Total colorblindness

Image 10.10
Someone no cone cells, damaged cone cells, or only one kind of cone cell will have trouble telling all the colors apart.

Reading colorful visualizations would also be a big challenge for someone who can't see color at all. The example in Image 10.11 shows how colors that look very different to someone with normal color vision can look exactly the same without color—especially if the colors are all the same darkness.

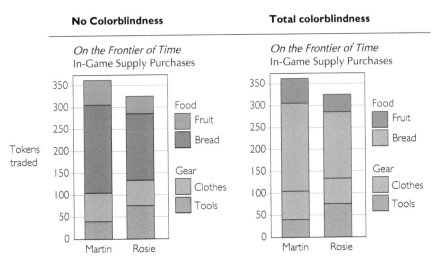

Image 10.11
Since all the colors in this visualization are of the same darkness, it would be very difficult for someone with total colorblindess to read.

How to be colorblind-friendly

At this point you might be wondering what to make of all this. How can we use everything we learned in the color chapters without leaving people behind? Don't worry, there are plenty of ways to make visualizations **colorblind-friendly**, meaning that even people with some kind of colorblindness can still tell the colors apart or understand the graph without needing to see the colors at all. In fact, we've already learned a few ways to be colorblind friendly without realizing it.

Mix up light and dark colors

The most important thing you can do to make a colorblind-friendly color palette is to include colors that are both light and dark. Instead of using colors that are all the same lightness or darkness, try to pick a mix of light, medium, and dark colors. For example, even if red and green can be difficult for some people to tell apart, *dark* red and *light* green will still appear different to everyone (Image 10.12).

Image 10.12
Choosing a combination of light and dark colors helps with colorblind-friendliness.

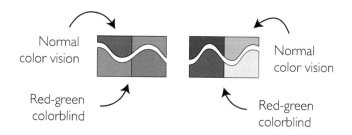

In a visualization, this might mean using dark colors for one group, and light colors for another. Or, if there are several categories, it could mean using white, a light color, a medium color, a dark color, and black. If you can still tell each color apart when you print the visualization in black and white then someone with red-green or blue-yellow colorblindness will likely be able to understand your graph, too.

Separate colors with white or black

No matter which colors you choose, outlining the shapes in a visualization with black or white can make it easier to tell where one shape ends and the next shape begins. This can be a big help for people who see fewer colors, but it's easier on the eyes for people with normal color vision, too. Take a look at the examples in Image 10.13.

	Smushed together	Separated by white	Separated by black

Normal color vision →

Red-green colorblind →

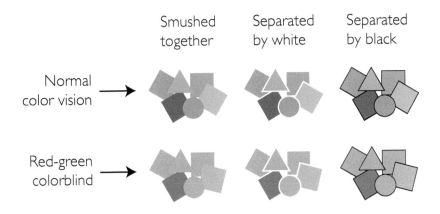

Image 10.13 *Drawing a white or black outline around the shapes in a visualization makes it easier to tell where one shape stops and the other one starts.*

The top row shows what the colorful shapes look like to someone with normal color vision; the bottom row shows how the same colors look to someone who is red-green colorblind. Without any borders around the shapes, it takes a lot of focus for *anyone* to pick out each shape on its own—either because the colors look either too similar or because they hurt your eyes! The shapes with borders, on the other hand, are easier to tell apart and don't clash as much. For visualizations like stacked bar charts and pie charts, then, black or white borders can help categories with similar colors to look separate, whatever the colors happen to be.

Use patterns and shapes

Patterns and shapes can also be a big help, particularly if you're not sure how someone else will see the colors in your color palette. Adding patterns to the example above would also help someone with red-green colorblindness tell the red and green squares apart—even if the colors look the same to them. Using light and dark colors as well as patterns makes the difference even clearer.

Everything we learned in the last chapter about using pattern and shapes in visualizations is still true. You can use similar-looking patterns or shapes to show groups that are related, and different-looking patterns and shapes to show groups that are totally separate. You can use patterns and shapes by themselves in a black and white visualization, or double up with colors like in the example in Image 10.14.

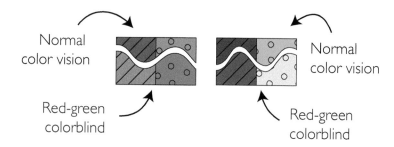

Image 10.14
Adding patterns to a visualization can make tricky colors easier to tell apart.

Normal color vision

Red-green colorblind

Normal color vision

Red-green colorblind

Pay attention to the legend

The legend's job is to tell us what each color, shape, or pattern means, but it's our job to make sure the legend is easy to use and colorblind-friendly. To do this, try to make the legend match the order of the colors in the visualization. That way, it's easier to find what each color means when you look back and forth between the visualization and the legend. If the colors in the legend look alike to someone who is colorblind, the order they're in will give them another way to tell them apart (Image 10.15).

Image 10.15
Matching the order of the legend to the order of the colors that it's the closest to make it easier to see where each color is used in the visualization.

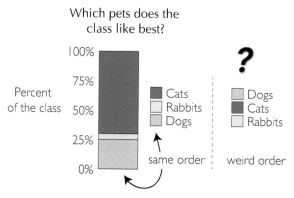

Which pets does the class like best?

In the visualization above, for example, the blue, green, and pink squares in the legend are in the same order as the blue, green, and pink stacks in the bar. Putting the legend in another order is more confusing and takes more work to understand whether you're colorblind or not.

Use notes and labels

Adding little notes or labels directly onto your visualization can go a long way towards colorblind-friendliness, too. If you're feeling unsure about the colors in your visualization, or if you're having trouble making patterns that you like, you can always point things out with words on your graph.

The stacked bar chart in Image 10.16, for example, doesn't have fancy patterns or a legend, but it *does* have labels. It's easy to see which stacks in the bars mean fruit, bread, clothes, or tools, as well as how those items are grouped together.

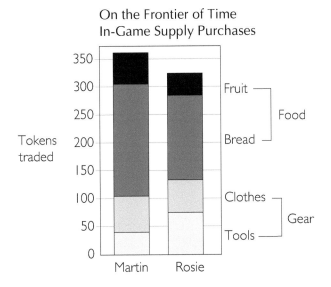

On the Frontier of Time
In-Game Supply Purchases

Image 10.16
This graph doesn't have a legend, but the labels tell us everything we need to know about what each stack in the stacked bars means.

We could label our pool temperature graph, too, to show which line belonged to each swimming pool. Labels like these are helpful if for some reason you can't change the colors or patterns of the lines, or if you just want to be sure that your visualization is clear (Image 10.17).

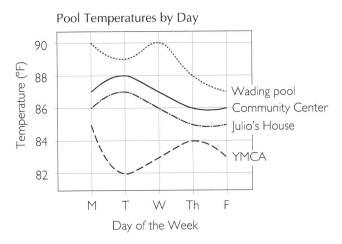

Pool Temperatures by Day

Image 10.17
Labeling each line makes it clear whose line is whose.

Colorblind-friendliness helps everyone

Even if you are able to see all colors easily, there are many reasons to make sure that the visualizations you make are colorblind-friendly. The first reason is basic kindness: you never really know how other people see things, and they might not even realize that they see colors differently than you do. A little extra care can go a long way towards making sure that no one is left out.

Secondly, using colors of different shades, lines of different patterns, points of different shapes, organized legends, and a few well-placed labels can make your visualizations easier to read for everyone. Just because a visualization *can* use color to tell things apart doesn't mean it's always the *best* or *only* way to do it. It's okay to show the same thing in a few different ways—like using colors *and* labels, or colors *and* patterns.

Thirdly, you might want to photocopy your visualization, print it, or present it on a projector in class. All of these can slightly change how the colors in your graph look. If you've already made sure that the colorful pieces are easy to tell apart regardless of the colors, then you'll have no problem sharing your work in new places. It's a win-win!

Chapter summary

In this chapter, we learned about color blindness and the many ways that people can see colors differently. Even if some people have a hard time telling certain colors apart, there are many ways to make visualizations colorblind-friendly. Picking a combination of light and dark colors makes confusing colors easier to pick out. Different shapes and patterns of points, lines, and areas don't rely on color vision at all. Using borders around the shapes in a visualization makes it easier to tell one shape from another. Being smart about legends and labels makes it easier to tell what is what. Thinking about colorblind-friendliness helps everyone because it makes sure our visualizations are as clear as possible in different situations.

It's your turn!

1. Fill in the visualization below in a colorblind-friendly way. That means that you should use:

   a. One light color and one dark color
   b. At least one pattern. You can use two patterns if you'd like!

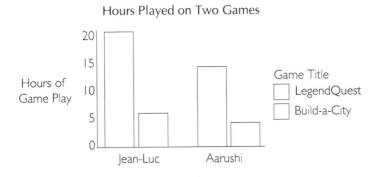

2. Make a colorblind-friendly line chart using data about your city.

   a. First, fill in the table below with the average monthly high and low temperatures for your city—this is something you can find online, or you can guess!
   b. Circle the highest High and the lowest Low so that you know how to number the y-axis.
   c. Then, make a line graph of the two amounts—one line for Low and one line for High—that doesn't have a legend but instead labels the lines directly.

Average Monthly High and Low Temperatures in _____		
Month	High (° _____)	Low (° _____)
January		
February		
March		
April		
May		
June		
July		
August		
September		
October		
November		
December		

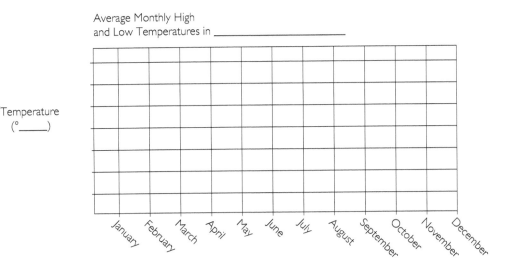

Average Monthly High
and Low Temperatures in _____

Temperature
(°___)

January February March April May June July August September October November December

3. The visualization below doesn't have any labels—it could be about anything! Use your imagination to create the following labels, so that the visualization has meaning. It can be about anything!

   a. A title
   b. Axis labels
   c. Axis title
   d. A legend

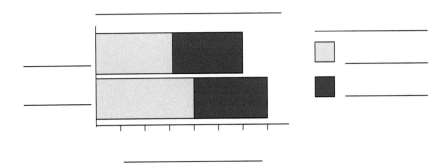

11 Angle

After spending so much time on color, we can finally move on to a totally different way of showing data—with angles. In many ways, **angles** are very much like lengths when it comes to how we can use them in a visualization. Just like longer bars in a bar chart mean more of something, changing angles to be wider or narrower can show different amounts. Also like length, you've probably already come across visualizations that use angle in your day-to-day life.

Examples from your everyday life. 166
Bending axes 167
Donut and meter charts 169
Using angle and position together 172
Using angle, position, and color. 175
Chapter summary 177
It's your turn!. 177

DOI: 10.1201/9781003309376-12

Examples from your everyday life

If you look carefully, data are represented with angles all around us. Perhaps the most common place to see angles in action is on clocks and watches. If you tell time using a clock with hands, you're really using the *angle* of each hand to read the hours, minutes, and seconds. Take a look at the watch shown in Image 11.1, for example. Do you know what time it is?

Image 11.1
The angles of a clock's hands are what tell us how many hours, minutes, and seconds have passed. This clock shows that it's 3:02 and 30 seconds.

We can see from the shorter hour hand that it's a tiny bit past three o'clock, or a quarter of the way through the twelve-hour day. The longer minute hand shows us how far past the hour it is—a little more than two minutes, to be exact, which is two sixtieths of the minutes in each hour. The red second hand shows that thirty seconds—or half of the seconds—have gone by during that minute. Putting it all together, we can tell from the three angles that it's 3:02 and 30 seconds.

Fuel gauges are another common place to see data shown with angles. Depending on the direction that the needle points and how slanted it is, we can decide if it's time to stop at the gas station.

On the fuel gauge shown in Image 11.2, the red needle is pointing up and to the right. Maybe we don't know exactly how many gallons of gas are left in the tank, but we can tell that the tank is more than half full. Since it's closer to the F for "full" than E for "empty", we can save a trip to the gas station for another day.

These are just two everyday objects that show data with angles, but there are countless more. Many kinds of meters, gauges, dials, knobs, and faucets tell us what's happening by the angle of a needle, marker, or handle. Take a look around you. Can you find anything else that uses angles to show data?

Bending axes

You'll remember that axes are the parts of a visualization that tell us the length, height, category, or position of the points, shapes, and lines in a graph. So far, we've only seen axes that are drawn with straight lines, but visualizations that use angle have axes, too… they're just bent!

The two graphs in Image 11.3 show how similar the axes are in bar charts and **pie charts**. Pie charts are circular graphs that use pie-shaped slices to show the parts of a whole—much like the layers in a stacked bar chart. We already know that a bar chart's axis must start at zero, and that the height of a stacked bar represents everything in a single group. Another way of saying *everything* is 100%.

Angle

Since pie charts are round, they can *only* show parts of a whole. Because of this, it's best to show your data as percentages or fractions. A pie chart's axis therefore starts at 0 or 0% and circles all the way around to 1 or 100%.

Image 11.3
Pie charts are really just stacked bar charts bent into a circle. A pie chart always shows 100%.

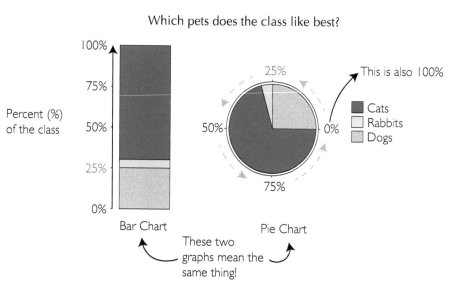

Notice how the pink slices of the bar chart and pie chart both show that 25% of the class like dogs the best. The pink slice is a quarter of the bar chart's height, and a quarter of the pie. When the pink, green, and blue slices are added together, they add up to 100% in both visualizations. The data for both charts are in Table 11.1.

Table 11.1
Classroom data about the most preferred pet

Which Pets Does the Class Like Best?

Pet	Count	Fraction	Percent
Cats	14	14/20	70%
Rabbits	1	1/20	5%
Dogs	5	5/20	25%
Total:	20	1	100%

The Pet variable is a categorical variable that shows the different types of pets. The Count variable is numerical—it shows the number of people who like each pet best. The Fraction variable shows the values from the Count variable as fractions, and the Percent variable turns the Fraction variable into percentages. The totals for each variable are written below the table. In fact, the Count, Fraction, and Percent variables are simply showing the same data in different ways.

Donut and meter charts

Pie charts aren't the only sweet way to show amounts with angles, though. There are **donut charts**, too! Donut charts are just pie charts with a donut hole cut out of the middle. Sometimes a caption or interesting value is written in the circle, and other times the circle is left blank. Take a look at donut chart in Image 11.4 about the sales at Sunny Sunshine's Gourmet Donuts. What does it tell you donut sales this week, and what *doesn't* it tell you?

Image 11.4
Donut charts are like pie charts with a hole in the middle. They always go to 100%, too.

The donut chart shows how popular each flavor of donut was this week at the donut shop. It looks like charcoal spice donuts were the most popular—they were half of what was sold! Sourdough was the least popular flavor. Carrot cake took second place at 40% of the sales. What we *can't* know from the visualization is how many people bought donuts at all—it could be ten or 5,000! Without any other labels or captions on the visualization, we can only know the percentage of people who bought each kind.

Lastly, **meter charts** are a third type of visualization that uses angles. Meter charts, which are sometimes called **gauge charts**, are named after things like electric meters and gas gauges. These visualizations are shaped like donut charts with a bite taken out. They're mostly used for showing progress toward a goal, or how empty, full, or extreme something is.

Angle

The meter chart in Image 11.5 uses angle and ordinal colors to show the temperature of coffee on a scale from Iced to Scalding. The lighter sections on the left side show the cooler temperatures like Iced and Cold. The darkest brown sections on the right show coffee that is piping hot. Everything else is somewhere in between.

Image 11.5
Gauge charts are like donut charts cut in half or with a bite taken out, and usually show how extreme something is or how much of something is left.

How do you like your coffee?

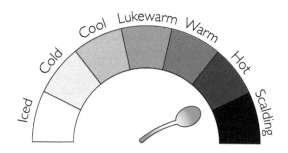

Depending on the angle of the spoon, someone can say exactly how hot they'd like their cup of joe. The spoon in the visualization is pointing almost all the way to the right, meaning slightly less than Scalding. Be careful!

The meter chart in Image 11.6 works in a similar way. Instead of using ordinal colors and a spoon, it uses two category colors—dark and light purple—to show exactly how close the annual clothes drive is to reaching its goal for winter coat donations. So far 714 coats have been donated, which is 71.4% of the way to the 1,000-coat goal.

Image 11.6
Meter charts can have categories, percentages, or numbers. They can use arrows (or spoons like in Image 11.5), or show amounts by filling in part of the half-circle.

Number of Coats Donated to
the Annual Clothes Drive

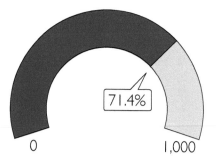

You might have guessed from the category colors, but the data from this chart are split into counts of Donated and Remaining coats. Like with the data about pets, the totals for each variable are tallied up at the bottom of Table 11.2.

Number of Coats Donated to the Annual Clothes Drive			
Category	Count	Fraction	Percent
Donated	714	714/1,000	71.4%
Remaining	286	286/1,000	28.6%
Total:	1,000	1	100%

Table 11.2
The count, fraction, and percent of coats that have been donated

As you can see, there are many ways to visualize data about fractions or percentages just by changing the shape of the axes. A stacked bar chart can be bent into a circular pie chart, which is just one donut hole away from a donut chart. Taking a piece out of a donut chart makes a meter chart. They all *can* show the same data, so it's up to you to pick the type of visualization that is the best for your idea.

Take a look at the different visualizations in Image 11.7. Do you think one way is better than the others? Do any of the visualizations help you understand the data more easily? Is there one that you like the best?

Image 11.7
There is often more than one way to show the same thing using a different type of visualization.

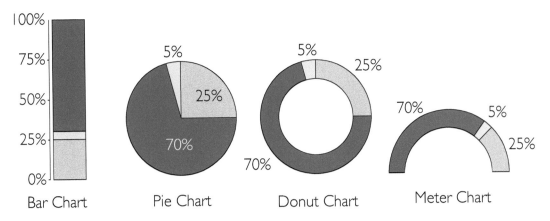

Using angle and position together

We've already used angle and color together a few times in this chapter, but that's not the only way to mix it up—angle and position make another good team. Take a look at the *very imaginary* map of wind patterns around the United States in Image 11.8, and especially at the big red arrow.

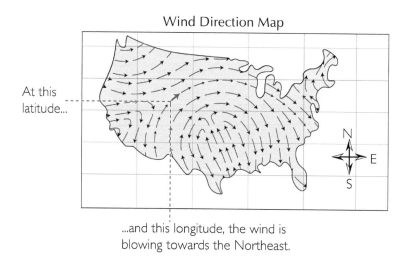

Image 11.8
Wind maps use position and angle to show the direction wind is blowing in a certain place.

Wind Direction Map

At this latitude...

...and this longitude, the wind is blowing towards the Northeast.

We don't normally think about maps as having x- and y-axes, but latitude and longitude lines are exactly that. Latitude lines run in the same direction as the Equator—like gridlines that go from east to west and stick out of the y-axis. Longitude lines run north to south like the gridlines that come from the x-axis.

The red arrow, then, has both a latitude and a longitude that tell us its position in the world. Since it is angled up and to the right, it *also* tells us a direction—northeast. This all means that in that exact spot, the wind is blowing northeast. Any of the other arrows on the map say the direction the wind is blowing in their position.

We could also use angle and position on a round graph. **Radar charts** (also called spider charts, web charts, star charts, or polar charts) are a type of visualization that use angle to show categories, and position to show amounts. The radar chart in Image 11.9 shows us two how two imaginary superheroes stack up against each other.

Image 11.9
*Radar charts use
angle to show
categories.*

A head-to-head battle between
Chart Wiz and **GRAPHTRON**!

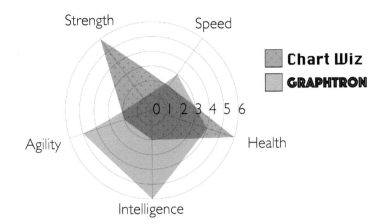

In this visualization, Chart Wiz is shown in patterned red and Graphtron is shown in blue. Each of their traits is shown around the circle. The lines that run from the center to the edge—these are called **spokes**, like on a bicycle—are separate axes for each trait. The position on the spoke shows the amount of each trait the hero has. While each trait runs from 0 (the very middle) to 6 in this example, the spokes on radar charts can show different amounts, too—they're different axes, after all.

We can see that Chart Wiz has a health score of six, whereas Graphtron only has a health score of four. Graphtron is smart though! He has an intelligence score of six, unlike Chart Wiz who only scores two in that area. Who do you think would win in a battle between the two of them?

Table 11.3 shows each of the variables visualized in the chart. The Hero variable is visualized using the category colors and patterns. The Trait variable is visualized with the angle—or the position along the bent category axis. The Score variable is shown by the position along each spoke.

Table 11.3
Each superhero has different traits. The Hero and Trait variables are categorical, and the score variable is numerical.

A Head-to-Head Battle between Chart Wiz and Graphtron		
Hero	**Trait**	**Score**
Chart Wiz	Agility	2
Chart Wiz	Strength	6
Chart Wiz	Speed	2
Chart Wiz	Health	6
Chart Wiz	Intelligence	2
Graphtron	Agility	5
Graphtron	Strength	1
Graphtron	Speed	3
Graphtron	Health	4
Graphtron	Intelligence	6

With these data in hand, we could make a grouped bar chart, too, like in Image 11.10.

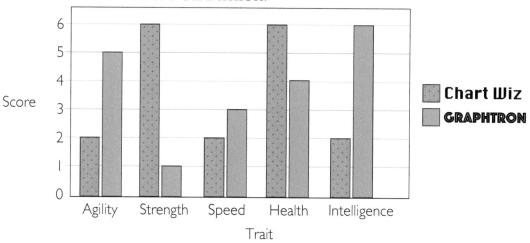

A head-to-head battle between
Chart Wiz and **GRAPHTRON**!

Image 11.10
The radar chart above can easily become a grouped bar chart. Here, the angle is replaced with position along the x-axis.

Flip back and forth between the two—can you see how they're similar? Do you think that one is easier to understand than the other, or that one is more interesting to look at? If you were to make your own version, which one would you make, or would you try something else altogether?

Using angle, position, *and* color

Finally, we could use angle to add to a visualization that already uses position and color for other variables. Think back to the heatmap visualization that showed the number of pages that Juanita and her friends read. Previously, each square was filled in with different colors to show a single number—just the pages from this week. Adding angled arrows to the squares lets us see another interesting fact about the readers. Now we can see if they read more or less this week than last week, too (Image 11.11)!

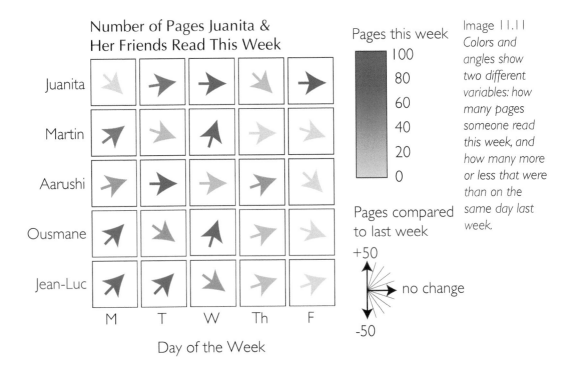

Image 11.11
Colors and angles show two different variables: how many pages someone read this week, and how many more or less that were than on the same day last week.

Take a look at Martin, for example. On Wednesday, we can see that he read around 90 pages because the arrow is bright red. Since it's pointing up at a steep angle, we can also tell that he read around 40 pages more than the Wednesday of last week. On Friday, however, his light-yellow arrow points down to tell us that he read fewer than ten pages, which is around ten less than he had read the previous Friday.

Can you write out the data for Ousmane by looking at the visualization? Don't worry about getting the exact values, just try to get close enough! Juanita's data for this graph are shown in Table 11.4 as an example.

Table 11.4
The number of pages that Juanita read last week compared to the week before

# of Pages Juanita & Her Friends Read This Week			
Person	Day	Pages Read	Week Change
Juanita	Monday	3	−25
Juanita	Tuesday	68	+5
Juanita	Wednesday	83	+0
Juanita	Thursday	19	−25
Juanita	Friday	100	+0

Flip the page upside down to see Ousmane's data. Did you get the values correct, or at least close? (Table 11.5)

Table 11.5
Ousmane's data from the visualization above

Person	Day	Pages Read	Week Change
Ousmane	Monday	16	+25
Ousmane	Tuesday	48	-25
Ousmane	Wednesday	82	+40
Ousmane	Thursday	31	+10
Ousmane	Friday	5	-10

With angles, we're starting to see how many ways there are to show the same data, and how we can mix-and-match different pieces to create visualizations of our own. There's almost always more than one way to visualize something, and as we saw in this chapter, you can learn different things from your data by seeing it in a new light. Like the words that we say or write, visualization gives us the tools to share our ideas without giving us a script—we get to decide the best way to tell our own data stories. In the final chapters, we'll learn about some of the more advanced ways of sharing data and how we can be the most honest and careful data visualizers.

Chapter Summary

Very similar to length, angle can be used in data visualizations to show quantities or amounts. Pie charts, donut charts, and meter charts are really just stacked bar charts that have been bent—but remember that they should always add up to 100%. Radar charts use angle to show categories and position to show amounts. You can also use angle with position to create charts that show movement, direction, or change—on maps and on graphs with number axes, as well as on visualizations with category axes.

It's your turn!

1. As we learned, pie charts are just stacked bar charts that have been bent into a circle.

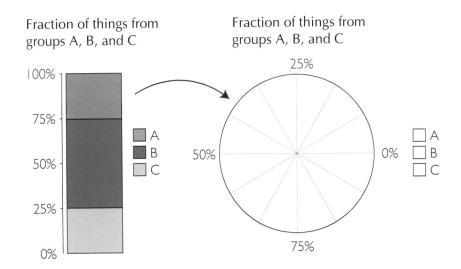

Fraction of things from groups A, B, and C

Fraction of things from groups A, B, and C

a. Color in the empty pie chart so that it matches the amounts shown in the bar chart. You can use different colors if you'd like as long as the legend still makes sense.

b. Which chart do you like better? Do you think that one is easier to understand than another?

2. Using the data in the table, color in the donut chart below to show the percentage of people who prefer each sweet treat. Make sure that you fill in the legend, too, so that it is clear what each color means.

Which sweet treats are our favorites?			
Treat	Count	Fraction	Percent
Cake	4	4/20	20%
Pie	9	9/20	45%
Ice cream	2	2/20	10%
Candy	5	5/20	25%

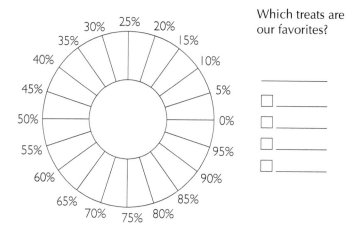

Which treats are our favorites?

3. Create a radar chart showing how much you and one friend like each subject in school.

a. First, rate each subject from one to five and put those data into the table. Ask a friend for their ratings, too.
b. Visualize your scores on the radar chart.
c. Make sure to fill in the legend.
d. What does the radar chart tell you about what you like to learn, and how that is different or the same as your friend?

How much do you like each school subject? (1–5)		
Subject	**Your Rating**	**_____'s Rating**
Math		
Science		
Geography		
English		
Music		

How much do you like each
school subject?

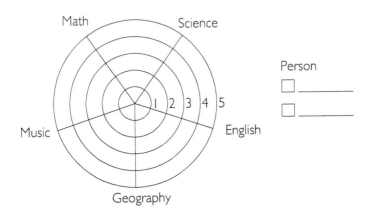

Person

☐ _____

☐ _____

12 Connections and networks

Many of the ways we've learned to visualize data help us to show *how much* of something, like numbers of people, temperatures, or scoops of ice cream. We've also seen a few ways to show who's who and different categories by using shapes, colors, patterns, and positions. In this chapter, we'll learn how to make visualizations that show the relationships between things, too.

Networks and trees 182
Trees of all shapes and sizes. 184
Parallel coordinate graphs 189
Sankey diagrams 190
Chord diagrams 192
Chapter summary 196
It's your turn!. 196

DOI: 10.1201/9781003309376-13

Networks and trees

When you hear the words *relationship* and *connection*, you might think about friendships, your family, or people that you know. Some of these relationships are very close, while others feel further away. You might be very connected to your best friend, but her cousin is just someone that you've heard about. None of the visualizations that we've studied so far have given us a way to show these relationships, though. For this type of data, we'll need a new type of graph altogether.

Image 12.1
Networks are made up of nodes that are linked together. Each node is a data point that might have several values. The links show how the nodes are connected.

Networks or **network graphs** show relationships between things using **nodes** and **links**. Nodes are similar to the points on a scatterplot—they show one data point each. Links are the lines or arrows that show how the nodes connect or relate to each other. In illustration in Image 12.1, the red node connects to two blue nodes with two links.

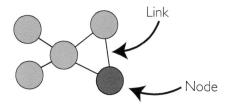

Let's do a more interesting example. The next visualization is a network graph that shows who knows whom. The four people in the middle of the graph all know each other because they're in the same class. They don't, however, know each other's friends from outside of school. Quiana, for example, knows Julio, but none of the other people Julio knows. Julio is part of a tight group where everyone knows each other. Alex knows loads of people, too, but it looks like they're part of different sports teams or clubs that don't share many of the same members (Image 12.2).

Who knows whom?

Alex's friends don't
know each other.

Julio's friends all
know each other.

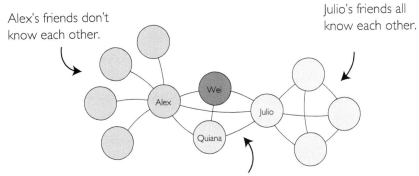

Image 12.2
*This group of
people is a
network. Each
person is a node,
and they are
linked together if
they know each
other.*

This link shows that Quiana and
Julio know each other.

In this version of the network graph, each link shows a relationship that goes both directions—Quiana knows Wei, and Wei knows Quiana. These are called **undirected** graphs because the links don't go in one particular direction. However, this is not true in all networks!

Think about pizza delivery: When your pizza arrives for the party, do you get in the car and drive it back to the shop? No, of course not! The pizza only travels one way. Some relationships only go in one direction, too, and a network graph can show that. Networks that have links pointing in only one direction are called **directed** networks. Often, directed networks are shown using little arrows, like in this version of the graph from above (Image 12.3).

Who is friends with whom?

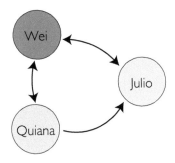

Image 12.3
*Directed
networks use
arrows to show
connections that
only go in one
direction.*

This version doesn't only show if people *know* each other, it shows if they are *friends*. Unfortunately, the arrows show that even if Quiana and Julio know each other, their friendship doesn't go in both directions. Quiana thinks of Julio a friend, but not the other way around. Hopefully they've just had an argument and can make it up soon! In the meantime, it's a good thing that both Julio and Quiana are on good terms with Wei.

Trees of all shapes and sizes

One kind of network that you might know about already is a family tree. Family trees show how each person in a family is related, whether or not they are parents, children, cousins, or siblings, and if they're part of the family through birth or a partnership. Take a look at the visualization in Image 12.4 showing Rosie's family tree.

Rosie's Family Tree

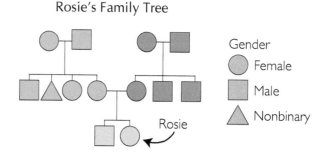

Image 12.4
*Family trees are
a special kind of
network graphs
called trees.*

The top row shows Rosie's grandparents, then her parents, aunts, and uncles on the next row, and finally Rosie and her brother on the bottom row. The links show us how each person is related to the next. Parents are connected to each other with their own links to show that they're connected but not related. Siblings, like Rosie and her brother or Rosie's aunts and uncles from either side of the family, all link up to the same two parents instead of connecting to each other.

In this family tree, the shapes tell us the gender of each family member, and the colors help us see the different sides of Rosie's family more easily. We can see that Rosie has one brother, and that her moms come from families of three and four siblings.

Just like Rosie's family tree, **trees** are a special kind of network all to themselves. All trees are networks, but not all networks are trees. Unlike the graph about who knows whom, you can only move between two nodes in a tree by taking a single path. For example, you can *only* connect Rosie to her grandfather on the purple side of the family by going through her mom on the right. To get from Julio to Wei, however, you can move your pencil along the graph straight from one to the next *or* by going all the way around through Quiana and Alex. Trees are also always undirected networks—like the branches on real trees in nature—so the graph about who is friends with whom is also definitely not a tree.

Family relationships aren't the only thing we can visualize with trees, though. In fact, trees are great at showing all kinds of data with different levels that are similar to grandparents, parents, and children.

In the last chapter about angles, we made a pie chart about the different pets that people in the class liked the best. As you might remember, pie charts and stacked bars are both good at showing the percentage or fraction of things, but not the best for showing the actual amounts. The visualizations in Image 12.5 tell us that 70% of the class liked cats the best, but what kind of cats? How many people? Who liked them? We need a different visualization to answer these questions.

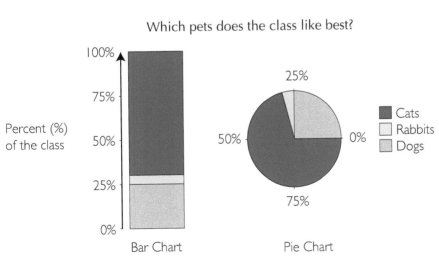

Image 12.5
Bar charts and pie charts show data after it has been added up, but they don't show each data point from every category. We can see how many people liked cats the best, but not who they were or the kinds of cats.

Take the **icicle chart** in Image 12.6, for example. Icicle charts show how different groups break down into smaller and smaller parts by putting all of the parts from one big group into the same row or column. In this chart, the first column shows us the categories that are in the bar chart and pie chart: dogs, rabbits, and cats. The second column shows us the breed of each dog, rabbit, or cat that people liked. The third column shows the person who liked that particular animal. What does this have to do with trees, though?

Which pets does the class like best?

Image 12.6
Each column in the icicle chart shows a different level of detail. The first column shows the biggest grouping, and the last column shows each person.

Animal	Breed	Person
Dogs	Golden Retriever	Lorenzo
		Veronica
		Juanita
	Corgi	Sophia
	Pomeranian	Rita
Rabbits	Angora	Marina
Cats	Calico	Julio
		Wei
		Alex
		Charlie
	British Shorthair	Quiana
		Gabrielle
		Rosie
		Serena
		Martin
	Bengal	Aarushi
		Ousmane
		Jean-Luc
	Hairless	Kwesi
	Persian	Ahmad

Everything! The *data* in the icicle chart actually form a tree shape, even if the visualization is suspiciously square. Since there are different levels of data that branch out into smaller and smaller groups, the data themselves are organized like a tree.

We can see the tree shape more clearly if we draw this data set to look like an actual tree. In the illustration in Image 12.7, you can see that the three biggest branches represent dogs, rabbits, and cats. From there, each branch splits off into breeds. The leaves, also called **leaf nodes** because they come at the end of each branch, represent the person who liked that type of pet.

Which pets do my friends like best?

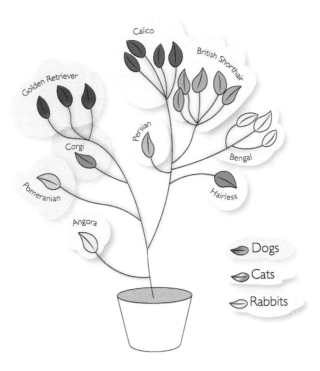

Image 12.7
The same data that made the stacked bar chart, pie chart, and icicle chart, can be visualized as a tree because each level branches into smaller and smaller groups. Starting with the animal— dogs, cats, or rabbits—the tree branches into the breed, and then to each person as a leaf node.

Funnily enough, many visualizations that show tree data don't look anything like the maple tree growing outside or the picture of the potted plant. **Tree maps** are one of them. Tree maps show networks by arranging rectangular branches and leaf nodes into a big block. Each branch in a tree map is packed with leaf nodes of the same color. Sometimes, the leaf nodes are in different sizes to show different amounts. Since they're quite complicated to draw, tree maps are usually made and looked at on computers. The tree map in Image 12.8 shows the same data from the icicle chart and tree illustration.

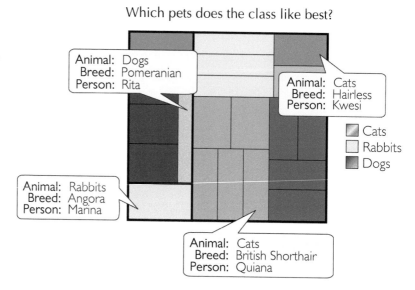

Which pets does the class like best?

Animal: Dogs
Breed: Pomeranian
Person: Rita

Animal: Cats
Breed: Hairless
Person: Kwesi

☑ Cats
☐ Rabbits
■ Dogs

Animal: Rabbits
Breed: Angora
Person: Marina

Animal: Cats
Breed: British Shorthair
Person: Quiana

The blue block of rectangles shows the branch with all the cat lovers, and each shade of blue shows a different breed. You can tell that most people prefer cats because the blue area is the biggest. You can see that the green rectangle is the smallest and doesn't have any rectangles inside it—it only represents Marina who likes Angora rabbits. In this tree map, the leaf nodes are actually all the same area even though they're slightly different shapes. This is because they're all showing one person. If the data were about something else, the leaf nodes could be different sizes to show different amounts.

It will come as no surprise that there is a rounder way to show this data set, too. We could take the original icicle chart and wrap it into a circle! This type of visualization is called a **sunburst chart** where the center is either a pie chart or a donut chart of the biggest categories surrounded in donuts that show each of the other levels. The outside donut has the leaf nodes—which in this case are each person (Image 12.9).

Which pets does the class like best?

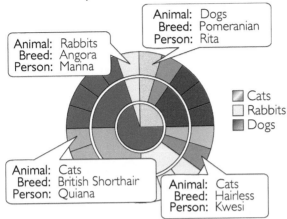

Animal: Dogs
Breed: Pomeranian
Person: Rita

Animal: Rabbits
Breed: Angora
Person: Marina

☐ Cats
☐ Rabbits
■ Dogs

Animal: Cats
Breed: British Shorthair
Person: Quiana

Animal: Cats
Breed: Hairless
Person: Kwesi

Image 12.9
*Wrapping an
icicle chart into
a circle makes a
sunburst chart.*

Look at the sunburst chart and compare it to the icicle chart, tree illustration, and tree map on the previous pages. Do you find that one graph is easier to understand than the other? Can you think of reasons why you would use an icicle chart instead of a sunburst chart or a tree map? When would you choose use a sunburst chart? A tree map?

Parallel coordinate graphs

Another visualization we made in the last chapter was about two superheroes, Chart Wiz and Graphtron, who battled it out a radar chart. The heroes' traits were shown around the edge of the biggest circle, and each spoke was a separate axis showing the amount of each trait they had (Image 12.10).

A head-to-head battle between
Chart Wiz and **GRAPHTRON**!

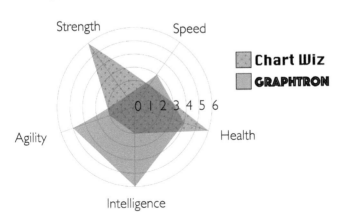

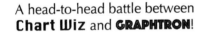

Strength

Speed

■ **Chart Wiz**

☐ **GRAPHTRON**

0 1 2 3 4 5 6

Agility

Health

Intelligence

Image 12.10
*Radar charts
use angles and
connections to
show who's who,
and what
they're like.*

In a way, radar charts also use connections to show us groups or categories. Connecting each spoke together makes a unique shape for each group. Round charts make it hard to compare each spoke side by side, though, so you might want another way to visualize the same data. If we wanted a different way to show the connections between the heroes' traits, we could make a **parallel coordinates** chart.

Like the spokes in radar charts, parallel coordinate charts also use different axes for each variable—they're just side by side instead. This means that each axis can show the same or different values. Agility could range from 0 to 6, for example, while Intelligence could go from 40 to 100. The lines that connect each point on every axis are like the special shapes in the radar charts—they help us pick out the values for a single group or category (Image 12.11).

Image 12.11
Parallel coordinate charts are like radar charts that have been unwrapped. Now, each superhero has its own line instead of a unique shape.

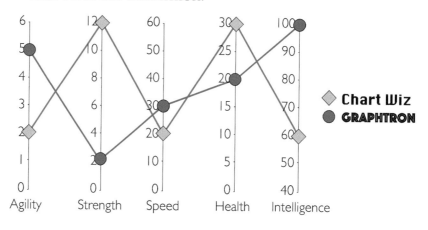

This parallel coordinate chart makes it easy for us to see that Chart Wiz has fairly low agility, speed, and intelligence (ouch!), but is quite strong and healthy. Graphtron, on the other hand, is pretty weak, but agile, fast, healthy, and smart.

Sankey diagrams

The last two types of connection visualizations show us changes over time or changes from situation to situation.

Sankey diagrams show how different groups of things change in number over time or at different stages. Just like in networks, they use links and nodes. In Sankey diagrams, the links are thick lines that look like rivers flowing from one place to the next. The nodes are labels at each stage. Sankey diagrams are another type of chart that is mostly created on a computer, but you can try drawing them on your own, too.

Sankey diagrams can be a bit confusing to read, so let's look at a simple example first. In Image 12.12, only one section of the visualization is colored in so that we can see exactly what's happening.

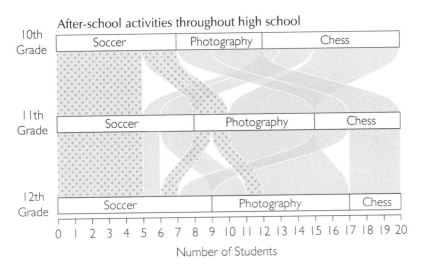

Image 12.12
Sankey diagrams like this one show how groups of things change in number over time or at different stages.

Pay attention to the yellow spotted links first. In this diagram we can see that seven students started out playing soccer in the 10th grade. We know this because the yellow links below the Soccer label—which is a node—run from zero on the x-axis all the way to seven.

We can also see that five of the students kept playing soccer in 11th grade, too, because the yellow link is five students wide once it gets to the 11th grade node. The other two students joined the photography club. When it came time for 12th grade, all five soccer players kept playing soccer, and one of the two photographers stayed in photography club. The other photographer went back to soccer.

We can see what happened with the other activities by looking at the same visualization in full color (Image 12.13).

Image 12.13
The differently-colored links in a Sankey diagram help us follow a single group as it splits up over time.

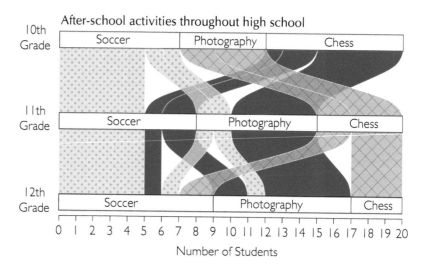

Take a look at Photography in green—five students started with photography in 10th grade, and then they all moved over to chess club in 11th grade. Three of them kept playing chess in 12th grade, and the other two tried out for soccer.

Chord diagrams

Chord diagrams are like round Sankey diagrams. Since they are round, each link can only connect one node to another, or loop around to connect a single node back to itself. Unlike Sankey diagrams, the links in chord diagrams can't make several stops like going from 10th grade to 11th grade to 12th grade. Instead, they can only make one stop, like going from 10th grade to 11th grade, or 11th grade to 12th grade.

The numbers on a chord diagram are also a bit different. Unlike the numerical axis on a Sankey diagram, the numbers at each node on a chord diagram count the number of people or things that are coming *and* going. Like we did with the Sankey diagram, let's look at an example that's only partly colored in to help this all make sense. Pay attention to the purple parts of Image 12.14 for now.

How 20 classmates felt at the beginning and end of the day

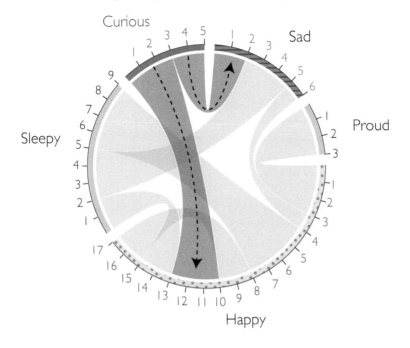

Image 12.14
Chord diagrams show where different categories start and stop.

The chord diagram above shows how the 20 classmates felt at the beginning of the day and the end of the day. The purple areas show two **chords**—which are the links in a chord diagram—that add up to the five students who arrived at school feeling curious. We know that they *started* the day like this because the Curious node and chords are both purple. In chord diagrams, the chords *start* from the node that they match in color. The chords end on nodes of different colors, or loop back to the same node if nothing changed.

The purple chords show us that two of the students *left* school feeling sad, and three left feeling happy. We know this because the purple Curious chord that goes to the blue Sad node is two people wide, and the purple Curious chord that goes to the yellow Happy node is three people wide.

The data for this chord diagram are in Table 12.1.

Table 12.1
How many people started and ended the day with different moods?

How 20 Classmates Felt at the Beginning and End of the Day		
Beginning	**End**	**Count**
Happy	Sad	1
Happy	Sleepy	4
Happy	Proud	3
Happy	Happy	2
Sleepy	Happy	2
Sleepy	Sad	3
Curious	Happy	3
Curious	Sad	2

If we color in the Happy chords we can start to see even more. The numbers on the Happy node go all the way up to 17. That's because ten people started the day feeling happy, five people ended the day feeling happy, and two people started *and* ended the day happy. Since the numbers at each node count the number of people that are coming *and* going, the students who start *and* end the day happy appear twice at that node. Adding up all the numbers around the whole chord diagram will equal 40—two feelings for each person (Image 12.15).

Image 12.15
Chords can start and end at the same node, so make sure you're counting stops at that node instead of people or things.

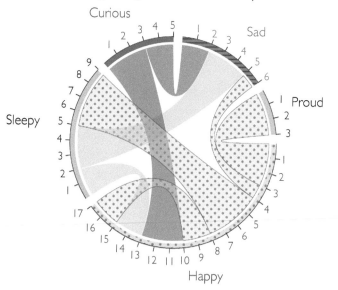

How 20 Classmates Felt at the Beginning and End of the Day

The full-color version of the chord diagram should make a bit more sense now. We can see in Image 12.16 that no one came to school feeling sad because there aren't any blue chords that match the blue Sad node. Unfortunately, six people *ended up* feeling sad. It must've been a tough day for a lot of people. We can also see that three people began the day feeling happy and all three of them ended the day feeling proud. Can you tell how many people felt sleepy at one point or another during the day? How many of them started the day feeling sleepy?

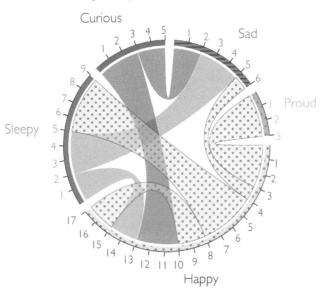

How 20 Classmates Felt at the Beginning and End of the Day

Image 12.16
The differently-colored chords in a chord diagram show us where things that started in one place ended up.

The network visualizations we learned in this chapter are unlike any other kind of visualization we've seen so far, and we wouldn't have been able to understand them as well if we hadn't already learned so much about colors, shapes, positions, size, and lines. The relationships that we see in network charts of all kinds show us once again how many ways there are to visualize data, and how creative you can be in showing the world what you know. You should pat yourself on the back, too, because networks are an important and challenging type of visualization to understand!

Chapter summary

Connections in data visualizations show us how things are related. Networks use links and nodes to show relationships and whether or not those relationships go in both directions. Trees are a kind of network where the relationships branch into smaller and smaller groups. Trees can be drawn as networks, icicle charts, tree maps, sunburst charts, or even actual trees! Connections also connect the dots between different axes in radar charts and parallel coordinates charts. Sankey diagrams show how much of something travel from one point to the next (and the next...), whereas chord diagrams show how many things started and ended at different places. It's *all* connected.

It's your turn!

1. Draw your family tree—or invent a family of imaginary characters. It should include at least ten people, two groups (colors or shapes), and three generations. Make sure that you include a legend for the shapes or colors that you use. Then:

   a. Label yourself (or your favorite character) on the family tree.

   b. What group or groups are you (or they) a part of?

   c. Label your (or their) parents.

   d. What group or groups are *they* part of?

2. Score three different animals—real or imaginary—on three variables: cuteness, ferocity, and athleticism.

Comparison of Three Animals			
Animal	Cuteness	Ferocity	Athleticism

a. Use those data to create a parallel coordinate chart comparing the animals.
b. Fill in the legend with the shapes and colors you use to represent each animal.
c. Which animal would make the best pet? Did your answer change after you drew the parallel coordinates graph?

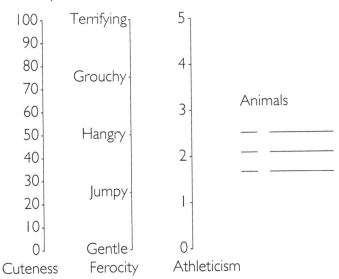

Comparison of Three Animals

3. Color in this tree map to show the data in the network. Make sure to fill in the legend with your color choices.

a. What does the tree map tell you that the network graph does not?

b. Of the people who do artistic activities, who seems to spend the most time?

c. Which types of activities do people spend the same amount of time on? Why might this be?

Weekly time spent doing
different after-school activities

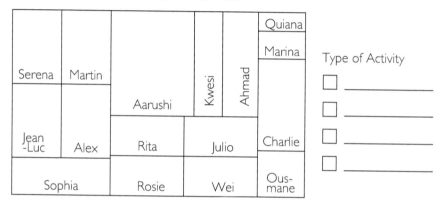

Who participates in different types of
after-school activities?

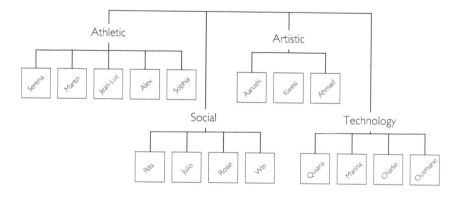

13 Visualization whoopsies

As we've seen throughout this book, data visualization is an almost magical way to share what we know. Showing data with shapes and colors makes it easier to find patterns that are hard to see in a table or data set. In fact, data visualization is *so* good at uncovering patterns and helping us make comparisons that it's possible to say things that aren't totally true. In this chapter, we'll learn how to make sure our visualizations are truthful and honest, and how to watch out for visualizations that might give us the wrong idea. As the saying goes, "With great power comes great responsibility!"

You can't always believe your eyes 200
Double axes 201
Backward axes 205
Bar charts that don't start at zero 206
Very tall or flat graphs 208
Using extra dimensions for no reason 209
Sometimes 3D does make sense 213
Not telling the whole story 214

DOI: 10.1201/9781003309376-14

Visualization whoopsies

Just plain wrong, aka lying 216
Chapter summary 219
It's your turn! 220

Note: You'll see some visualizations in this chapter marked with a warning sign. Watch out! These are examples of what **not** to do.

You can't always believe your eyes

Take the graph in Image 13.1, for example. Without looking too carefully, would you say that the temperature was increasing or decreasing?

Image 13.1
An innocent line graph… or is it?

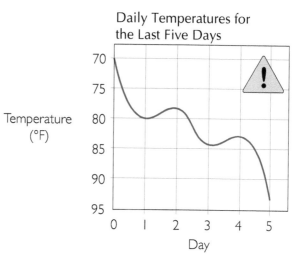

Of course, *you* knew to be careful, but at first glance, it could easily look like the temperature had gone down over the last five days. The line starts out much higher than it ends, doesn't it? The catch is that the y-axis that shows Temperature going from high to low, which is backward from what we'd normally expect. That could be a real problem for someone not paying attention!

Now quickly look at the next chart (Image 13.2). Which dog weighed more, Bingo or Princess?

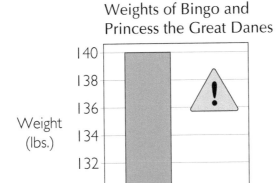

Weights of Bingo and Princess the Great Danes

If you weren't already on the lookout, you might assume that Bingo was almost eight times heavier than Princess because his blue bar was so much longer. Really though, he's only about 12 pounds heavier. Princess is nearly 130 pounds herself—they're Great Danes after all! We learned early on that bar charts use length to show amounts, but that only works if the axis starts at zero. Otherwise, we end up with a confusing visualization like this one where the length of the bar is not the same as the quantity it shows.

Unfortunately, these are just a few of the ways that we can accidentally make a visualization that is confusing or wrong. Even worse, they are ways that someone could give us the wrong idea on purpose. Let's learn what to look out for so that our visualizations are truthful and we don't get fooled.

Double axes

One of the most common ways that people accidentally create confusing visualizations is by using *two* y-axes for two different variables. Take, for example, Table 13.1 that shows the grades Jean-Luc got on his weekly math quizzes compared to the price of one gallon of milk at the store that week.

Table 13.1
*Some data just
aren't related,
even if they are
in the same
table.*

Jean-Luc's Math Quiz Grades and Milk Prices for the Last Six Weeks		
Quiz #	Gallon Price	Quiz Grade
1	$4.85	95
2	$4.89	87
3	$4.89	85
4	$4.93	81
5	$4.96	82
6	$4.99	76

Out of curiosity, we might try putting these data on the same graph to see if they show any patterns—because that's what visualization is good for, right? The graph in Image 13.3 does just that. The red values on the left for Jean-Luc's grades go with the red line, and the blue values on the right for milk prices go with the blue line. The axes both show reasonable values for each variable, so there's no harm done, right?

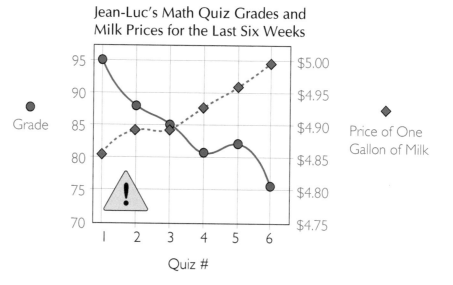

Image 13.3
*Using two y-axes
on the same
graph can make
it look like the
two lines are
related when
they might not
have anything
to do with each
other.*

Not quite. For one thing, nothing special happened when Jean-Luc got an 85 on his quiz that would make milk cost $4.90 per gallon—this is where the two lines cross. In the same way, nothing about Jean-Luc's grades going down would make milk more or less expensive. Jean-Luc's quiz grades have absolutely nothing to do with what the grocery store charges for a gallon of milk—so it's not great that the visualization makes us think they do.

There's another problem, though, that's even sneakier. Using the same data from the table and *only* changing the axes makes the same graph look completely different! Take a look at the version in Image 13.4 where the two y-axes have both been stretched out to start at lower values and end at higher values than before. The light red and blue rectangles show the values from the old axes.

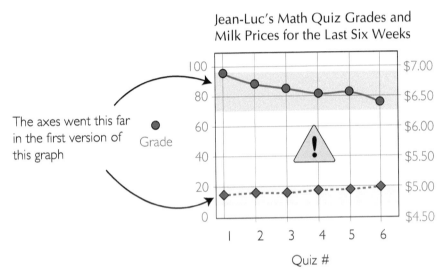

Jean-Luc's Math Quiz Grades and
Milk Prices for the Last Six Weeks

The axes went this far in the first version of this graph

Grade

Price of One Gallon of Milk

Quiz #

What do you notice? Suddenly, it doesn't look so much like Jean-Luc's falling grades make milk more expensive. The lines never cross, either. Milk prices don't seem to change much at all now! What can we do, then, if we want to show two variables at the same time without making them seem more—or less—related than they really are?

One good way is to make separate graphs or small multiples so that each variable has its own axis. Sure, you can still see that Jean-Luc's quiz grades are going down while milk prices are going up. However, since they are different graphs, it doesn't seem as if one is *causing* the other. We can see that both things are happening and decide for ourselves if they are related (Image 13.5).

Image 13.5
*Two small graphs
can do the job
of two y-axes on
the same graph,
without the
confusion.*

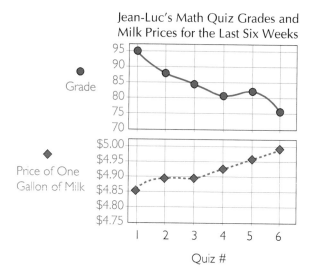

Another possibility is to turn the second y-axis into the x-axis of a connected scatterplot. We learned about these visualizations in chapter about position. The numbers that *were* the x-axis can be written directly onto the graph. In our example, that would look like this (Image 13.6):

Image 13.6
*Connected
scatterplots can
show how two
variables are
related over time
without using
two y-axes.*

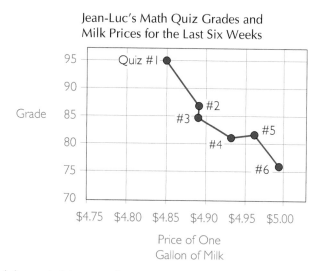

You could read this graph as saying, "During Week 1 milk was $4.85 per gallon, and Jean-Luc got a 95 on his math quiz. On week six, milk cost almost $5.00 per gallon and Jean-Luc got a 76 on his quiz. In general, Jean-Luc's grades went down and milk became more and more expensive."

Graphs like this *do* still show a relationship between the two variables, but having them on the x- and y-axis instead of on two y-axes makes it clearer that they're separate from each other. We can still decide for ourselves if Jean-Luc's quizzes have anything to do with milk prices, or if they just so happen to be changing at the same time.

Backward axes

Just when you think it couldn't get worse, you might come across a visualization like the one we saw at the beginning of the chapter where the y-axis goes in an unexpected order—from high to low, instead of the usual low to high (Image 13.7).

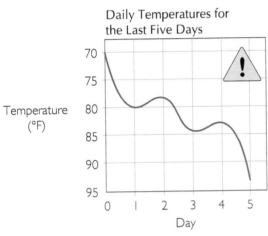

Image 13.7
A y-axis that puts the highest numbers at the bottom shows increasing values as low on the page.

At first glance it would be easy to miss that the axis is flipped, and you might walk away thinking that the temperature had gone down. Really, the graph should have looked like Image 13.8, where the higher temperatures are at higher positions on the page.

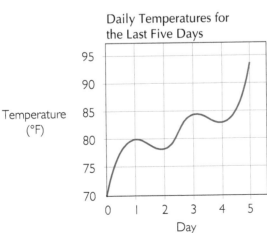

Image 13.8
Flipping the y-axis from Image 13.7 makes this graph easier to understand.

Of course, you might come across a good reason to use an axis that goes from high to low, but in those cases it's best to make it *very* clear that the axis is unusual. The visualization in Image 13.9, for example, shows Aarushi's apple pie competition placings for the past five years. Since 1st place is the best and highest placing, it's at the top instead of the bottom where 1 would usually go. An extra arrow is drawn beside the y-axis to make it clear that the axis is different than you might expect.

Image 13.9
Depending on your data, sometimes it might make sense to use a y-axis that puts the highest values at the bottom.

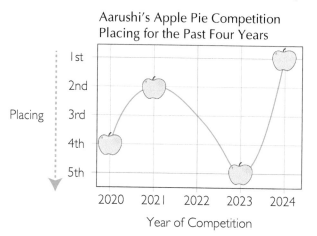

Bar charts that don't start at zero

Let's also take a closer look at the graph we saw a few pages ago about Bingo and Princess the Great Danes. In the confusing version of the graph, Bingo first appears to be *gigantic* compared to Princess. It's not until you look closely at the axes that you might realize that Princess is a big dog, too! Bingo is 140 lbs., but Princess isn't far behind at 129 lbs. (Image 13.10).

Image 13.10
Bar charts are supposed to use length to show amounts, so the y-axis must always start at zero.

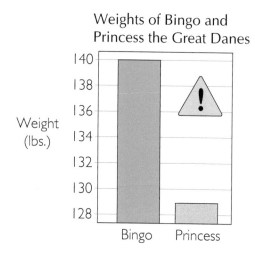

If we made the same graph with a y-axis that starts at zero, we can see how similar the two dogs are. The graph in Image 13.11 still shows that there is a small difference between them, but it's much closer to what they're like in real life.

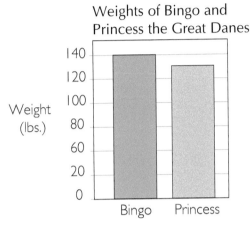

This is why we always start bar charts at zero—because they use length to show an amount, we should be able to compare lengths in a way that makes sense. Comparing the lengths in the first graph gives the wrong idea, but the second graph tells us what we need to know.

If it is more important to show the difference between each dog or the exact amount that each one weighs, you could make a scatter plot instead of a bar chart. In the scatterplot in Image 13.12, the y-axis is the same as the confusing bar chart. However, since it uses dots and not bars, it's okay to start the y-axis at something other than zero. Points don't rely on the length of anything to show data—they use position—so points can go along any axis.

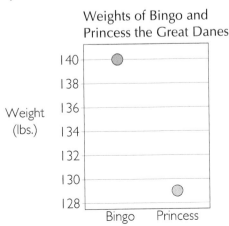

Very tall or flat graphs

Sometimes even the shape of the graph itself can change how we see the data that it shows. Table 13.2, for example, shows Gabrielle's height from the ages of 8 to 13.

Table 13.2
Gabrielle's heights from age 8 to 13

Gabrielle's Height over Time	
Age	Height (inches)
8	49
9	51
10	55
11	59
12	60
13	62

Using the exact same data, we could plot them on a graph that was either short and flat or tall and thin (Image 13.13).

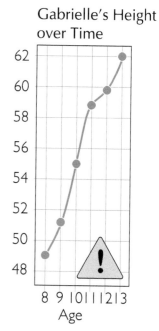

Image 13.13
Short and flat graphs make lines look less dramatic. Did Gabrielle even grow? Tall and thin graphs, on the other hand, make lines look very dramatic!

In the version on the left, it doesn't look like Gabrielle grew that much at all—the line only goes up a little bit. In the second graph, it looks like she grew quite a bit—the line is very steep! The real answer is somewhere in the middle, like we could see in a squarer visualization (Image 13.14).

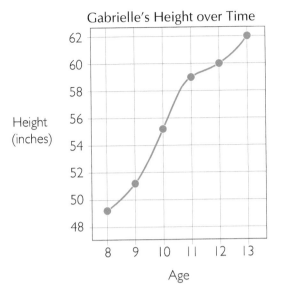

Gabrielle's Height over Time

Does this mean that we should never make tall or flat graphs? No, certainly not. It only means that if we see a graph that is stretched out in one way or the other, we should be careful to think about how the shape of the graph could change how we see the data. Tall and thin graphs usually make patterns look more dramatic, while flat graphs make lines or patterns look, well, flat.

Using extra dimensions for no reason

Speaking of the size or shape of a graph, how a graph looks on the page—whether it looks flat or popped out—can also change how we see the data it's showing. In other words, the **dimensions** of a visualization can make it confusing if they aren't used wisely.

When we talk about the *dimensions* of something we usually mean how tall, wide, and deep it is. You might see the *dimensions* of a thing you're shopping for online in a diagram that looks like Image 13.15.

**Big Gray Block:
Product Dimensions**

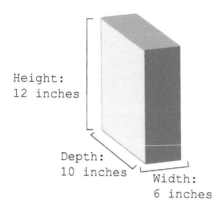

Image 13.15
*Height, width,
and depth are
the dimensions
of an object.*

The diagram tells us that the Big Gray Block is twelve inches tall, six inches wide, and ten inches deep. Since each of the three measurements is one of its dimensions, we can say that this object is three dimensional, or 3D.

A picture on a page only has height and width, however. That's two dimensions, or 2D, such as Image 13.16.

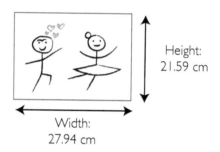

Image 13.16
*A flat picture
only has two
dimensions,
height, and width.*

And you might've seen this coming, a line only has a length, so it's one dimension, or 1D (Image 13.17).

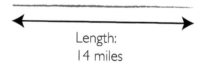

Image 13.17
*A line only has
one dimension,
length.*

In data visualization, though, the word **dimension** means more than just how much space something takes up. It also means how many variables are shown and *how* they are shown. Take the stacked bar chart in Image 13.18, for example, about our old friends Chart Wiz and Graphtron.

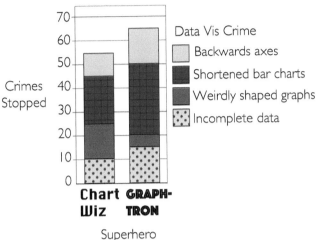

Data Vis Crimes Stopped by
Chart Wiz and **GRAPHTRON!**

Image 13.18
The image is on a two dimensional page, but it has three dimensions of data—Superhero, Crimes Stopped, and Visualization Crime.

In one sense, this image is in 2D because it's drawn with flat rectangles. In another sense, the visualization is actually *three dimensions* because it shows three dimensions of data—or variables! We can count them:

1. The Superhero dimension shown on the x-axis
2. The Crimes Stopped dimension shown on the y-axis
3. The Data Vis Crime dimension shown as color

But what if we put the bars in 3D, too? It would look like Image 13.19.

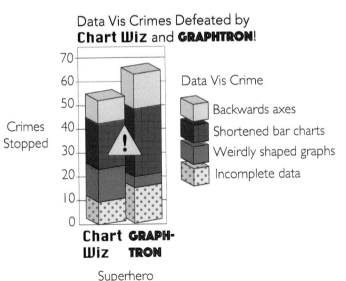

Data Vis Crimes Defeated by
Chart Wiz and **GRAPHTRON!**

Image 13.19
They do look cool, but the depth that makes these bars look 3D doesn't mean anything, and only makes it harder to read the visualization.

Now the bars have height, width, color, *and* depth. Not only are they on the x-axis and y-axis, but they're also on a new axis called the **z-axis**. The z-axis goes back into the page away from you and out of the page toward you. And, truth be told, it's been there all along—we just haven't used it to make any of our visualizations (Image 13.20).

Image 13.20
Two axes create two dimensions of space. Three axes, including the z-axis, make three dimensions of space.

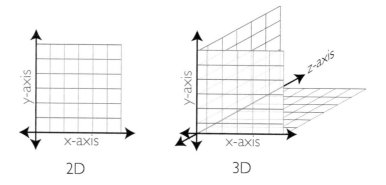

2D   3D

In the 3D version of the bar chart, we can still tell who stopped more crimes over all, but it's trickier to see *exactly* how many of each data vis crime the two superheroes stopped. It looks cool to see the graph in 3D, but adding depth to the bars isn't showing us anything more than the regular 2D bars. In fact, it makes it *harder* to read the visualization. Sadly, the depth doesn't mean anything—it's just an extra dimension for no reason.

Using an extra dimension to make round graphs 3D can be even more confusing because it can change how we see the angles. If we add depth to the pie chart about preferred pets, for example, we get Image 13.21.

Image 13.21
Putting a pie chart into 3D makes it harder to see the angles that show amounts.

Preferred Pets of My Friends

Sure, the labels help us know the amount that the shape represents, but just look at pink Dogs slice! Because the top part of the graph appears to be further away, it's hard to know what angle we're seeing… which is the whole *point* of a pie chart. Just like with the bar chart above, the extra dimension—adding in depth to make the pie chart 3D—doesn't mean anything and only makes the graph harder to understand.

Sometimes 3D *does* make sense

Of course, sometimes making a 3D visualization is a great idea, and there are software programs that can make sure they're drawn accurately. If your data are about something that is wide, tall, and deep—like the actual World—then it makes a lot of sense to make a visualization in 3D. It's hard to draw every side of something that is 3D on a flat 2D picture, but a 3D visualization that you can move around on a screen would let you see all sides.

Visualizations in 3D are also useful if you have data that you'd like to show using position or length, but the x- and y-axes are being used for other variables. The z-axis is all yours! The same goes for visualizations that are just fine in 2D, but you want to make a certain variable stand out more by using position or length on top of something like color or size.

Think back to the heatmap about the number of pages that a few classmates read one week. It's already great in 2D, but showing the number of pages with color *and* height makes the high and low values stand out even more (Image 13.22).

Image 13.22
The number of pages each person read are shown with color and height in this 3D version of the heatmap visualization.

Finally, 3D visualizations can be dramatic, interesting, and inspiring! Some can even be viewed in virtual reality, or look like they are made out of real materials. Visualizations like these let you experience the data in new ways and can make a big impression on the people seeing them.

Ruling out all 3D visualizations, then, is a little too strict. The most important thing to remember is that while 3D graphs can be interesting and useful in some cases, they can be confusing when they aren't made for a good reason. When in doubt, don't bother with 3D if the extra dimension doesn't mean anything, and be careful about reading 3D graphs if you're not sure why they are in 3D.

Not telling the whole story

If you'd only ever eaten one piece of cake and it was *terrible*, then you might think that all cake was disgusting. Fortunately, you've probably had enough different kinds of cake to know that most are excellent, and a few just aren't your favorite.

In a way, the data that we show in a visualization can be like tasting cake. If we only show a tiny bit of data, the people looking at our visualization might think that they know the whole story—but the whole story might be quite different!

In the graph in Image 13.23, for example, we see a very lonely scatterplot showing the number of soccer games played according to an athlete's age. The single point on the graph shows that someone who is 16 years old played 25 games this season. That sounds like a lot!

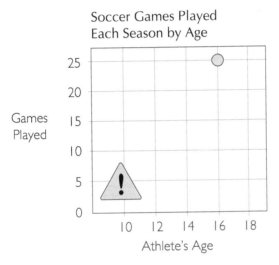

Image 13.23
It's hard to know what a graph means if only a tiny amount of data are shown.

A graph with more data, on the other hand, would give us a much better idea if this was a normal number of games per season for a 16-year-old to play (Image 13.24).

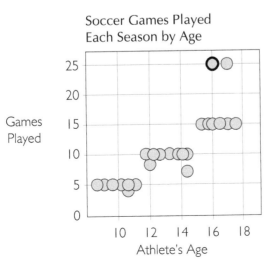

Image 13.24
Showing complete data lets us see where each point stands compared to the others.

In this version of the graph, we can see that very few athletes played 25 games in their season. In fact, it seems that the number of games someone plays really depends on their age. The youngest athletes play about five games per season—but maybe miss one from time to time. Among the older teenagers, all but two athletes played 15 games during the season. The athlete from the original graph must've been on two teams or in a different league that plays more games, perhaps with the other athlete that played 25 games.

When you make visualizations for yourself, try to use as much useful data as possible so that your graph shows the big picture. And, when you look at other peoples' visualizations, ask yourself if any other data would help you to understand the situation better. Sometimes what you don't know *can* hurt you—or at the very least deceive you!

Just plain wrong, aka *lying*

Until now, all of the confusing visualizations that we've seen are often just honest goofs. Most people want to do the right thing, but it's easy to make mistakes if you're still learning. Unfortunately, you may occasionally run into graphs that are wrong on purpose—so wrong, in fact, that you won't believe someone dared to make it.

This can happen if someone wants to make a point about something that the data don't show, or if someone wants to hide something in the data that they don't like. Let's be clear: Making confusing visualizations on purpose is the same as lying. Sadly enough, the few bad apples that choose to do this make it harder to trust data visualization everywhere. Take this graph for example, about the number of points scored by several people in a basketball game (Image 13.25).

Points Scored in the Basketball Game

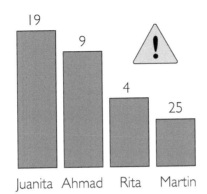

*Image 13.25
Oh, no! The heights of the bars are entirely wrong! Lies!*

For someone who wasn't good at reading data visualizations, they might think that Juanita scored the most points because her bar is the tallest and comes first. They might also think that Martin scored the fewest points because his bar is last and is the shortest. *We* know that that's not true, however, because there's no way that Juanita—who scored 19 points according to the labels—should have a *taller* bar than Martin who scored 25 points.

This is a case of a visualization that is totally incorrect, and will definitely give people the wrong idea. Visualizations should be as truthful and clear as possible, and that means using shapes, colors, and axes that match the *true* values in the data.

Just to make ourselves feel better after seeing all these confusing situations, let's look at what the correct version of this graph should be (Image 13.26).

Points Scored in the Basketball Game

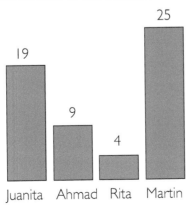

*Image 13.26
Bar charts use length to show amounts, so the lengths of the bars must mach the quantity even if there are labels.*

Ah, *much* better! We can now see that Juanita actually scored the second-most points, and Martin took first place. Rita and Ahmad were on defense, so they were the lowest scorers.

Before you get discouraged by what we've learned in this chapter, remember that you can't fix a problem that you don't know about. We all make mistakes at one point or another, so don't be too hard on yourself or anyone else if you notice something fishy in a visualization. It's easy to get carried away when you're trying to share something exciting or make a chart look good. Instead, use what we've learned to make your own visualizations as strong as possible, and help your friends or people you work with to create their best work, too. It never hurts to have someone double-check your designs to make sure that they are saying what you think. In the end, visualization is *so* good at sharing information quickly that we all need to be careful that we're sharing and understanding the truth.

Chapter summary

There are many ways that visualizations can leave us with the wrong idea, either accidentally or on purpose. Using two y-axes for unrelated data is quite common, but can make us believe that two things are closely related when they might not be. Flipping the direction of an axis can also cause confusion; we're used to seeing axes that go from low to high, so writing them in the opposite order can be confusing. Shortening axes on bar charts so that they don't start at zero is a problem because it makes it impossible to compare the lengths of the full bars. Squishing the entire graph to be either short and flat or tall and thin can make us *think* that the data are more or less dramatic than they really are. Adding an extra dimension to make a graph 3D for no reason makes it harder to read the graph and changes the way we see angles and lengths. Showing only a small piece of a visualization can cause us to think that we know the whole story when we really don't. And finally, making graphs that are not truthful to the data can give people an entirely wrong understanding of what is really happening.

It's your turn!

Take a look at the following three graphs and answer parts a, b, and c for each one.

1. Weight of Alex's Hamster vs Traffic Accidents in Their City

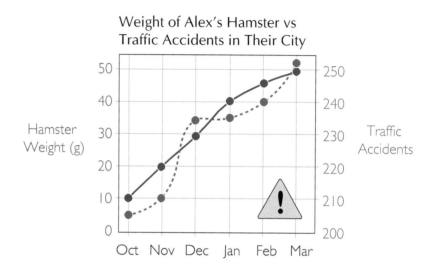

a. What about this visualization could be confusing?
b. How might someone misunderstand the meaning of the visualization?
c. Try redrawing the visualization to be less confusing. What did you change?

Weight of Alex's Hamster vs Traffic Accidents in Their City		
Month	Hamster Weight	Traffic Accidents
October	10	205
November	20	210
December	30	235
January	40	236
February	46	240
March	49	252

2. Text Messages Sent on Saturday

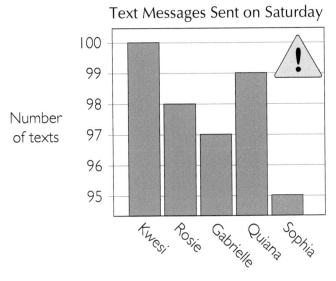

Text Messages Sent on Saturday

a. What about this visualization could be confusing?
b. How might someone misunderstand the meaning of the visualization?
c. Try redrawing the visualization to be less confusing. What did you change?

Text Messages Sent on Saturday	
Person	Texts
Kwesi	100
Rosie	98
Gabrielle	97
Quiana	99
Sophia	95

3. Holiday Lattes Sold at the Coffee Shop

Holiday Lattes Sold at the Coffee Shop

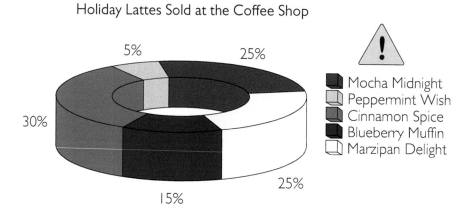

a. What about this visualization could be confusing?
b. How might someone misunderstand the meaning of the visualization?
c. Try redrawing the visualization to be less confusing. What did you change?

Holiday Lattes Sold at the Coffee Shop	
Latte Flavor	Percent
Mocha Midnight	25%
Peppermint Wish	5%
Cinnamon Spice	30%
Blueberry Muffin	15%
Marzipan Delight	25%

14 Sound and touch

Everything we've learned up to this point has been about showing different types of data with shapes and colors that we can see—aka, data *visualization*. Without knowing it though, we've really been learning something bigger than simply picking color palettes and connecting dots: we've learned how to match data to one of our human senses, sight. Sight isn't our only sense though—we can hear and touch, too—which means that there are other senses that we can use to understand data without seeing a single thing. In this chapter we'll learn how to share data in ways that can be heard and felt.

Data you can hear. 224
Pitch 224
Instrument 227
Volume 228
Other types of data sonification 230
Data you can touch. 231
Texture 231
Temperature. 233

DOI: 10.1201/9781003309376-15

Weight 234
Other types of data physicalization 235
Sharing data in more ways 237
Chapter summary 237
It's your turn!. 238

Data you can hear

You've likely heard and understood data without even realizing it. Does your microwave beep when the time is up, and then beep differently to remind you that your food is getting cold? Have you heard the crosswalk chirp when it's safe to cross, and then make another sound when you only have a few seconds left? Do you know what it sounds like to dial a phone number that you have memorized? Even though these are simple examples, they are all places where sound is being used to share data. In other words, these are **data sonifications**.

Much like data visualization, data *sonification* uses different sounds to play data out loud. Instead of seeing patterns with our eyes, a data sonification lets us listen to patterns with our ears. There are several ways to *sonify* data, so let's use a few visualizations from other chapters to understand how a visualization can become a sonification. Make sure to have the audio files ready! They can be found on the book's webpage, www.routledge.com/9781032301006.

Pitch

You might remember the data visualizations we made about sales from Lorenzo and Wei's lemonade stands. On the five days that their stands were both open, they recorded data about the temperature outside and the amount of money that they brought in. The data looked like Table 14.1.

Table 14.1
On each of the
five days that
Lorenzo and
Wei both sold
lemonade they
recorded the
temperature
outside and the
sales from their
stands

Profits from Lemonade Sales by Temperature and Person			
Person	**Day**	**Sales**	**Temperature (°F)**
Lorenzo	Monday	$3.75	86
Lorenzo	Tuesday	$5.00	93
Lorenzo	Wednesday	$3.75	95
Lorenzo	Thursday	$1.25	72
Lorenzo	Friday	$2.50	88
Wei	Monday	$0.50	73
Wei	Tuesday	$2.25	77
Wei	Wednesday	$2.25	84
Wei	Thursday	$4.75	89
Wei	Friday	$5.00	96

A line graph of Lorenzo's sales for each day shows us a line that climbs up and then falls, only to swing back up a bit at the end (Image 14.1).

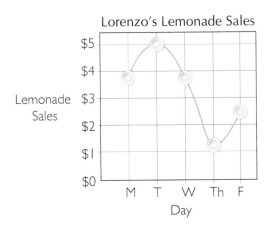

Lorenzo's Lemonade Sales

Image 14.1
Lorenzo's
lemonade sales
during the week
started out by
going up, but
then went down.
They ended
lower than they
started.

There are two variables in the line graph above—Day and Sales. Since the Day variable only lists the week days in order, we can sonify the Sales variable to hear how the values go up and down. Give the first sonification a listen.

▶ *Sonification 14.1: Lorenzo's lemonade sales*

Can you hear how the **pitch**—how high or low the note sounds—goes up and down? Does the pitch seem to match the position of the line in the line graph? Count the number of notes—did you notice that there are five, one for each day?

Without looking back at the data set or ahead to the next visualization, try listening to a sonification of Wei's lemonade sales, too. You might want to listen a few times to make sure you hear how the notes go up or down in pitch.

▶ *Sonification 14.2: Wei's lemonade sales*

If you listen carefully, you'll hear that the pitch of the notes starts out low and gets higher and higher throughout the week. The second and third note are the same. The last note is the highest, which means that Wei made the most money selling lemonade on the last day.

Now look at the line chart of Wei's data. Does this match what you heard (Image 14.2)?

Image 14.2
Wei's lemonade sales went up all week!

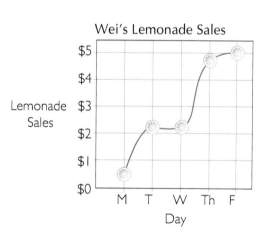

In these two examples, the pitch of the sounds in the sonification replaces the position of the points on the y-axis in the visualization. In other words, the higher up the points are on the graph, the higher pitched the notes sound.

Instrument

Putting both Lorenzo's and Wei's data on the same graph makes a multiple line graph, and usually multiple line graphs use different colors or patterns to tell the lines apart. Sounds don't have colors, though, so each person's data need to sound different to be understandable in a data sonification.

The way something sounds—kind of like its voice—is called **timbre** (pronounced *TAM-ber*). Different instruments sound unique even when they are playing the same note because they have different timbres. For example, listen to these three instruments playing the same scale. Are you able to tell them apart?

▶ *Sonification 14.3: The C major scale played on a piano.*

▶ *Sonification 14.4: The C major scale played on a trumpet.*

▶ *Sonification 14.5: The C major scale played on a violin.*

Now, give a few listens to the sonification of Lorenzo and Wei's data together. You can first try to figure out which two instruments are playing. Then, try to guess who is who. Do you hear Wei's data going up, and Lorenzo's data flowing up and down?

▶ *Sonification 14.6: Lorenzo and Wei's lemonade sales*

Take a look at the multiple line graph of the same data in Image 14.3, and try playing the sonification again while you look at it. Does the sonification make it easier to understand the visualization? Does it make it harder? Did you notice anything in the sonification that made you curious to see the visualization?

Image 14.3
Lorenzo and Wei's lemonade sales went up and down at different times during the week. In the sonification of these data, you can hear each instrument go up or down depending on the person it represents.

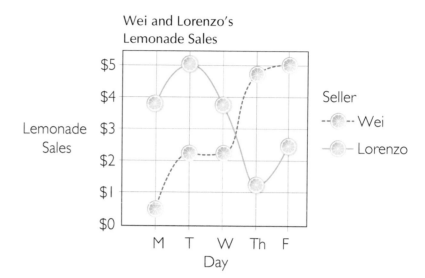

Wei and Lorenzo's Lemonade Sales

In this example, the timbre of each instrument in the sonification replaces the categorical color in the visualization. Different timbres or instruments could also replace different shapes or patterns that are used to show categories in a visualization.

Volume

When we learned about visualizations that use area and size, we looked at a data set that recorded how much certain classmates liked playing video games. We made two visualizations of these data. First, we made a packed circle chart of these data that used small circles to show small values, and larger circles to show larger values (Image 14.4).

Image 14.4
Packed circle charts use area to show amounts. Smaller areas mean less, and larger areas mean more.

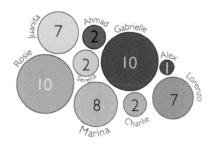

How Much Several Classmates Like Playing Video Games (1 - 10)

We also used the same data to make a bar chart where the lengths of the bars showed the values instead (Image 14.5).

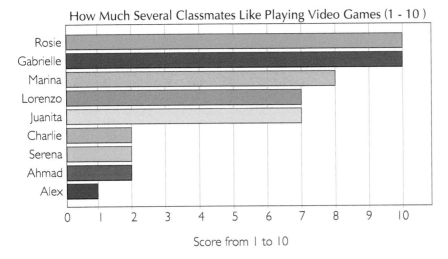

How Much Several Classmates Like Playing Video Games (1 - 10)

Image 14.5
A bar chart uses length to show values. Shorter bars mean less, and longer bars mean more.

To make a sonification of these visualizations, we need something that can sound *more* or *less* or *longer* or *shorter*. We could use pitch like in the first example, or we could use **volume**. Sounds with a high volume are loud, while sounds with a low volume are quiet.

In the next sonification, the volume of the sounds replaces the length of the bars or the areas of the circles. Give it a few listens:

▶ *Sonification 14.7: Video game data using volume*

Can you hear the difference in volume between each note? Are you able to tell *how much* more or less one person likes video games by listening to the sonification alone? Do you have an easier time understanding the visualization? Did the sonification make you notice any patterns that you hadn't seen in the visualization?

Now, listen to the same data in a sonification that uses pitch instead of volume.

▶ *Sonification 14.8: Video game data using pitch*

Is it easier to compare the score for each person in the sonification that uses volume or pitch? Did you have an easier time visualizing the values in your mind with one or the other?

There are no right answers to these questions; just take a moment to think about what *you* notice.

Other types of data sonification

Pitch, timbre, and volume are some of the most obvious ways of adjusting sounds to make a data sonification, but there are others ways of sonifying data that might surprise you. For example, data that are visualized using different positions on an axis or colors in a color gradient could be sonified with sounds that come from different distances or directions. Low values might sound far away, very far to the left, or sound like they're coming from below. High values might sound very close, far to the right, or seem to be coming from above.

Visualizations using length or area could be sonified by changing the duration of the notes. Long bars or large areas could be replaced with slow, steady notes. Short bars and small areas could be replaced with short, choppy notes.

Depending on what your visualization is about, you might choose colors and a style that feel happy, sad, scary, or excited. A sonification, on the other hand, could use instruments and rhythms from certain kinds of music that make us feel these emotions—like slow trombone sounds for something a bit dreary, or a melodious strings ensemble for something inspiring.

You don't need instruments or special equipment to create data sonifications, either. Your voice is already great at changing pitch, being quiet or loud, and showing emotion. On top of that, you can click your tongue, smack your lips, burp, whistle, wheeze, and growl—all for free. Just like in visualization, there are many different ways to share data with sound. To get started though, you can experiment with the replacements from Table 14.2 in your own data sonifications.

Visualization		Sonification
length or angle	→	pitch, volume, duration, distance, or direction
size or area	→	pitch, volume, duration, distance, or direction
position	→	pitch, volume, distance, or direction
gradients	→	pitch, volume, distance, or direction
ordinal colors	→	pitch, distance, or direction
categorical colors	→	instrument or timbre
color palette and style	→	musical genre, instrument, or timbre
shapes and patterns	→	instrument or timbre
connections	→	distance, direction, or timbre

Table 14.2 *Replacing visualization with sonification*

Data you can touch

Have you ever felt a page of braille—the tiny bumps that allow people to read with their fingers? Or, have you felt around for a certain piece of clothing in a drawer rather than turning on the lights so that you can see them? Have you held your hand on the crosswalk button and noticed it buzzing when it's time to cross? These are all examples of ways that we collect data with our sense of touch instead of by what we can see. If we can collect data with touch then we can share it that way, too. This is called **data physicalization**.

Texture

When we learned how to use angles for data visualization, we saw a meter chart that uses angles and ordinal colors to show how hot a cup of coffee is. The darker brown and further to the right the spoon points, the hotter the coffee (Image 14.6).

Image 14.6
*Angle and color
show coffee
at different
temperatures.*

How do you like your coffee?

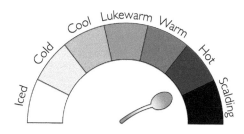

But how could we turn this data visualization into a data physical-ization? It'd be the most obvious to use different temperatures to share data about temperature—and we'll make a physicaliza-tion that uses temperature soon. For this example, though, let's imagine something more unexpected like different textures.

In the physicalization illustrated in Image 14.7, the smoothness or roughness of the materials gives an unusual way of thinking about temperature. The feeling of shiny aluminum foil means the cold-est iced coffee, while a spiky cheese grater means the hottest of hot—ouch! The rougher the texture, the higher the temperature.

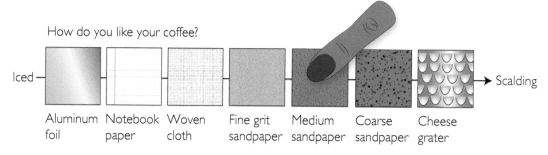

How do you like your coffee?

Iced —   → Scalding

| Aluminum foil | Notebook paper | Woven cloth | Fine grit sandpaper | Medium sandpaper | Coarse sandpaper | Cheese grater |

Image 14.7
*Different
textures of
materials
let us feel
temperature
data in a new
way.*

Here, texture in the physicalization replaces the ordinal colors from the visualization. Depending on the textures, they could also replace categorical colors and shapes.

You obviously won't be able to feel the textures by touching the picture, but gather few different materials that you find around the house or in your classroom. Grab things like printer paper, construction paper, cloth, or plastic bags. Close your eyes, and try to put them in an order. Can you tell them apart? How did you sort them? Did some feel similar to the others?

Temperature

Now let's try using temperature in a physicalization, too. This time, let's look back at the data about the number of pages that Juanita read during a school week. The heatmap visualization that we made with these data looked like Image 14.8.

Number of Pages Juanita Read This Week

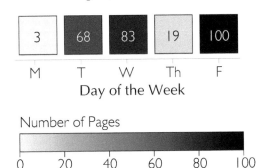

Image 14.8
A light-to-dark color gradient shows low numbers as lighter green and high numbers are dark green or black.

In the visualization, the gradient runs from light green to black, where the lower numbers are lighter and the higher numbers are darker. It would be tricky to make a gradient of textures—though maybe not impossible—but pretty easy to set up a few glasses of water that have been brought to different temperatures like in Image 14.9.

Number of Pages Juanita Read This Week
1 C = 1 page

Image 14.9
Different temperatures of water allow you to feel the number of pages Juanita read. Hotter water means more pages and colder water means fewer pages.

This physicalization replaces the gradient colors from the visualization with temperature. Each page that Juanita read is represented with one degree in temperature. When she only read three pages on Monday, the cup of water is 3°C, which means it's close to freezing. On Friday when she read 100 pages, the water is 100°C—boiling!

Touching each glass would let you know roughly how many pages she'd read each day. Like with the color gradient, it still might be helpful to show the actual numbers, but the physicalization would be a totally new way to experience these data. Temperature replaced color here, but it could also replace position, length, angle, size, or area in a visualization.

Weight

Have you ever had two boxes of cereal or pasta in the pantry—one open, and one new? Maybe you reached for the new one, realized it was too heavy, and put it back to grab the open box. If you've ever done something like that, then you used weight understand a quantity of something without counting or looking at it.

In data visualization, bar charts are great at showing amounts and letting us compare between different groups. Longer bars mean more, while shorter bars mean less. In the example about the long jump competition, we used the length of each bar to know how far each person had jumped. Gabrielle has the longest bar that goes until the number 10 on the x-axis, so we know that she jumped the furthest (Image 14.10).

Image 14.10
Bar charts use length to show amounts. Here, the lengths of the bars show distances.

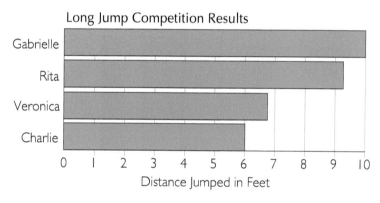

To physicalize these data, we could replace the length of the bars in the visualization with weight. For example, each bar from the bar chart could be physicalized as a small pile of black-eyed peas. The heavier the pile, the longer the long jump. The physicalization illustrated in Image 14.11 uses one ounce of beans for every 10 feet, or 0.10 oz. for each foot.

Long Jump Competition Results
Distances measured in weights of black-eyed peas

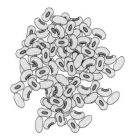

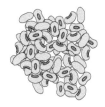

Gabrielle
10 feet = 1.00 oz.

Rita
9.25feet = 0.93 oz.

Veronica
6.75 feet = .68 oz.

Charlie
6 feet = 0.60 oz.

You can use any kind of bean, grain, or nut to try this example at home—you'll just need a food scale to measure the weights. Putting the beans in small paper cups will make less of a mess. Can you feel the difference between Charlie and Gabrielle's pile? What about Rita and Gabrielle? If you put the piles in a different order, is it still easy to tell who is who?

The weights of the beans in the physicalization replace the length of the bars in the visualization, but weight could also replace numerical colors, position, length, angle, area, or size.

Image 14.11
A physicalization using the weight of beans to represent data measured in feet, with 1 oz. of beans for each 10 feet.

Other types of data physicalization

Texture, temperature, and weight might be some of the easier physicalizations to make at home, but they're not the only ones!

The strength of magnets, for example, could replace the connections in a network visualization. Stronger magnets could represent more important links, and magnets that push away from each other or don't stick to different materials could represent nodes that do not connect. Different types of tape or Velcro could work the same way.

Sound and touch

The squishiness or firmness of materials or springs could replace categorical or ordinal colors, or even shapes and patterns. Low values or categories could be squishy like clay, Jell-O, or weak springs, while strong springs and solid materials might represent high values. If the materials feel different enough, they could stand for separate categories entirely.

Instead of using certain colors or styles in a visualization, the materials in a physicalization could hint at what the data are about, too. Metals and stones, for example, would make sense for data about construction, while velvet and silk would make more sense for a project about royalty.

Of course, you can physicalize some visualizations without changing much at all. You could line up blocks in different positions along a measuring tape instead of drawing bars on an axis. Rather than making a bubble chart or a scatterplot with different shapes, you could collect or build objects in several shapes and sizes. You could even connect pieces together with wire or string to make a network.

You'll surely discover new ways to share data through touch, but you can try the replacements in Table 14.3 if you need ideas.

Table 14.3
*Replacing
visualization with
physicalization*

Visualization	Physicalization
length or angle →	Temperature, weight, position, or prize
size or area →	Temperature, weight, position, or prize
position →	Temperature, weight, position, or prize
gradients →	Temperature, weight, position, or prize
ordinal colors →	Texture or squishiness
categorical colors →	Texture, squishiness, material, or shape
color palette and style →	Material
shapes and patterns →	Texture, squishiness, material, or shape
connections →	Magnetism or stickiness

Sharing data in more ways

Earlier in this book we learned about colorblindness and that some people have a hard time telling certain colors apart. We also learned that it was useful to make colorblind-friendly visualizations even if *you* can see colors easily. Not only is it good to make sure that colorblind people aren't left out from understanding your visualization, but the things that make a visualization more color-blind-friendly often make it clearer for everyone anyway.

In a similar way, data sonification and data physicalization share data with people who can't see at all or can't see well. However, that doesn't mean that people who can see won't appreciate listening to data or feeling it with their hands. Sometimes it's nice to think about things in a new way.

Maybe you're a musician and you've always been good at hearing patterns, for example. Or, maybe you do pottery and often use your sense of touch to notice interesting differences. Perhaps you have a hard time paying attention to a busy visualization, but seeing *and* hearing the data help you to follow along. We all experience the world differently, but sonification and physicalization give us more ways to share data with even more people.

Chapter summary

Data sonification puts different types of data to sound. Changing pitch lets us hear different values as high or low notes. Different instruments or timbres let us tell different groups or categories apart. Adjusting the volume of a sound to be louder or softer can tell us how much or little of something there is.

Data physicalization puts data to things we can touch. The texture of a material lets us feel different categories or amounts. Different temperatures or weights can tell us how much of something there is.

It's your turn!

In the following exercises you'll try making your own data soni-fication and data physicalization. You'll then let someone else hear or feel what you've made and ask them a few questions about what they notice.

Note: If you aren't able to make the sonification or physicalization with the suggested materials, feel free to get creative and make them with something else. You can also answer the questions for yourself if it's not a good time to ask someone else to participate. If you are deaf or hard of hearing you are welcome to make two physicalizations or remake the visualization in a different way.

1. Make a sonification that replaces the lengths in the following bar chart with high and low pitches.

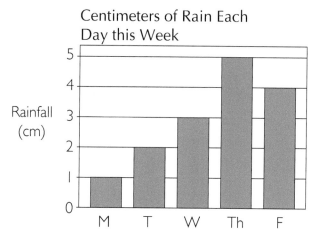

Centimeters of Rain Each Day this Week

a. If you play an instrument, you can use the first, second, third, fourth, and fifth note of a scale. You can also use your own voice—some people call this *punk sonification*!

If you don't play an instrument or feel comfortable singing, you can fill a few cups with different amounts of water so that they make different sounds when you lightly tap them with a spoon. The more water you add, the lower the pitch will be. Sort the cups in order so that you can create a data sonification of the bar chart.

Play the sonification for yourself. Write a few sentences about how you made your sonification and what you hear.

b. Find a friend or family member to listen to your data sonification. Don't show them the visualization! Tell them what the sonification is about, something like, "This sonification is about the amount of rainfall in centimeters each day this week. The first note is on Monday, and the last note is on Friday."

Play your sonification and have them guess which days had the most and least rain. Record their answer and why they thought that.

c. Now, tell them the highest and lowest values and what it means to go up or down in pitch. Something like, "Now, I'll tell you that the driest day had one centimeter and the rainiest day had five centimeters of rain. Higher numbers have higher sounds."

Play your sonification again, and have them guess the value for each day. Write down their guesses. Were they right?

d. Show them the visualization that you turned into a sonification. Record how they react to seeing the visualization.

2. Make a physicalization that replaces the categorical colors in the following visualization with different textures of paper.

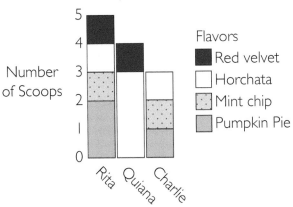

Number of Scoops and Flavors
on Three People's Ice Cream Cones

a. Find four different types of papers or materials that you can cut up. You might use printer paper, construction paper, aluminum foil, pieces of plastic bag, cloth, duct tape, or something else you find around the house. Write down which material will replace each color.

    Cut the materials into small pieces that are about an inch wide. Make as many squares as there are scoops of ice cream in the visualization. For example, Rita had two scoops of pumpkin pie ice cream and Charlie had one, so you'll need to make three squares of material to represent pumpkin pie ice cream.

b. Organize your pieces of materials into little piles, so that each pile shows the types of ice cream that each person had.

    Close your eyes and feel each pile. Can you get a good idea of who had what, and who had the most?

c. Find a friend or family member to try out your data physicalization—but don't show them the visualization or physicalization before you begin! You may need to cover your physicalization with a towel or box so that it stays hidden.

    Tell the other person what the physicalization is about. You might say something like, "This is a data physicalization about the different kinds of ice cream scoops that three people had." Explain what each material means.

    Have them close their eyes and feel each pile of material. Write down what they experience and if they are able to say how many scoops of each ice cream flavor there are in each pile.

d. Now, show them the visualization that you turned into a physicalization. Record how they react to seeing the visualization.

15 Wrapping up

If we picture ourselves as mechanics in an auto shop, this book is like a trusty tool box. Stocked with a gleaming set of screwdrivers, wrenches, bolts, and gaskets, it gives us endless possibilities of things to build. Sports car? No problem. Minivan? Done. Lifted pickup with a flaming exhaust? If you insist…

We don't actually have the tools to build cars, but we do have something just as fun and a little less messy: the tools to create data visualizations. Our toolbox holds things like shapes, colors, axes, variables, and legends, and we've seen a glimpse of the things we can make with them. In this chapter, we'll look back at what we've learned and how it all fits together. We'll see why it's so important to use the right tool for the job, what can go wrong if you don't, and how the right data visualization can be a dream car for people and purposes of all kinds.

DOI: 10.1201/9781003309376-16

Encoding all along 242
Making comparisons 242
Messing with encodings. 244
Know your purpose 250
Know your audience. 252
Putting it all together 253
Congratulations and good luck!. 254
Chapter summary 255
It's your turn!. 255

Encoding all along

We haven't used these exact words yet, but the shapes, angles, positions, colors, sizes, sounds, and textures that we've been using to share data are all different **encodings** or **mappings**. Either word is fine, but we'll stick with *encode* to keep things simple. To *encode* something means to put it into a new format so that it can be shared and understood. Like the word *encode* sounds, encoding data means putting it *in code.* You might use Morse Code to *encode* a message into dots and dashes, or *encode* categories in a visualization as color or shapes.

Chapter by chapter, we've learned which data types each encoding is good or not so good at showing, as well as the visualizations that can be made with them. We've also seen how some encodings can be put together into a single visualization, like how many graphs have two variables encoded with position on the x- and y-axes, and another variable encoded with something like color, size, shape, or length.

Making comparisons

We haven't been encoding data for no reason, though! Instead, we've used encodings to create full visualizations that help us make comparisons. Who has the most ice cream or read the fewest pages? How much more ice cream, and how many fewer pages? Which pool is usually the warmest, and how steady is the temperature over time? Who sold more lemonade in large or small cups? Which word was used the most often in a story? All of these questions ask us to compare one thing to another, and picking the right encodings for each data type lets us create visualizations that do just that.

Image 15.1 lists the visual encodings that we've learned about and says how good they are for making comparisons with each type of data. Some encodings work well for all data types, like position along an axis. Other encodings are only okay at sharing exact values that we can easily compare, like angle or color for numerical data. These encodings should be used with good legends and labels to make sure that the values are clear. The red sad faces show the encodings that are pretty bad at making comparisons, like length or size for categorical data.

Which encodings are good at showing each data type?

	Numerical	Categorical	Ordinal
Length	😊 Great	😞 Bad	😐 Okay
Size	😐 Okay	😞 Bad	😐 Okay
Position	😊 Great	😊 Great	😊 Great
Color	😐 Okay	😊 Great	😐 Okay
Brightness	😐 Okay	😞 Bad	😐 Okay
Shapes	😞 Bad	😊 Great	😞 Bad
Patterns	😞 Bad	😊 Great	😐 Okay
Angles	😐 Okay	😞 Bad	😞 Bad

Image 15.1
Not all encodings work for each data type. Some are great, while others are terrible. Some encodings work just okay, and might need a little extra labeling to be useful.

Most of the visualizations that we've made so far have used Great or Okay encodings, so we're no strangers to how good visualization *can* be at sharing data. What we haven't seen, however, is what happens when the encodings aren't so great. As always, let's do a few examples to see for ourselves why the right—or wrong—encodings make such a big difference in a visualization.

Messing with encodings

Back in Chapter 5 we made a few visualizations about the delays for each bus in three different bus lines on a particular Monday. The data about the buses looked like Table 15.1.

Table 15.1
The bus delay data. The Bus Number variable is ordinal, the Bus Line Variable is categorical, and the Delay variable is numerical.

Monday's Bus Delays (in Minutes)					
Bus Number	Bus Line	Delay	Bus Number	Bus Line	Delay
1	Red	4	6	Blue	7.2
2	Red	10.3	7	Blue	9.4
3	Red	7.4	8	Blue	8
4	Red	8	9	Blue	12.5
5	Red	5.6	1	Orange	2.6
6	Red	11.5	2	Orange	4.8
7	Red	0.9	3	Orange	0.8
8	Red	–	4	Orange	7.3
9	Red	–	5	Orange	2
1	Blue	4.3	6	Orange	1.6
2	Blue	10.9	7	Orange	1
3	Blue	6.5	8	Orange	3.3
4	Blue	9	9	Orange	–
5	Blue	5			

In our visualizations about these data, the numerical Delay variable is encoded as the position of the points the on the y-axis. The categorical Bus Line variable is **double-encoded** as color and as the position of each point on the x-axis. *Double encoding* means using two encodings to show the same variable. We didn't need to make each bus a different color—they are already in different positions—but the colors make the graph a little easier to read (Image 15.2).

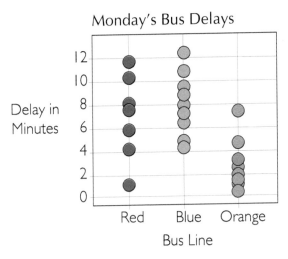

These encodings make it easy to compare the overall lateness of one bus line to the others, and to compare the difference between the latest and timeliest buses on the same routes. This isn't the only way to visualize these data, though!

In the visualization in Image 15.3, the encodings have changed. By encoding the Delay variable as *height* rather than position, we could have a grouped bar chart instead. The bars in each Bus Line are arranged in order of the Bus Number variable.

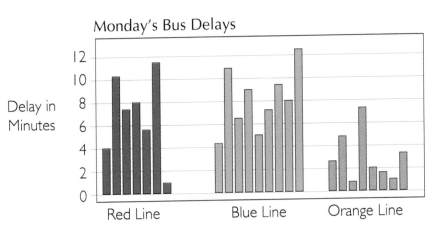

Already, the visualization above looks completely different than the strip plot! It's still easy to compare the lateness of each bus line overall to the other bus lines, as well as the lateness of each single bus to the others—just like the strip plot. However, this version also tells us that the very late buses seem to be spread out during the day, which we couldn't know in the first chart. In other words, it lets us compare the order of the buses to their lateness.

Now, what if we added the bars together and made a bar chart that compares the *total* amount of delay for each bus line? That would look like Image 15.4.

Image 15.4
Adding up the total amount of delay for each day makes a different version of the first bar chart.

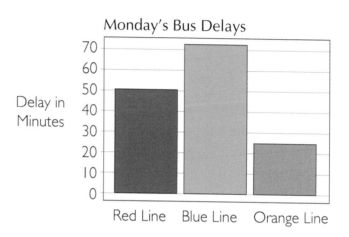

This visualization still uses length to encode lateness so that we can see which Bus Line caused the most delay overall. The Blue Line totaled more than 70 minutes of delays on Monday, towering over the Orange Line's 25 minutes. We can't, however, compare the number of busses in each bus line. That comparison might be useful for understanding why the Blue Line caused so much more delay than the others. We also can't compare the lateness of a single bus to the others like we could in the first two visualizations.

Bending these bars into a pie chart like in Image 15.5 would mean encoding Delay as angle instead of length—and would tell us yet another story. Do you have an idea of what we can compare with the pie chart that we couldn't in the last visualization? Fractions! The pie chart lets us compare the fractions of the total delays on Monday caused by each bus line. We can see that the Blue Line caused as much lateness as both the Red and Orange lines combined.

Monday's Bus Delays

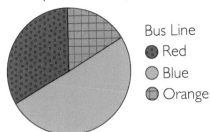

Bus Line
- ● Red
- ○ Blue
- ◐ Orange

Image 15.5
Pie charts make it easier to see fractions than bar charts.

But wait, there's more! We could make a multiple line chart, too, by encoding the Bus Number and its Delay with positions on each axis. The Bus Line can be *triple*-encoded as color, shape, and line pattern. These encodings make it easier to compare the number of buses in each line because we can notice where each line on the visualization stops. We can also compare the delays for the 1st through 9th buses of the day across each of the three bus lines. We can now see that the first buses of the day were fairly on time, but that there was a big difference in how late the 6th bus from each line was. Even if it was possible to make this comparison with the grouped bar chart, it was harder because the bars for the 1st, 2nd, or 9th busses in each Bus Line weren't side-by-side (Image 15.6).

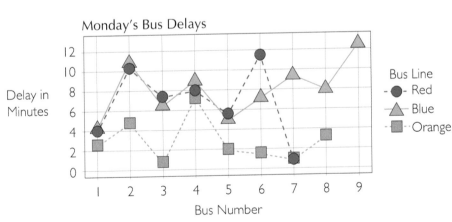

Image 15.6
Multiple line charts make it easier to compare values from different groups at the same position.

Like we did with the pie chart, wrapping the multiple line chart into a few radar charts would give us a new way to compare the bus lines to each other. In the radar charts in Image 15.7, we can see the big blue blob showing the Blue Line's delays, and the tight little knot for the timelier Orange Line. The Red Line has a long spike for the 6th bus. What we *can't* see so well is that each line had a different number of buses, or who had the latest first or last bus of the day. In fact, the radar charts don't really help us make any good comparisons apart from the shapes looking somewhat bigger or smaller than the others.

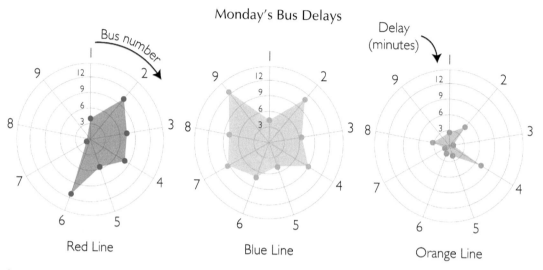

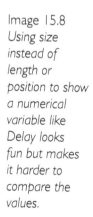

Image 15.7 Small multiples of radar charts show the shape of each bus's delays.

Since we've already used position, length, and angle to encode the Delay variable, we could try encoding it with size, too. Putting the Bus Number on the x-axis like we did in the multiple line graph, the Bus Line on the y-axis, and encoding Delay with size makes a bubble chart (Image 15.8).

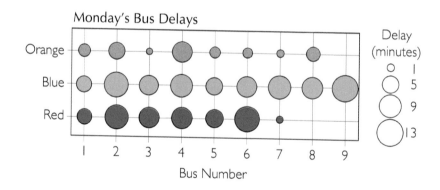

Image 15.8 Using size instead of length or position to show a numerical variable like Delay looks fun but makes it harder to compare the values.

On the one hand, this version makes it easy to see which bus line had the most buses, and the dots aren't on top of each other like they were in the multiple line chart or the strip plot. On the other hand, it makes it harder to compare the delays for each bus than it was in the visualizations that used length or position. Like we learned in Chapter 4, size encodings are best for giving an *idea* of how much more or less something is, but they aren't great at showing exact amounts.

We still haven't done anything interesting with color either, so let's see what happens if we encode Delay with color instead of size. In the heat map in Image 15.9, we can still compare the number of buses that each line ran on Monday, and the light-to-dark gradient makes it pretty easy to spot the latest and timeliest buses. It's might be a tiny bit easier to compare delays with this heat map than it was in the bubble chart, but it's still difficult to compare exactly *how* different the delays were by looking at the colors alone.

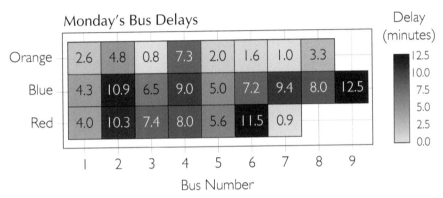

Image 15.9
Heat maps make it easy to pick out "hot spots" but harder to compare amounts.

And for a grand finale, let's do something that's downright weird. Let's put the Delay variable on the x-axis. The Bus Line variable can be encoded with different shapes. The Bus Number variable can be shown in color as if it were a numerical variable... even though it's really an ordinal variable with no Bus Number 2½ or 0. The y-axis can disappear so that it doesn't matter how far up or down the shapes are on the graph. It's a masterpiece of chaos (Image 15.10)!

Image 15.10
Position is one of the best encodings for variables of all data types, and not using it when you could can spell disaster for a visualization.

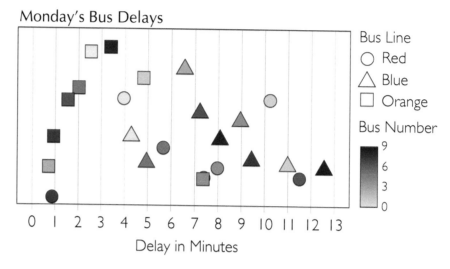

This visualization is hilarious but completely useless. Which bus line had the worst delays? Were the buses that came earlier in the day more on time than the ones later in the day? Which was the latest bus line in general? It's tough to answer *any* of these questions, or make any good comparisons, even though this graph visualizes exactly the same data that we saw in the original strip plot.

And *that* is why it's important to be careful about choosing the right encodings for your visualization. Sure, you can make a random visualization by throwing together a few careless encodings, but why? You want something useful that helps you answer specific questions or make interesting comparisons. Picking from the best encodings for each data type—starting with the variables you want to compare—is a much better idea.

Know your purpose

Visualization can't happen without encodings, but there are a few more things to think about before you pick up your pencil. Just like you would if you were designing a car, you need to know *why* you're making a visualization. Sports cars and minivans are both cars, but people use them for very different reasons. In general, there are three reasons that you might make a visualization, and each of these reasons will change the kinds of comparisons that you want to make.

Exploratory visualization

If you have a new data set and you're not sure what the values look like, you might make a few **exploratory visualizations** to get a good idea of what it's about. *Exploratory visualizations* help you *explore* the data, and usually let you see many data points at once. Said another way, exploratory visualizations let you compare the values within a variable and between variables. A scatterplot, for example, will show you if there are any big patterns or groups that you didn't notice in the rows and columns of a data table. It might also show you values that doesn't look quite right so that you check that your data are correct.

Exploratory visualizations are often just for you and the people you're working with while you wrap your head around the data. They can be a little messy and a don't need to be perfect. It's all part of the process!

Presentation visualization

Once you've done a little exploring, you'll know what's interesting about your data and what you want to share with others. At this point, you're ready to make a visualization for presentation. Presentation visualizations are for other people who haven't seen your data or your exploratory visualizations. They don't know what's interesting about your data, so they need your visualization to help them learn.

Presentation visuals should make it as easy as possible for someone to understand what you're telling them. That means the titles, axis labels, legends, and captions should be useful and clear. Now is the time to pay special attention to colorblind-friendliness, and to choose encodings that will help people make the comparisons that you want them to make.

Artistic visualization

Finally, some visualizations are mostly about making people *feel* a certain way, just like a painting or a song would do. We'll call these artistic visualizations. Of course, these visualizations should still be correct and honest, but artistic visualizations use style and flair to attract attention or make people feel curiosity, excitement, or awe. Encodings like color, brightness, and size are right at home in artistic visualizations because they can be so beautiful and dramatic.

Data sonification, data physicalization, and 3D visualization are great examples of where artistic visualization shines. Perhaps you make a 3D visualization that looks futuristic or other-worldly. Or, maybe you make a sonification that encodes your data with music from a harp. A physicalization made from glass and plastic could be an art installation about climate change or trash in the ocean. The possibilities are endless for using visualization to make powerful art.

Know your audience

Along with knowing the purpose of your visualization—exploratory, presentation, or artistic—you'll also want to think about the audience for your work. Knowing who is a visualization is for will help you create something that is useful and understandable to them.

You yourself are one possible audience. If you are making an exploratory visualization or just creating something for fun, you can do whatever you want—the floor is yours! Use silly colors, draw it in sidewalk chalk, make a sonification with a kazoo... *you* decide. Making visualizations for yourself without worrying about what other people think or need is a great way to practice new skills, try out new encodings, and do a little bit of experimenting.

After you've had some fun, you might go on to make a visualization for other people to use. That means you'll need to think about *who* will see the visualization, *what* you want to tell them, and *how* good their visual literacy is. A scientist, for example, will be pretty good at understanding whatever kind of visualization that you show her. A five-year-old kid, on the other hand, might have more fun with a simple visualization like a pictograph chart.

Different people will want to make different comparisons, too, and it's your job as a data visualizer to figure out what those comparisons are. After all, the question isn't, "How can I show my data?" because there are *loads* of ways to do that. Rather, the question is "How can I show what my audience cares about in my data?" Answering this question is one of the hardest parts of data visualization, but with a little practice you'll get better at stepping into other peoples' shoes and seeing the world from their perspective. It will become a superpower!

Putting it all together

It took us a whole book to get here, but we finally have all of the pieces to make a data visualization from start to finish. We've seen how many ways there are to visualize the same data—and how quickly things can go sideways. We've also taken a step back to decide the purpose of a visualization, who it's for, and what they're interested in. Since there are so many things to think about when creating a data visualization, we need a plan to make sure nothing gets missed. In other words,

Step 1: Collect or find data. Gather as much data as you can to tell a complete story.

Step 2: Arrange the data into a table with one column for each variable. Make sure that the values in a variable are all the same data type.

Step 3: Decide what type of visualization you are making—exploratory, presentation, or artistic—as well as who your audience is.

Step 4: Describe what you want to visualize as a comparison. For example, "Compare the number of pages read each day by five different people" or "Compare the heights of people sitting at the same table."

Step 5: Pick encodings that help you to best make the comparison, paying special attention to the data types for each variable. Choose the strongest encodings—like position—for your most important variables first. Don't use up the strongest encodings on less important variables.

Step 6: Visualize it! Use the encodings you've picked to draw your visualization—in pencil, on a tablet, or with code on a computer. Or, sonify or physicalize with whatever you have around. Your visualization might be one of the many that we learned about, or it could be something entirely new.

Step 7: Add titles, labels, legends, and a caption to the visualization that describe what the visualization shows and how to read it.

Step 8: Take a step back and pretend that you are seeing your visualization for the first time, or show it to someone and ask for their thoughts. Does it say what you wanted to show? If you're happy with your visualization, stop here. You did it! If you think something could be better, start over at Step 3 and think about what you want to change.

Congratulations and good luck!

Take a moment to sit back, put your feet up, and give yourself a big high-five. It was only a few chapters ago that we learned what the words *data* and *visualization* meant—and look how far we've come! We visualized with color and shapes, lengths and angles, and even used our ears and hands to share data in new ways. Most importantly though, we learned how to *think* about data and how to make it talk.

The rest of your visualization journey is up to you. Try some things for yourself, make a mess, and share what you make when you're ready. Notice the visualizations around you, and think about what they tell you—or the secrets that they keep. The world is big and full of mystery, but visualization is something special for all of us to make sense of it. So go forth and visualize! This book will be here if you need it.

Good luck!

Chapter summary

Encodings are the different ways of visualizing, sonifying, and physicalizing data, like position, length, color, pitch, or weight. It's important to know what each encoding is good at so that you can select the best encodings for each variable in your visualization. Knowing the purpose of your visualization and the people who might see it can change the comparison you decide show and the encodings that you choose.

It's your turn!

1. Use the data set below for this exercise.

Rescue Dogs at Dos Reñas Dog Sanctuary						
Name	Weight (lbs.)	Height (inches)	Age	Gender	Coat	Energy
Otis	11	8	Senior	Female	Curly	Low
Sunny	12	10	Puppy	Female	Medium	High
Freida	23	12	Senior	Female	Long	Low
Rosita	27	17	Adult	Female	Medium	Low
Gertie	31	14	Senior	Female	Curly	Medium
Lorraine	40	21	Puppy	Female	Medium	High
Buddy	45	18	Puppy	Male	Long	High
Moose	80	30	Puppy	Male	Short	High
Paws	52	25	Adult	Male	Short	Medium
Rex	60	20	Senior	Male	Curly	Low
George	70	19	Adult	Male	Short	High
Scout	74	25	Adult	Female	Short	Medium
Hazel	81	20	Adult	Female	Curly	High
Princess	129	33	Adult	Female	Short	Low
Bingo	141	35	Senior	Male	Short	Low

a. Give the data type for each variable.

Variable	Data Type
Name:	_____
Weight:	_____
Height:	_____
Age:	_____
Gender:	_____
Coat:	_____
Energy:	_____

b. Write out a comparison that you think would be interesting to make using these data.
c. Make a visualization that lets you make this comparison.
d. List the encodings that you used for each variable that is in your visualization.

Variable	Encoding
Name:	_____
Weight:	_____
Height:	_____
Age:	_____
Gender:	_____
Coat:	_____
Energy:	_____

e. Now make another visualization by picking whatever encodings you want for the same variables.

f. List the encodings for this new visualization.

Variable	Encoding
Name:	_____
Weight:	_____
Height:	_____
Age:	_____
Gender:	_____
Coat:	_____
Energy:	_____

g. Find a friend, family member, or neighbor to look at your visualizations. Show them the second visualization, and ask them what they think it is about. Then, show them the one you made first. What do they say? Do they like one better than the other? Is one funny, but one useful?

Appendix 1: Glossary of words

Area   The amount of space a shape takes up if it is flat on page.

Axis   The part of a data visualization that tells quantities or categories using position.

Axis break   A zig-zag or slash on an axis that shows that the axis labels don't start at zero or that there is a gap in the values.

Axis labels   The numbers or words below or beside an axis that explain what the positions on the axis mean.

Axis title   The word or phrase below or beside an axis that tells which variable the axis shows.

Caption   A description of a visualization that explains what the visualization is about and how to understand it.

Categorical data   Data that can be split up into clear groups where no group is more, less, before, or after any other group. Also called nominal data.

Cells   The smallest living pieces of the body. Each part of the body is made up of a different type of cell.

Chord   The thick ribbon of color that is a link in a chord diagram.

Color palette   A collection of colors for a certain purpose. Categorical data are best shown with a color palette that has different-looking colors. Ordinal data are best shown with a color palette that shows an ordering.

Cone cells   The cells in the eye that detect different colors of light. Most people have three types of cone cells that see mostly blue, green, or red light.

Continuous   Spaced evenly apart with fractions in between. Color gradients can show numerical data because they are both continuous.

Contour map   A type of visualization that uses lines, curves, and colors to show the hills and valleys of a landscape.

Data   Pieces of information that are observed, measured, and recorded about any topic.

Data physicalization   Sharing data with different textures, weights, temperatures, or anything else that you can feel.

Data point   One single piece of data that has one value from each variable in the data set. Also called a datum. Usually one row in a data table.

Data sonification   Putting data to sounds of different pitches, volumes, timbres, and anything else you can hear.

Data visualization   Showing data using things we can see like shapes and colors.

Dimension   How something is measured in space or a variable and how it is shown in a visualization. For objects in the real world, dimensions include height, width, and length. For visualizations, dimensions could be the use of color for temperature or the x-axis for the date.

Directed   Pointing a specific way. In networks, a graph is directed if the links show the direction that a relationship goes. Most of the time, directed networks use arrows.

Diverging   Going in opposite directions. Diverging color palettes and gradients show data that go in opposite directions by changing from a dark color, to very light, to another dark color.

Double encoding   Using two encodings to show the same variable. See Encoding for more.

Encoding   In visualization, the ways of sharing data so that it can be seen, heard, or felt—like color, position, length, pitch, or temperature—are called encodings. Some encodings work better than other for different data types. Also called mapping.

Exploratory visualization   Charts and graphs that are created to help you understand the values in your data and become familiar with it.

Gradient   Colors that blend smoothing from one to the next.

Gridlines   Thin lines that run back and forth or up and down across a visualization that make it easier to see where a position on the graph is compared to the axes.

Interval data   Data, like dates and times, that fall in an order and are evenly spaced by an amount that can be measured. Unlike numerical data, interval data don't have a definite starting point.

Jittering   Slightly moving points on a visualization so that they do not overlap. Points can only be moved in a direction that doesn't change their meaning.

Key   The part of a data visualization that explains the meanings of the different colors or shapes. Also called a legend.

Legend   The part of a data visualization that explains the meanings of the different colors or shapes. Also called a key.

Links   The parts of a network graph that connect nodes to each other. Depending on the relationships between the nodes, the links might be lines or arrows.

Mapping   In visualization, the ways of sharing data so that it can be seen, heard, or felt—like color, position, length, pitch, or temperature—are called mappings. Some mappings work better than other for different data types. Also called encoding.

Nodes   The parts of a network graph that are connected or related to each other.

Nominal data   Data that can be split up into clear groups where no group is more, less, before, or after any other group. Also called categorical data.

Numerical data   Data that are made of entirely numbers that aren't split into different groups. Zero means there is absolutely none of whatever is measured. Also called ratio or quantitative data.

Opacity   How hard it is to see through something. If something is fully opaque or at full opacity, then it's impossible to see through. The opposite of transparency.

Ordinal data   Data that can be split into different groups as well as put into a specific order. Each group comes before or after the others, or is greater or less than the others. The distance between categories can't be measured.

Palette   A collection of colors for a certain purpose. Categorical data are best shown with a color palette that has different-looking colors. Ordinal data are best shown with a color palette that shows an ordering.

Physicalization   Sharing data with different textures, weights, temperatures, or anything else that you can feel. Also called data physicalization.

Pitch   How high and squeaky, or low and rumbly a sound is.

Position   The place of something on a visualization compared to the axes.

Quantitative data   Data that are made of entirely numbers that aren't split into different groups. Zero means there is absolutely none of whatever is measured. Also called ratio or numerical data.

Ratio data   Data that are made of entirely numbers that aren't split into different groups. Zero means there is absolutely none of whatever is measured. Also called numerical or quantitative data.

Rod cells   The types of cells in the eye that help us see in dim light. Rod cells do not help us see color.

Sonification   Putting data to sounds of different pitches, volumes, timbres, and anything else you can hear. Also called data sonification.

Spoke   The axes of a radar chart that run from the center of the graph to the outside edge. They are called spokes because they look like the spokes on a bicycle wheel.

Table   A way of organizing data so that each variable is in a column (up and down), and each data point has its own row (left to right).

Tick marks Short dashes that stick out of an axis to show exactly where each possible value on the axis falls.

Transparency How see-through something is. Something that is fully transparent is totally clear. The opposite of opacity.

Undirected Not pointing in a particular way. In networks, a graph is undirected if the links only show connection and not which way the relationship goes.

Variable Data about one specific subject, often recorded in columns of a data table.

Visual literacy How well someone is able to read and understand the meaning of a visualization, as well as create a data visualization that others are able to use.

Visualization Showing data using things we can see like shapes and colors. Also called data visualization.

Appendix 2: Glossary of graphs

Bar chart

Bar charts (Chapter 3) use the length or height of rectangles to show quantities in different categories. Each bar starts at zero and represents one category. Bars can go from left to right or from bottom to top. Bar charts that measure from bottom to top are sometimes called **column charts**.

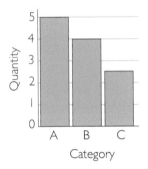

You can read the bar chart above as saying, "There are five things in Category A, four things in Category B, and 2½ things in Category C."

Bee swarm chart

Bee swarm charts (Chapter 5) use the position of points to show quantities in different categories. The points in bee swarm plots are jittered, meaning that they are moved to the right and left to make room for each other—no points overlap like in **strip plots**. The widest bunches in the graph have many values that are similar to each other.

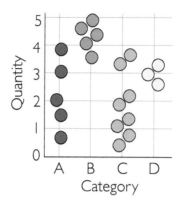

Read the bee swarm chart above as saying, "The points in Category A are quite spread out—some show quantities that are less than one while others show almost four. The points in Category D, however, are grouped together around a quantity of three."

Bubble chart

Bubble charts (Chapter 5) use position to show two quantities and size to show a quantity or order. You can read a bubble chart just like a scatterplot, except the size the points—which are called bubbles—has meaning, too.

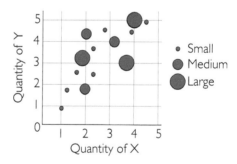

Read the bubble chart above as saying, "In general, the more of X there was, the more Y there was, too. The red bubble shows a data point that has four of X and five of Y, and is the largest size."

Chord diagram

Chord diagrams (Chapter 12) use connections to show how different groups of things move from one place or situation to the next. Like networks, chord diagrams have **links** and **nodes**. The links are the thick ribbons of color, called **chords**, and the nodes are the colorful pieces of pizza crust around the edge. The thicker the chord, the more of something there is moving from one place to another.

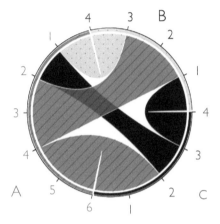

You can read this chord diagram as saying, "Two things moved from A to B. Two things moved from A to C. One thing moved from B to A. One thing moved from C to A. One thing moved from C to B."

Column chart

See **bar chart**.

Connected scatterplot

Connected scatterplots (Chapter 5) use position and arrows to show quantities in an order. You can read a connected scatterplot like a scatterplot and line chart put together, following the arrows from one point to the next.

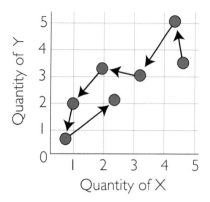

Read the connected scatterplot above as saying, "In general, the more of X there was, the more Y there was, too. The first point in the data set is in the top right corner, and the last point is near the middle of the graph."

Donut chart

Donut charts (Chapter 11) use angle and color to show how something is made up of smaller categories, very much like **percent bar charts**. Donut charts always add up to 100%. Large bites of a donut mean that the there is a lot of a category; small bites mean that there is only a little. Donut charts are the same as **pie charts** except for the donut hole in the center!

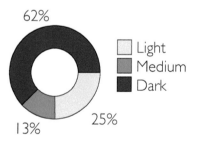

Read the donut chart above as saying, "25% the things being counted are light, 13% are medium, and most of the things—62%—are dark."

Dot plot

Dot plots (Chapter 2) use the heights of stacks of dots to show frequencies. The x-axis shows different values or ranges of values, and the y-axis shows often those values happened.

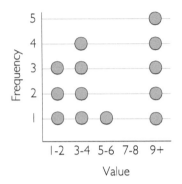

You can read this dot plot as saying, "Something happened 1–2 times three times. Nothing ever happened 7–8 times. Most often, something happened 9+ times."

Dumbbell chart

Dumbbell charts (Chapter 3) use the distance between two points to show before-and-after quantities in different categories, or to compare the quantities of two things in different categories.

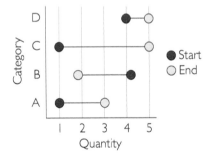

You can read this dumbbell chart as saying, "Category A started with one thing and ended with three things. Category C had the biggest change because it started with one thing and ended with five things. Category B is the only category that started higher than it ended."

Gantt chart

Gantt charts (Chapter 3) use rectangles of different lengths to show durations of time for different activities. The length of the bar shows how long something lasted.

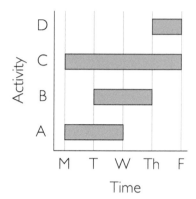

You can read this Gantt chart as saying, "Activity A started on Monday and went until Wednesday. Activity C started on Monday and went until Friday. Activity D didn't start until Thursday and ended the next day."

Grouped bar chart

Grouped bar charts (Chapter 6) use length and color to show quantities of things that are in two categories at the same time. Each cluster of bars represents a single category, and each single bar shows the smaller groups within the bigger category.

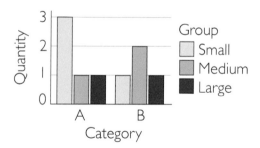

You can read the grouped bar chart above as saying, "In Category A there are three small things, one medium thing, and one large thing, for a total of five things altogether. In

Category B there are four total things, but one is small, two are medium, and one is large."

Heat map

Heat maps (Chapter 7) use color and position to show quantities across categories or levels.

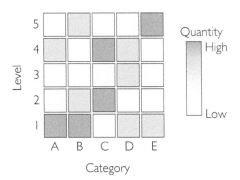

Read this heat map as saying, "In Category C, Level 4, there is the highest quantity of something. We know this because that square is the darkest color, and the legend shows that darker shades of yellow mean higher quantities. In Category D, Level 2, there is very little something because the square is very light yellow."

Icicle chart

Icicle charts (Chapter 12) show tree data by arranging rectangles from left to right or top to bottom in order of the branches in the data. The rectangles at the bottom or right of the icicle chart are the **leaf nodes**; they don't branch into any other nodes.

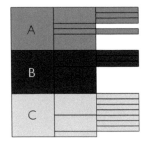

You can read this icicle chart as saying, "Branches A, B, and C make up the whole tree. Within Branch A, there are two large branches and two small branches. One of the large branches splits off into three leaf nodes, while the other large branch is a leaf node itself."

Line chart

Line charts (Chapter 5) use the position of lines compared to the x and y axes to show how two quantities of things change at the same time. **Multiple line charts** have more than one line and a legend to explain what each line means.

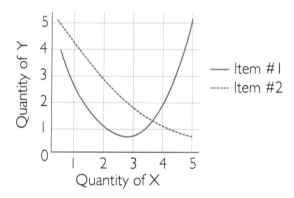

Read the line chart above as saying, "As Item #1 gets more and more of X, it loses some Y—until it has around three of X. After that, more X means more Y for Item #1. For Item #2, on the other hand, having more of X always means having less of Y."

Meter chart

Meter charts (Chapter 11) use angle and sometimes color to show amounts of something or progress toward a goal.

You can read the meter chart above as saying, "Something is on level two out of six," or "Someone has two of six possible things."

Network graph

Network graphs (Chapter 12) use **links** and **nodes** to show connections or relationships between things or categories. If the links connecting the nodes are arrows, then the connection only goes in one direction. If links are lines, the connection goes both ways. Each node represents one data point. Also called node-link diagrams.

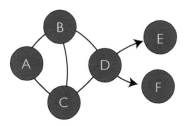

You can read this network as saying, "A is connected to B and C, and those relationships go both ways. B and C are both connected to A, D, and to each other. D is connected to E and F, but those relationships only go one way. E and F are not connected to each other."

Node-link diagram

See **network graph**.

Packed circle chart

Packed circle charts (Chapter 4) use circles of different sizes to show different amounts in different categories. The circles are bunched as tightly together as possible, but it doesn't matter where in the visualization they are.

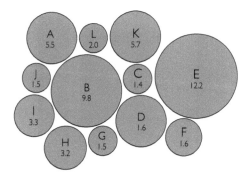

You can read this packed circle chart as saying, "Category B has more than Category A, but Category E has more than everyone. Category C has the least."

Parallel coordinates chart

Parallel coordinates charts (Chapter 12) use position and connection to show multiple values for the same data point. The axes in a parallel coordinate chart can have different values or be different data types altogether.

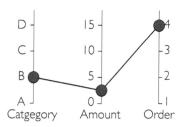

Read this parallel coordinates chart as saying, "Something was in Category B, had an amount of 2½, and was 4th in order."

Percent bar chart

Percent bar charts (Chapter 11) are **stacked bar charts** that always go from 0% to 100%. They use length and color to show how different categories are made up of smaller groups. All of the bars in a percent bar chart are the same height because they show fractions instead of counts.

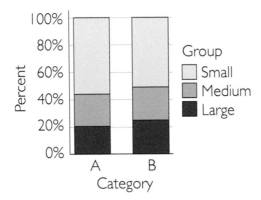

You can read the percent bar chart above as saying, "Category A is made up of 20% large things, 25% medium things, and 55% small things. Category B is up of 25% large things, 25% medium things, and 50% small things."

Pictograph chart

Pictograph charts (Chapter 3) use the height of stacks or length of rows of pictures or symbols to show amounts. Taller stacks mean more, and shorter stacks mean less. The pictures can represent one thing or multiple things.

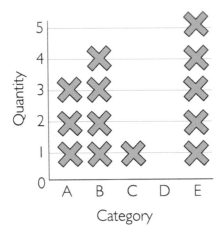

You can read the pictograph chart above as saying, "Category A had three of something, while Category D had nothing."

Pie chart

Pie charts (Chapter 11) use angle and color to show how something is made up of smaller categories, very much like **percent bar charts**. Pie charts always add up to 100%. Large slices of pie mean that the there is a lot of something in that category; small slices mean that there is a little.

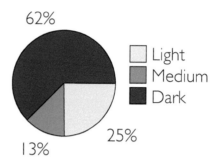

You can read the pie chart above as saying, "25% the things being counted were light. 13% of them were somewhere in the middle. Most of the things—62%—were dark."

Radar chart

Radar charts (Chapter 11) use angle and position to show quantities in different categories. If you imagine that a radar chart is a like a bicycle wheel, each **spoke** on the chart represents a single category with its own axis. The distance from the center on each spoke shows the amount in that category. Also called spider charts, web charts, star charts, or polar charts.

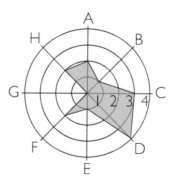

Read this radar chart as saying, "There were two things in Category A, one thing in Category B, and three things in Category C. Nothing is in Category G."

Sankey diagram

Sankey diagrams (Chapter 12) use connections to show how different groups of things change in number over time or at different stages. Just like networks, Sankey diagrams are made with **links** and **nodes**. The links are the thick ribbons of color, and the nodes are the labels for each group.

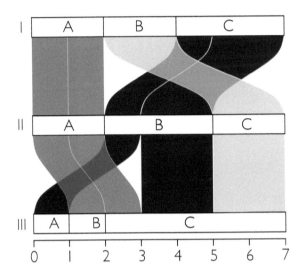

Read the Sankey diagram above as saying, "Two things started in group A at stage I, and then *stayed* in group A at stage II. After that, one thing went to group B and the other went to group C. Two things started in group B, both went to group C, and then both stayed in group C. Three things started in group C. Two of those went to group B and then back to group C. One of them went to group B and then to group A."

Scatterplot

Scatterplots (Chapter 5) use position to show two quantities at once—one variable per axis. Usually, the points or shapes on a scatterplot that are closer to the left side of the x-axis represent a smaller amount or earlier time than the points or shapes that are further to the right. Similarly, the points that are closer to the top along the y-axis usually mean larger amounts or later times than the ones that are lower down.

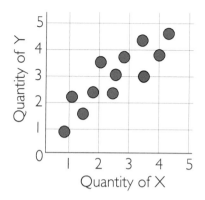

Read the scatterplot above as saying, "In general, the more of X there was, the more Y there was, too. The red point shows something that had 3½ of X and three of Y."

Stacked bar chart

Stacked bar charts (Chapter 6) use length or height of rectangles to show quantities of things that are in two or more categories or groups at the same time. Each bar represents a single category, and each stack in that bar shows the smaller groups within that category.

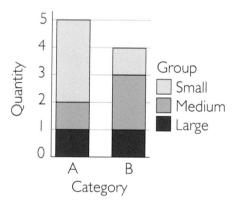

You can read the stacked bar chart above as saying, "In Category A there is one large thing, one medium thing, and three small things, for a total of five things altogether. In Category B there are four total things, but one is small, two are medium, and one is large."

Strip plot

Strip plots (Chapter 5) use the position of points to show quantities in different categories. Often, the points in a strip plot are a bit transparent so that you can still see them if they are crowded together.

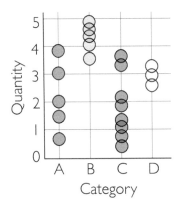

Read the strip plot above as saying, "The points in Category A are quite spread out—some show quantities of less than one while others show quantities of almost four. The points in Category D, however, are grouped together at around three."

Sunburst chart

Sunburst charts (Chapter 12) show tree data by branching off into smaller and smaller **nodes**, starting from the center. Different colors help to tell each branch apart. The outside ring of a sunburst chart shows the **leaf nodes** in the data. Sunburst charts are like round **icicle charts**.

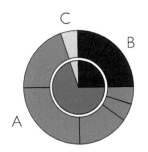

You can read this sunburst chart as saying, "Group A branches off into three large leaf nodes and two small leaf nodes. Group C only branches off to a single leaf node."

Tree graph

Tree graphs (Chapter 12) are a special type of **network graph** that shows tree data by connecting **nodes** with **links**. Tree data can be either **directed** or **undirected**, but there is always only one way to get between two nodes. The nodes that are only connected to one other node are called leaf nodes.

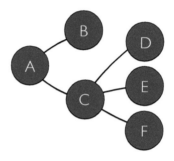

You can read this tree graph as saying, "A is connected to B and C. B is a leaf node, but C is connected to D, E, and F."

Tree map

Tree maps (Chapter 12) use rectangles of different colors to show how the nodes in tree data are related, and size to show how the quantities in each **node** compare to each other. Each branch in the tree data is shown in a different color. The smallest rectangles are the **leaf nodes**.

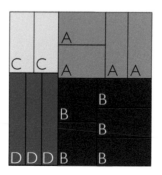

You can read this tree map as saying, "The overall tree branched into four branches: A, B, C, and D. Branch B had five leaf nodes of about the same size. Added together, Branch B was more than 1/4th of the full tree. Branch C only had two leaf nodes, and together they were only a small portion of the whole tree."

Word cloud

Word clouds (Chapter 4) use size show how often different words appear in a story, book, or article. The larger the letters in a word, the more often it appears. The order and direction of the words don't matter, like in a **packed circle chart**.

You can read this word cloud as saying, "The words *sentence, verb, and word* were the most common in this story. The word *name* was not used very often."

Appendix 3: Solutions guide

Chapter 1

There are endless ways to answer these questions, so these solutions are just suggestions. The most important thing is that the data types are correct.

1. Examples of numerical data:

    - Prices: $2.00, $2.30, $1.29
    - Heights: 53 inches, 49 inches, 59 inches

2. Examples of categorical data:

    - Football teams: Seahawks, Patriots, Titans
    - Cities: San Francisco, Topeka, St. Paul

3. Examples of ordinal data:

    - Ratings: good, better, best
    - Speeds: crawl, walk, run

4a. Your table will look different if you chose different items and different prices, but the important thing is that the item and its price are on the same row.

My Shopping List		
Item	Price	weight (oz.)
Cereal	$4.50	8
Carrots	$3.23	16
Ketchup	$2.22	12
Oatmeal	$4.00	32
Peanut butter	$4.30	16

4b. A good additional variable would be Weight, measured in ounces. Other possible variables are container size (small, medium large), shelf height (bottom, middle, top), or who the product is being purchased for (sister, mother, self).

Chapter 2

1a. Do you mark your height on the back of a door in your home? That's a data visualization!

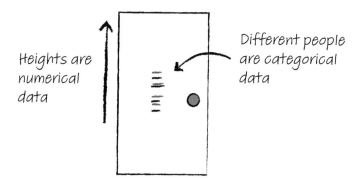

Heights are numerical data

Different people are categorical data

1b. Heights are numerical data because they are measured in numbers. If more than one person's heights are shown, then the peoples' names or the colors that they're marked with are categorical data.

2a. Waste bins are often in three different colors: black or gray for trash, blue for recycling, and green or brown for food and yard waste.

The types of waste that go in each bin are categorical data, shown as different colors.

2b. The types of waste are categorical data shown as different colors.

Chapter 3

1a. The first part of the question asked to count up the shapes. Each row shows the color and shape to count. The counts are:

Number and Color of Shapes		
Color	Shape	Count
White	Δ	5
White	X	4
White	O	3
Blue	Δ	4
Blue	X	3
Blue	O	3
Black	Δ	1
Black	X	3
Black	O	4

1b. A stacked bar chart of these data would look something
like this:

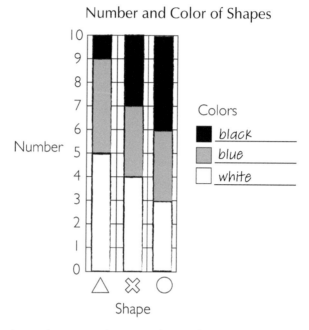

Number and Color of Shapes

Colors

black

blue

white

Your bar chart might put the colors in a different order,
use different colors, or be filled with different patterns like
stripes or polka dots. The important thing is that the colors
are in the same order in each bar, and that the lengths of
each stack are correct.

2. Your graph should look something like the one below.
You might have used a different color, or even a different
color for each person. You might have also decided to put
the bars in a different order, maybe fastest to slowest, or
slowest to fastest. The important thing is that each person
has their own bar that shows their mile run time.

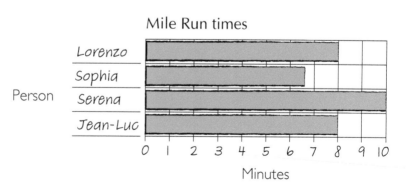

Mile Run times

3a. This is just an example of what you might put for your daily schedule. Someone else's day might look very different!

My Daily Schedule		
Activity	Start time	Time
Breakfast	7:15 am	8:00 am
Morning run	8:00 am	8:30 am
Working	9:00 am	4:00 pm
Dinner time!	7:00 pm	8:00 pm
Relaxing	8:00 pm	9:30 pm
Bedtime routine	9:30 pm	9:45 pm

3b. The Gantt chart for the schedule above could look like this:

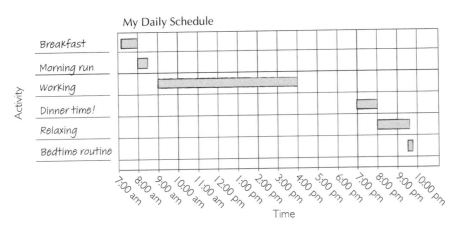

You might decide to use different colors or patterns in the bars, and of course your activities might be different. You might also choose different times to put on the x-axis... for example if you wake up earlier than 7 am or go to bed later than 10 pm. The important thing is that the amount of time shown for each activity matches the data in your table.

Chapter 4

1a, 1b. You might have used a different shape or a different color in your visualization, but the important thing is that you use one shape in different sizes. The shapes in the legend should start small for 1 and get bigger and bigger until the biggest shape that represents 6.

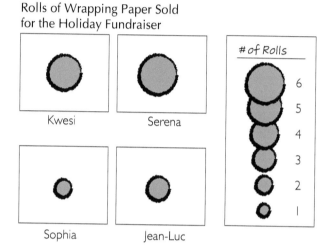

Rolls of Wrapping Paper Sold for the Holiday Fundraiser

1c. You might have used different colors for your bar chart, or made the bars thicker or thinner, but the important thing is that each bar shows the correct value.

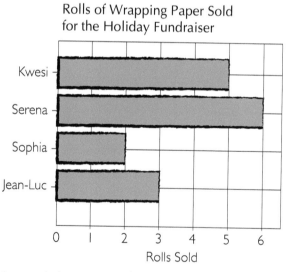

Rolls of Wrapping Paper Sold for the Holiday Fundraiser

1d. There's no right answer here! Perhaps you like the visualization in part 1a. the best, or maybe you prefer the bar chart. Either way, it's important to think about why you like one or the other, and which one you think other people might prefer. To most people, the bar chart will be easier to understand because it uses different lengths to show data instead of different sizes.

2a. Making word clouds by hand can be tricky, so don't worry if your letters are a little bit outside of the box, or a little too far inside. You can use capital letters or lower case. The important thing is that the words that appeared more often in the story have bigger letters than the words that didn't appear very often.

DARK 10	SQUEAK 6
CREAKY 9	JUMP 5
DOORS 8	FOG 4
QUIET 7	GIGGLE 4
	CRUMPLE 3

2b. You might have used different colors or only one color, but the important thing is that the words are close together without overlapping. You can arrange them however you'd like!

2c. Since this word cloud is about an imaginary story, it's up to you what you think it's about. It looks like it might be about a haunted house since there are words like "dark" and "creaky" as well as "giggle" and "crumple". Did someone go trick-or-treating?

Chapter 5

1a., 1b. Your graph might look a bit different if you used different colors or different shapes, but the important thing is that each point shows the correct week and number of roses and that the points are connected to make a line chart.

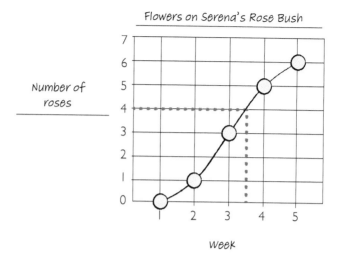

Flowers on Serena's Rose Bush

Number of roses

week

1c. Serena's rose bush seems to be growing! It has more flowers every week. Many people will have an easier time understanding the visualization than the table, but you might prefer the table.

1d. If you draw a dashed line above 3½ on the x-axis, it crosses the gridline that goes to the 4 on the y-axis. We can guess that Serena had about 4 roses by 3½ weeks.

2a., 2b. You might use different colors for the bubbles or put weight on the y-axis instead of the x-axis, but the important thing is that the bubbles show the right values for each dog.

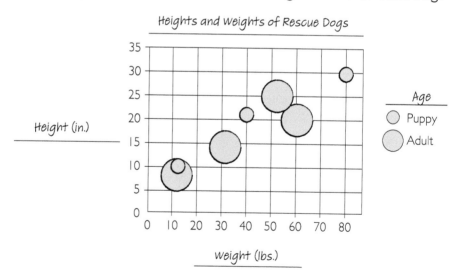

Heights and Weights of Rescue Dogs

Height (in.)

weight (lbs.)

Age
○ Puppy
◯ Adult

2c. Adult dogs are *sometimes* bigger than puppies, but there are small adult dogs, too. However, one puppy was much further to the right than the others—Moose is one heavy puppy!

3a. Your visualization might be a bit different if you used different colors or jittered the points in a different way. The important thing is that the points are at the right position on the y-axis—the right height to show the correct test score. Of course, the scores should go with the correct teacher, too!

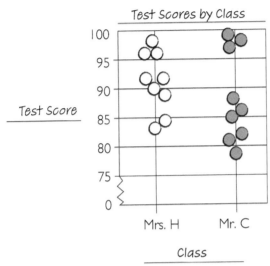

3b. The classes did about the same, but the lowest scores were in Mr. Chen's class. However, the highest score was also in Mr. Chen's class! You might decide that one class did better than other, but the important thing is that you explain why you think what you think.

Chapter 6

1a. You might've chosen different colors to show each fruit, but the important thing is that the colors are possible for each one. For example, you might've picked green for an unripe banana, but not blue!

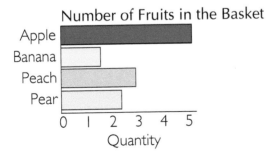

1b. You might choose different categorical colors for this visualization, but the important thing is that they all look different from each other.

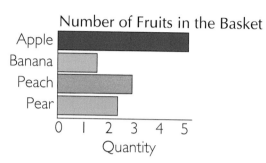

Number of Fruits in the Basket

1c. There's no one right answer to this question, but you might find the visualization from part a. to be easier to use because the colors make more sense for what they are showing. On the other hand, you might like your answer for part b. better if the colors are easier for you to tell apart.

2a. Kwesi spends the most time in the shower because his dark yellow bar is the longest.

2b. Marina has the shortest trip to school because her dark blue bar is the shortest.

2c. Kwesi spends the longest getting ready in the morning and traveling to school. His stacked bar is the longest.

2d. Breakfast and travel are the longest stacks in the three stacked bars, but it depends on the person. Kwesi spends a similar amount of time at breakfast and traveling, but Ahmad has a short breakfast and a long trip to school. Marina has a long breakfast and a short trip.

3a. Your names and numbers will be different, but the important thing is that you put data for yourself and four other people.

How Many Cousins Do People Have?	
Person	Number of Cousins
Me	8
Veronica	9
Alex	3
Rosie	12
Martin	5

3b., 3c. The important thing for this question is that the bars are the correct length and that the bar showing your data is a different color than the others.

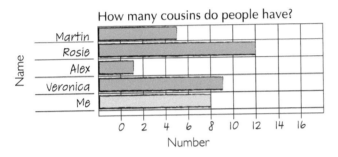

How many cousins do people have?

Chapter 7

1a. This is a low-middle-high or diverging gradient that flows from black to white to red. White is the middle color that could represent the speed limit.

1b. You might choose different numbers, but the important thing is that the middle number shows a reasonable speed limit and the other numbers are higher or lower than the middle by the same amount.

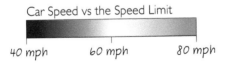

Car Speed vs the Speed Limit

40 mph   60 mph   80 mph

2a. This is a low-to-high gradient that runs from a light color to a dark color. The lightest color shows the least amount of time, and the darkest color show the longest amount of time.

2b. You might choose different numbers, but the important thing is that they are in order and spaced out evenly.

Seconds in the Microwave

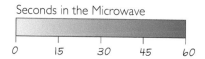

0   15   30   45   60

3a. This is a multi-color or rainbow gradient that runs between pink, purple, blue, green, and yellow. Each color shows a different number of feet of snow, and the shades in between show how close the amount is to a round number.

3b. You could've chosen other values, but the important thing is that the numbers are in order and evenly spaced.

Forecasted Feet of Snow

0   1   2   3   4

3c. This might not the best kind of gradient to show feet of snow because the different colors make each amount seem very different from the next instead of being continuous. Some values stand out more than others in an uneven way. On the other hand, this gradient might work well if it's important to see when the snow was reaching a round number, like one or two feet.

3d. A low-to-high gradient might make more sense for these data, or a diverging gradient if there is an important amount of snow to watch out for.

Chapter 8

1a. You might have chosen different colors, but the important thing is that you picked one color and made it lighter and darker or brighter and darker. In this solution, the light green gets darker and darker as the ratings go up.

1b. Your graph will look different if you picked different colors in part a. The important thing is that the bars are the correct heights and that the colors you chose are in order on the graph and in the legend.

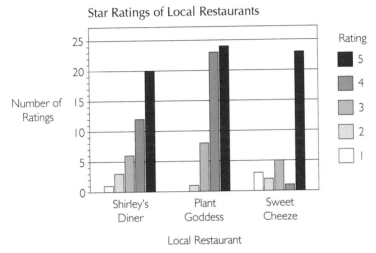

Star Ratings of Local Restaurants

1c. Looking at the graph, it looks like Plant Goddess is the most popular. It has the most five-star reviews as well as the most four-star reviews. It doesn't have any one-star reviews.

2a. Your colors might be different, but the important thing is that there are seven colors with three going one way, three going the other way, and a middle color gluing them together.

Grades on Last Week's Math Test

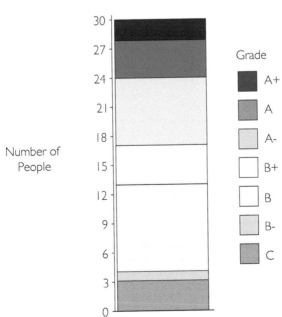

2b. There isn't one right answer to this question. You might think that the Math test was hard because many people got B's and Cs. Or, you might think that it was easy because so many people got A's. You might also decide that it was fair! The important thing is that you make your decision using the data shown in the visualization.

2c. The colors for A+ and C are similar because they are the darkest and are at the ends of the gradient.

2d. The colors for A− and B are similar to each other because they are both close to the middle and the lightest.

3. For a., b., c., and d., the colors you pick might be different depending on the crayons, markers, or pencils that you use. The important thing is that the colors step smoothly from one to the next as best as possible.

Chapter 9

1a. You could pick a variety of shapes, but in this solution, Quiana is shown with circles and Ahmad is shown with triangles. The important thing is that the shapes look different from each other.

1b. Dotted, dashed, or solid, you could pick any number of patterns to draw Quiana and Ahmad's lines. This graph uses a solid line for Quiana and dotted line for Ahmad. The important thing is that the lines are easy to tell apart.

1c. Your shapes and lines might be different, but the important thing is that the legend shows what both the shapes
and the lines mean.

1d. Your title might be a little different, but the important
thing is that it explains what the graph is about.

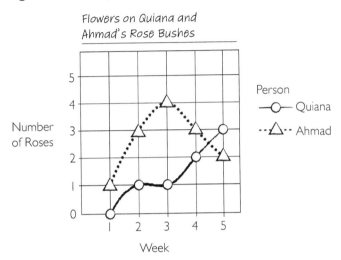

Flowers on Quiana and
Ahmad's Rose Bushes

2a. Your patterns might be different, but the important thing
is that you can tell them all apart and that the city cars look
different than the off-road cars. In this graph, the city cars
have different types of dots and the off-road cars have
different types of lines.

Different Types of Cars on My Street

2b. Your legend will look different if you used different patterns, but it should match the patterns in the graph as
much as possible.

Chapter 10

1a., 1b. This is just one way of coloring in the bars, but the important thing is that there is a light and dark color *and* a pattern. You could also use two patterns and different colors—even a light and dark shade of the same color, like light and dark blue.

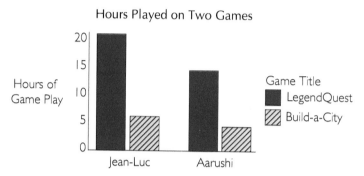

2a., 2b. The temperatures in your city (real or imaginary) might be different than these values. You can choose to use Fahrenheit or Celsius. Depending on your data, the highest and lowest values that you circled will be different.

Average Monthly High and Low Temperatures in Seattle, Washington		
Month	High (°F)	Low (°F)
January	47	39
February	49	40
March	52	42
April	57	45
May	63	50
June	66	54
July	72	57
August	72	57
September	67	55
October	59	50
November	51	43
December	46	39

2c. Since 72 was the highest and 39 was the lowest, the y-axis can go a little above and below those values. The y-axis in this graph runs from 20 to 80, but your graph will be different if the highest and lowest temperatures are different.

Instead of using a legend, the lines are labeled at the end. You could also label them on top of the graph close to each line.

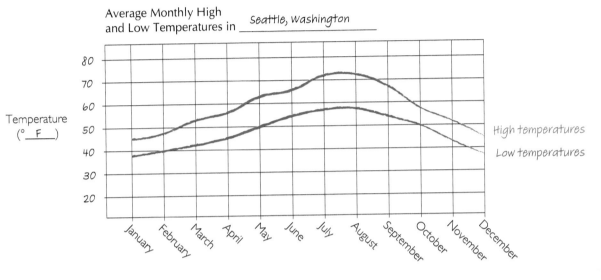

Average Monthly High and Low Temperatures in _Seattle, Washington_

Temperature (°_F_)

High temperatures

Low temperatures

3a., 3b., 3c., 3d. There are endless ways to label this graph! The important thing is that each blank or tick mark has a value and that the graph makes sense.

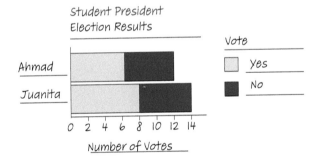

Student President Election Results

Ahmad

Juanita

0 2 4 6 8 10 12 14

Number of Votes

Vote

☐ Yes

■ No

Chapter 11

1a. The slices could be in any order or on any part of the pie. The important thing is that groups A and C take up a quarter of the pie, while group B takes up half.

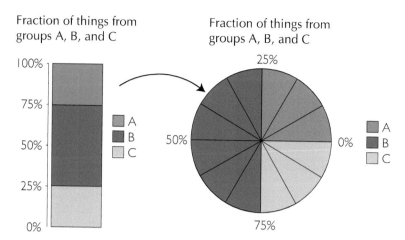

1b. There's no right or wrong answer to this question! Some people might prefer the bar chart because it's easier to see the values on the y-axis. Other people might prefer the pie chart for these data because it's more obvious that group B is half of the pie.

2. The slices could be in any order or any place on the pie, but the important thing is that they show the correct amounts.

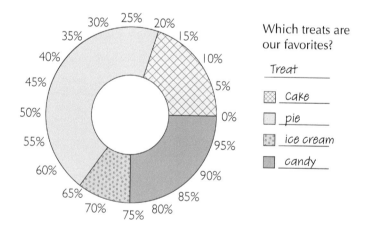

3a. This is just one way to fill in the table, but your answers will be different. The important thing is that the values are between 1 and 5.

How much do you like each school subject? (1–5)		
Subject	Your Rating	*wei*'s Rating
Math	4	2
Science	5	4
Geography	4	4
English	3	5
Music	4	3

3b., 3c. It doesn't matter whose shape is on top, or even if it is colored in. You can put points in each corner, or not! The important thing is that you can tell each person's shape apart.

How much do you like each school subject?

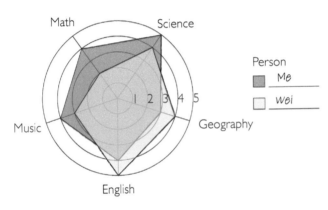

3d. From this radar chart, you could see that I like Science more than Wei, but that she likes English more. You can see that we both like most subjects quite a lot, and neither of us gave any subjects a low rating.

Chapter 12

1a. This family tree shows the eye color of each person in Sophia's family. Sophia is shown at the bottom with her three other siblings. Your tree will look different, but the important thing is that you or a favorite character is labeled, that there are at least two different groups across the ten people and three generations.

Sophia's Family Tree

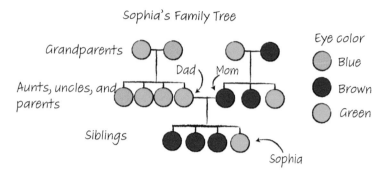

1b. Sophia is part of the group with green eyes. Your answer will be different, but the important thing is that you know the group that you or a favorite character is part of and that the group is shown in the legend.

1c. Sophia's mom is shown above Sophia's row, beside her dad. The important thing is that the parents are above you or the character and that they are connected to each other to show a relationship.

1d. Sophia's mom is part of the group with brown eyes. Her dad is part of the group with green eyes. Your answer will be different, but the important thing is that you know their groups and that the groups are shown in the legend.

2a., 2b. Any animals are fine, and the data are just based on how you think of them. The important thing is that the values fit on each axis.

Comparison of Three Animals			
Animal	Cuteness	Ferocity	Athleticism
Chinchilla	100	Jumpy	4
Chihuahua	80	Grouchy	2
Chicken	70	Gentle	1

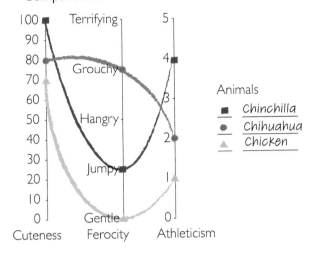

Comparison of Three Animals

2c. Looking at this visualization, chickens seem like pretty good pets! They're very cute, very gentle, and not very athletic… so they won't run away. Chinchillas are also cute, but this graph shows that they are grouchy and athletic, so they might be hard to keep track of in the house.

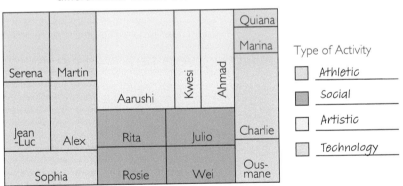

Weekly time spent doing different after-school activities

3a. The tree map shows more about how much time the people spent on different activities, and how much time they spent altogether. The tree only showed the types of activities people did.

3b. Aarushi spends the most time doing artistic activities each week because her leaf in the tree map is the largest.

3c. People spend the same amount of time on social activities, perhaps because they're hanging out together!

People also spend similar amounts of time during athletic activities, maybe because they are playing on the same team or at the same sports events.

Chapter 13

1a. This graph could be confusing because it has two y-axes for different things: hamster weight and number of traffic accidents. Each axis starts and ends at different amounts.

1b. Someone might think that Alex's hamster getting heavier over time was the cause of more traffic accidents. Or, they might think that traffic accidents caused their hamster to grow.

1c. On option is to split the visualization up into two parts so that it is very clear which measurements go with each y-axis. Using two smaller graphs also makes it seem less like one measurement is causing the other—it just looks like they increased at the same time for one reason or another.

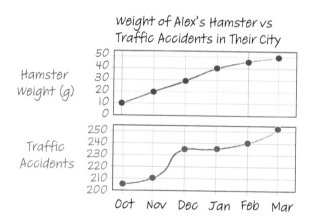

You also could have made a connected scatterplot, like this:

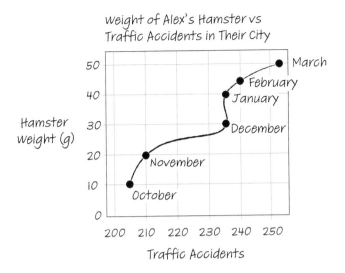

weight of Alex's Hamster vs
Traffic Accidents in Their City

Hamster weight (g)

Traffic Accidents

Instead of having two y-axes, the Traffic Accidents values are on the x-axis. The months are labeled on each point. This lets us see that the hamster grew at the same time that traffic accidents were increasing, but keeps the separate measurements on different axes.

2a. It's confusing that this visualization is a bar chart with the y-axis starting at 95. Bar charts use the lengths of the bars to show amounts, so starting at 95 makes it hard to compare the different amounts.

2b. Someone might think that Kwesi sent many more messages than everyone else, even though they all were pretty chatty. Someone might also think that Sophia had kept to herself, even though she still sent many texts.

2c. It would be much better to start the y-axis at zero since this is a bar chart. This will let someone compare the lengths of the bars to understand how each person was different from the other. Like this:

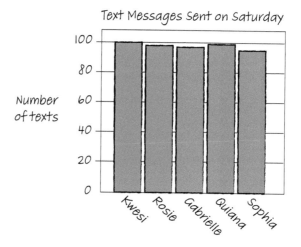

You might also choose to use the same y-axis, but make a scatterplot instead. This would let someone see the real amounts more clearly as well as who sent the most and fewest messages.

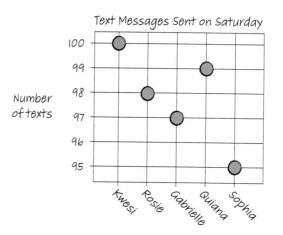

3a. It could be confusing that this visualization is in 3D because it's harder to see the angles that make each portion of the donut chart.

3b. Someone might look at this graph and not notice that Cinnamon Spice was the most popular latte flavor, or think that Blueberry Muffin was more popular than it really is. The graph is in 3D and tilted back, so it's hard to compare the slices to each other.

3c. The best way to make this visualization less confusing is to make it 2D—just flat on the page. It could be a donut chart or a pie chart… or a bar chart!

The most important thing is that the graph doesn't have more dimensions than the data. The data in this graph have two dimensions (flavor and percentage), but the 3D graph has three dimensions (flavor, percentage, and the thickness of the donut).

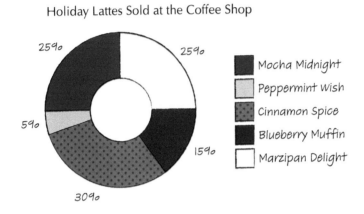

Holiday Lattes Sold at the Coffee Shop

Chapter 14

1a. Your sonification might sound different from another person's depending on the instrument or materials that you use. The important thing is that different values are different pitches, and that higher values have higher pitches than lower values.

1b. There isn't a right or wrong answer for this part of the exercise. The important thing is that you give your friend or family member a chance to hear the sonification and describe what they hear. This will help you understand what other people think and feel when they listen to a sonification for the first time.

1c. It's okay if your listener didn't get the right answers. The important thing is that you give them a chance to hear what data sound like when they have a little bit more information.

1d. This part of the exercise helps you think about how someone might hear and see the same information in different ways. Did they like the sonification better? Was the visualization clearer? There isn't a right or wrong answer here, either!

2a. Your physicalization will be unique to you depending on the materials you choose. The important thing is that the four materials feel different from each other and that you've cut the correct number of squares for each flavor of ice cream. You should have two squares of red velvet, five squares of horchata, two squares of mint chip, and three squares of pumpkin pie.

2b. There isn't one right answer to this question. The important thing is that you feel the differences between each material and think about how it is to feel data in this way.

2c. It's okay if the other person guesses incorrectly. The important thing is that they have a chance to experience the data with their hands, and that you have a chance to observe someone getting data through their sense of touch. Did they have a difficult or confusing time? Was it easy? Did it make them curious about anything?

2d. There isn't a right answer to this part of the exercise. The important thing is that you get to see how someone feels about taking in data with their hands instead of their eyes.

Chapter 15

1a.

Name:	Categorical
Weight:	Numerical
Height:	Numerical
Age:	Numerical
Gender:	Categorical
Coat:	Ordinal
Energy:	Ordinal

1b. Your answer might be different, but some interesting comparisons could be:

- Compare the weight of tall dogs to the weight of short dogs.
- Compare the height or weight of female dogs to male dogs.
- Compare coats of different ages of dogs or different genders.
- Compare the energy of dogs of different ages.

1c, 1d. Depending on the comparison you want to make and the encodings you choose, your visualization could look like anything! The important thing is that you choose encodings that are good for each variable's data type and the comparison you want to make.

1e, 1f. Depending on the comparison you want to make and the encodings you choose, your visualization could look like anything! The important thing is that you choose encodings that aren't great for each data type and aren't very helpful for making the same comparison in 1c.

1g. It all depends on who sees your visualizations and what they were about, but the important thing is that you hear from someone else what it's like to see a poorly-encoded visualization *and* a well-encoded visualization.

Bibliography

As its title says, this book was written for people of all ages or most ages, at least. Many fascinating books and scientific papers have come before it, though, and their authors' hard work and discoveries made this book possible. This section shares a few resources from my personal list of references that you might find interesting. Some are written for everyday learners, while others were published with scientists and scholars in mind.

The works below are organized by subject and how technical they are:

◗ **Mild:** Nice and light.

◗◗ **Medium**: Getting up there…

◗◗◗ **Hot:** Serious business!

Color

Borland, D., & Taylor II, R. M. (2007). Rainbow Color Map (still) considered harmful. *IEEE Computer Graphics and Applications*, *27*(2), 14–17. https://doi.org/10.1109/mcg.2007.323435. ◗◗

Liu, Y., & Heer, J. (2018). Somewhere over the rainbow: An empirical assessment of quantitative Colormaps. *Proceedings of the 2018 CHI Conference on Human Factors in Computing Systems*, (598), 1–12. https://doi.org/10.1145/3173574.3174172. ◗◗◗

Thyng, K., Greene, C., Hetland, R., Zimmerle, H., & DiMarco, S. (2016). True colors of oceanography: Guidelines for effective and accurate Colormap selection. *Oceanography*, *29*(3), 9–13. https://doi.org/10.5670/oceanog.2016.66. ◗◗

Data Sonification

Geere, D., & Quick, M. (2023a). Loud Numbers. https://www.loudnumbers. net/. ◗

Geere, D., & Quick, M. (2023b). Loud Numbers. *Podcast.* https://www.loud-numbers.net/podcast. ◗

Data Physicalization

Jansen, Y., Dragicevic, P., Isenberg, P., Alexander, J., Karnik, A., Kildal, J., Subramanian, S., & Hornbæk, K. (2015). Opportunities and challenges for data physicalization. *Proceedings of the 33rd Annual ACM Conference on Human Factors in Computing Systems.* https://doi. org/10.1145/2702123.2702180. ◗◗

Deceptiveness

Cairo, A. (2020). *How charts lie: Getting smarter about visual information.* W. W. Norton & Company. ◗

McNutt, A., Kindlmann, G., & Correll, M. (2020). Surfacing visualization mirages. *Proceedings of the 2020 CHI Conference on Human Factors in Computing Systems.* https://doi.org/10.1145/3313831.3376420. ◗◗◗

Pandey, A. V., Manivannan, A., Nov, O., Satterthwaite, M., & Bertini, E. (2014). The persuasive power of data visualization. *IEEE Transactions on Visualization and Computer Graphics, 20*(12), 2211–2220. https:// doi.org/10.1109/tvcg.2014.2346419. ◗◗

Pandey, A. V., Rall, K., Satterthwaite, M. L., Nov, O., & Bertini, E. (2015). How deceptive are deceptive visualizations? *Proceedings of the 33rd Annual ACM Conference on Human Factors in Computing Systems.* https://doi.org/10.1145/2702123.2702608. ◗◗

General Textbooks

Bertin, J., & Berg, W. J. (2011). *Semiology of graphics: Diagrams, networks, maps.* ESRI Press. ◗◗◗

Few, S. (2012). *Show me the numbers: Designing tables and graphs to enlighten.* Analytics Press. ◗◗

Munzner, T. (2015). *Visualization analysis & design.* CRC Press. ◗◗

Steele, J., & Iliinsky, N. (2010). *Beautiful visualization looking at data through the eyes of experts.* O'Reilly. ◗◗

Tufte, E. R. (2015). *The visual display of quantitative information.* Graphics Press. ◗◗

Wilkinson, L. (2012). *Grammar of graphics.* Springer. ◗◗◗

Perception

Cleveland, W. S., & McGill, R. (1984). Graphical perception: Theory, experimentation, and application to the development of graphical methods. *Journal of the American Statistical Association, 79*(387), 531–554. https://doi.org/10.1080/01621459.1984.10478080. ◗◗◗

Jordan, G., & Mollon, J. (2019). Tetrachromacy: The mysterious case of extra-ordinary color vision. *Current Opinion in Behavioral Sciences, 30*, 130–134. https://doi.org/10.1016/j.cobeha.2019.08.002. ◗◗◗

Ware, C. (2013). *Information visualization: Perception for design*. Morgan Kaufmann. ◗◗◗

Visualization for Kids

Krolik, J. (2021). Data Visualization for Kids. *Nightingale.* https://nightingaledvs.com/data-visualization-for-kids/. ◗

Schwabish, J. (2018). Teaching Data Visualization to Kids. *PolicyViz.* https://policyviz.com/2018/11/19/teaching-data-visualization-to-kids/. ◗◗

Shreiner, T. (2018). Data literacy for social studies: Examining the role of data visualizations in K-12 textbooks. *Theory and Research in Social Education, 46*(2), 194–231. ◗◗

Visual Literacy

Alper, B., Riche, N. H., Chevalier, F., Boy, J., & Sezgin, M. (2017). Visualization Literacy at Elementary School. *Proceedings of the 2017 CHI Conference on Human Factors in Computing Systems*, 5485–5497. https://doi.org/10.1145/3025453.3025877. ◗◗

Chevalier, F., Riche, N. H., Alper, B., Plaisant, C., Boy, J., & Elmqvist, N. (2018). Observations and reflections on visualization literacy in elementary school. *IEEE Computer Graphics and Applications, 38*(3), 21–29. https://doi.org/10.1109/MCG.2018.032421650. ◗◗

3D Visualization

Brown, D. (2023). Interactive & Ray Traced Data Visualization. https://morphcharts.com/. ◗

Miscellaneous Topics

Bartram, L., & Stone, M. C. (2011). Whisper, don't scream: Grids and transparency. *IEEE Transactions on Visualization and Computer Graphics, 17*(10), 1444–1458. https://doi.org/10.1109/tvcg.2010.237. ◗◗

Bibliography

Drucker, S. M., Fernandez, R., & Marshall, D. (2023). *SandDance*. https://www.microsoft.com/en-us/research/project/sanddance/.

Gleicher, M. (2018). Considerations for visualizing comparison. *IEEE Transactions on Visualization and Computer Graphics, 24*(1), 413–423. https://doi.org/10.1109/tvcg.2017.2744199. 🔥🔥🔥

Mackinlay, J. (1986). Automating the design of graphical presentations of relational information. *ACM Transactions on Graphics, 5*(2), 110–141. https://doi.org/10.1145/22949.22950. 🔥🔥

Park, D., Drucker, S. M., Fernandez, R., & Elmqvist, N. (2018). ATOM: A grammar for unit visualizations. *IEEE Transactions on Visualization and Computer Graphics, 24*(12), 3032–3043. https://doi.org/10.1109/tvcg.2017.2785807.

Stevens, S. S. (1946). On the theory of scales of measurement. *Science, 103*(2684), 677–680. https://doi.org/10.1126/science.103.2684.677. 🔥🔥

Wickham, H. (2010). A layered grammar of graphics. *Journal of Computational and Graphical Statistics, 19*, 3–28. 🔥

Acknowledgments

Thank you!

In no particular order, thank you to…

Tamara Munzner and Alberto Cairo for setting the bar and keeping it there, as well as their thorough edits and seasoned guidance,

Elliott Morsia for patiently answering thousands of emails about how to actually write a book,

Miguel Porlan for his persistence and creative vision in designing the cover,

Miriam Quick and Duncan Geere for generously sharing their knowledge of sonification,

Dave Brown for his input and technical support with 3D graphics,

Steven Drucker for his enthusiasm and championing of this whole idea,

Noah Iliinsky for his unlimited cheerleading and meticulous reviews,

Brock Craft for his pedagogical wisdom and coaching,

Acknowledgments

Diego Perez for his even-keeled and all-encompassing support throughout this project,

Sunny and Rosie for the comedic relief,

...and the countless friends, loved ones, colleagues, and students who helped shape and shepherd this project to fruition.

Index

Note: **Bold** page numbers refer to tables; *italic* page numbers refer to figures; underline refers to sonifications.

Aarushi (student) 6, *103,* **104,** *175,*
  206, 214
Ahmad (student) 6, 13, **13, 55,**
  55–58, 217, 218, 228, 229, 229
Alex (student) 5, **12, 22,** *23, 23, 24,*
  32, 34, 40, 40, **55,** *55–58, 71, 72,*
  72, 182, 183, 185, 228, 229, 229
angles
  bending axes 167–168, **168,** *168*
  donut charts *169, 169,* **171,** *171*
  in everyday life *166,* 166–167, *167*
  exercises 177–179
  meter charts 169–171, *170,*
    171, *171*
  pie charts 167–168, **168,** *168*
  and position together *172,*
    172–174, *173*
  position and color 175–176,
    175, **176**
  radar chart 172–173, *173*
  spokes 173
area 54; *see also* size
  exercises 62–65
  legends 56–57, *57*
  packed circle charts 55, *55, 56, 57*
  problem with *60,* 60–62, *61*
  proportional area chart 54, *54*
artistic visualizations 251–252
axis/axes 38
  axis labels 39–40, *40*
  axis titles 39–40, *40*
  backward axes 205–206, *205–206*
  break 84
  gridlines 41, *41*

position *68,* 68–69, *69*
tick marks *41,* 41
x-axis 39, *39, 212*
y-axis 39, *39, 212*
z-axis 212, *212*

bars 33
bar charts 33–35, *33–35*
  axes 39, *39*
  in 3D 211, *211, 212, 214*
  column charts 33, *33*
  grouped bar charts 93, *93*
  stacked bar charts 35–37,
    36, *36, 37, 142, 143,*
    211, 211
bee swarm plot 80, *80*
bending axes
  donut charts *169, 169,* **171,** *171*
  meter charts 169–171, *170,*
    171, *171*
  pie charts 167–168, *168*
  radar charts *172, 173, 189, 189,*
    248, 248
black-and-white colorblindness
  154–155, *155*
blueish light *149, 149*
blue-yellow colorblindness
  153–154, *153, 154*
bright-to-dark gradients 100–102,
  101, **102**
bright-to-dark palettes 115–116,
  116, 117
bubble charts 72–74, **73,** *73, 74,*
  248, 248

caption 42–43, *43*
categorical data 13, **13**; *see also*
    nominal data
categories
    axis 68, *68*
    colors 87, *87*
    lines 138, *138*
    position 68, *68*
    shapes 134–136, *135*
cells 148
Charlie (student) 6, 36, **36**, *37, 38,*
    39, 40, *40,* 41, *43,* 44, 54, *54,* 55,
    55, *55*–58, 69, 87, 88, 94, **94,** *94,*
    118, **119,** *119,* 120, 228, 229, 229,
    234, 235, *235*
chord diagrams 192–195, *193,* **194,**
    194–195
chords 193
color; *see specific terms*
colorblind friendly 155–159
    helps everyone 159–160
    legends 158, *158*
    light and dark colors 156, *156*
    notes and labels 158–159, *159*
    patterns and shapes 157, *158*
    separate colors with white/black
        156–157, *157*
colorblindness 147
    black-and-white colorblindness
        154–155, *155*
    blue-yellow colorblindness
        153–154, *153, 154*
    colorblind-friendliness helps
        everyone 159–160
    colorblind-friendly 155–159,
        156–159
    exercises 161–163
    how we see color 148–150,
        148–150
    red-green colorblindness
        152–153, *152–153*
    why it happens 150–151, *151*
color palette 86
    categorical 86–88, *87*
    colorblind friendly 156, *156*
    confusing palettes 87, 88, *87, 88,*
        119–120, *119–120*
    diverging color palettes
        120–123, 126

light–to–dark palettes; *see* low–
    to–high palettes
low–to–high ordinal palettes
    114–119
multi–color ordinal palettes
    124–125
    rainbow ordinal palettes 124–127
    stoplight colors 114, *114*
column charts 33
    x-axis 39, *39*
    y-axis 39, *39*
comparisons 242–243, *243,* 253
    exercises 255–258
cone cells 148–151, *149, 150*
    missing *151*
confusing visualizations
    backward axes 205–206, *205, 206*
    bar charts that don't start at zero
        206–207, *206*
    double/dual axes 201–203,
        202, 203
    extra dimensions 209–213,
        211, 212
    lying 216–217, *217*
    missing data 214–216, *215*
    tall or flat 208–209, *208*
connected scatterplot 76, *76,*
    204, *204*
connecting the dots 74–77, *75, 76*
    connected scatterplot 76, *76,*
        204, *204*
    line graph 74, *75*
    multiple line charts 90, 227, *228,*
        247, *247*
    parallel coordinate graphs
        189–190, *190*
connections and networks
    chord diagrams 192–195, *193,*
        194, *194–195*
    exercises 196–198
    family trees 184, *184*
    icicle charts 186, *186*
    parallel coordinate graphs
        189–190, *190*
    Sankey diagrams 190–192,
        191, 192
    sunburst chart 188, *189*
    tree maps 187–188, *188*
continuous 100

contour map 124–125, *125, 127*

crowded and overlapping points
 bee swarm plot 80, *80*
 jittering 79–80, *79*
 opacity 80, *80*
 opaque 80, *80*
 transparent 80, *80*

dashed and dotted lines *138, 139, 140*

data 9, 10
 collection 11–12, **11, 12**
 data point 10, *10,* **11**
 data set 10, *10*
 definition 9, 10
 exercises 16–17
 storage 10
 table 11, *11,* **12**
 types 12–15, **13–14**
 value 10, *10*
 variable 10, *10*

data collection 11–12, **12, 13**

data physicalization 231
 exercises 238–240
 temperature 233–234, *233*
 texture 231–232, *232*
 types of 235–236, **236**
 weight 234–235, *234–235*

data point 10, *10,* **11**

data set 10

data sonification 224–231, <u>225</u>, <u>226</u>, <u>227</u>, <u>229</u>, **231**
 exercises 238–240
 instrument 227, <u>227</u>
 other types 230
 pitch 224–226, <u>225, 226</u>
 types of **231**
 volume 228–229, <u>229</u>

data types
 categorical data 13, **13**
 interval data 14, **14**
 nominal data 13, **13**; *see also* categorical
 numerical data 12, **13**
 ordinal data 13, **14**
 quantitative data 12; *see also numerical data*
 ratio data 12; *see also* numerical data

data visualization 19; *see also specific terms*
 creation 253–254
 importance of 22–26, **22,** *23, 24*
 visual literacy 22

dimensions 209–213, *210–212; see also* 1D, 2D, and 3D

directed networks 183, *183*

diverging 104, *105, 106,* 109, *110*
 color palettes *120,* 120–121, **121,** *123, 123, 126, 127*
 gradients 104–106, *105,* **106,** *106,* **107**

donut charts *169,* 169, **171,** *171*

double axes 201–205, **202,** *202–203*

double-encoding 244, *245*

dumbbell charts 44–45, *45,* **45**

encodings 242, *243*
 changing encodings 244–250, **244,** *245–250*
 exercises 255–258

exercises
 angles 177–179
 area 62–65
 colors for categorical data 96–98
 colors for numerical data 111–112
 colors for ordinal data 128–131
 colorblind friendliness 161–163
 comparisons 255–258
 connections and networks 196–198
 data 16–17
 data physicalization 238–240
 data sonifications 238–240
 data visualizations around you 27
 encodings or mappings 255–258
 gradients 111–112
 length and height 48–51
 position 82–84
 shapes 144–145
 patterns 144–145
 size 62–65
 whoopsies 220–222

exploratory visualizations 251

facets/small multiples *124,* 123–124, *204, 248*

family trees 184, *184*

Gabrielle (student) 8, **55**, *55–58*, 94, **94**, *94*, 116, 118, **119**, *119, 120*, 208, **208**, *208–209*, 228, 229, <u>229,</u> *234*, 234, 235, *235*
Gantt chart 46, *46–47*, **46**
gauge charts 169–171, *170*, **171,** *171*; *see also* meter charts
gradients 100, *100*
    low–middle–high diverging 104–106, *105*, **106**, **107**
    low–to–high 100–103, *101–103*, **102–104**
    multi–color and rainbow *108–110*, 107–111
graph 19; *see also specific terms*
greenish light 149, *149*
gridlines 41, *41*, 43
grouped bar chart 93, *93*

heatmaps/heat maps 101, *101*, **102,** *103*, 106, 214, 233, 249, *249*

icicle chart 186, *186*
instrument <u>227</u>, *227–228*, *228*
interval data 14, **14**

Jean-Luc (student) 7, *103*, **104**, *175*, 201–205, **202**, *202–204*, 214
jittering 79–80, *79, 80*
Juanita (student) 5, **55**, *55–58*, 101, *101*, 102, **102,** *103*, 103, **104,** 108, 116, 174, 175, *175*, **176**, *214*, 217, *217*, 218, 228, 229, <u>229</u>, 233, *233*
Julio (student) 8, **13**, 106, *106*, **107**, *139, 140*, **141,** *141*, 142, 182, *183*, 183, 184, 185

key 37; *see also* legend
Kwesi (student) 5, **12, 22**, 23, *23*, 24, *32*, 34, *34*, 71, *72*, 151, 151, *188–189*

leaf nodes 187, *187*
legends 37–38, *38*
    colorblind friendly order 158, *158*
    example 38, *38*
    size 56–57, *57*
length and height 29
    axes 38–42, *39–41*
    bar chart 33–35, *33–35*

distance, change, and time 44–47, *45–47*, **45, 46**
dumbbell charts 44–45, *45*, **45**
exercises 48–51
Gantt chart 46–47, *46*, **46**
pictograph charts 32, *32*
stacked bar chart 35–37, **36,** *36*, *37*, 142, *143*, 211, *211*
light-to-dark gradients; *see low–to–high gradients*
light-to-dark palettes; *see low–to–high palettes*
line charts/line graphs 74, *75*
    multiple line charts 90, 227, *228*, 247, *247*
links 182, *182*
Lorenzo (student) 4, 13, **13, 55**, *55*, 56, *56–58*, 69, 70, **70**, *70*, 71, 72, *73*, **73,** 74, 75, *75, 75*, 76, 77, 88, *88*, **89,** 89, 90, 134, *134*, 135, *135*, 136, *136*, 137, **137**, 138, *138*, 224, 225, **225,** *225*, <u>225,</u> 227, <u>227</u>, *228*, 229, <u>229</u>
low-middle-high diverging gradients 104–106, *105*, **106**, **107**
low-middle-high diverging palettes *120*, 120–121, **121**, 123, *123*, 126, *127*
low-to-high gradients
    bright-to-dark 100–102, *101*, **102**
    light-to-dark 100–102, *101*, **102**
    two-color gradients *102*, 102–103, **104,** *103*
low-to-high ordinal palettes
    bright-to-dark palettes 115–116, *116*
    light-to-dark palettes 115–116, *116*
    two-color ordinal palettes *117*, 117–118, *118*, **119**

mappings 242
Marina (student) 6, 44, *45*, **45, 55,** *55–58*, 188, 188, 189, 228, 229, <u>229</u>
Martin (student) 8, 91, 92, *92*, **92,** 93, *93*, *103*, **104**, 142, *142*, 143, *153–155*, 159, 175, *175*, 217, 217, 218

meter charts 169–171, *170,* **171,** *171*

missing/unusual cone cells 150, *151*

Morse Code 242

multi–color and rainbow gradients *108–110,* 107–111

multi–color ordinal palettes 124–125, *125–127*

multiple line charts 90, 227, *228,* 247, *247*

network graphs 182–183, *182–183*

nodes 182, *182,* 191

nominal data 13; *see also* categorical data

notes and labels, colorblind–friendliness 158–159, *159*

numerical data 12, **13;** *see also* quantitative data/ratio data

continuous 100

exercises 111–112

gradients 100; *see also specific terms*

1D 210, *210*

opaque/opacity 80, *80*

ordinal color palettes

confusing palettes 119–120, *119–120*

exercises 128–131

low-middle-high diverging palettes *120–122, 123,* 126, *127*

low-to-high ordinal palettes 114–118, *116–118,* **119**

multi-color ordinal palettes 124–125, *125–127*

rainbow ordinal palettes 124–127, *125–127*

stoplight colors 114, *114*

ordinal data 13, **14**

Ousmane (student) 7, *103,* **104,** *175, 175,* 176, **176,** *214*

packed circle charts 55, *55,* 228, *228*

palette; *see* color palette

parallel coordinate charts 189–190, *190*

patterns and shapes, colorblindness 157, *158*

patterns and textures *142,* 142–143, *143*

physicalization 231–236, *232, 233, 235*

pictograph charts 32, *32*

pie charts 167–168, *168, 171,* 212, *212,* 213, 246, *247*

pitch 224–226, **225,** *225,* 225, 226

points 70

crowded and overlapping 79–81, *79–80*

data point 10

polar charts 172; *see also* radar charts

position

and angles *172,* 172–176, *173, 175,* **176**

axes 68, 68–69, *69*

bubble charts 72–74, **73,** *73, 74*

connected scatterplot 76, *76, 204*

crowded and overlapping points 79–81, *79–80*

exercises 82–84

line charts 74–77, *75, 76*

numerical and categorical variable 77–79, **78,** *78, 80*

scatterplots 69–72, **70,** *70–72*

presentation visualization 251

proportional area chart 54, *54*

quantitative data/ratio data 12

Quiana (student) 5, **36,** *36, 37, 38, 39, 40, 41, 43, 44,* 69, 86, 87, 88, *116,* 182, 183, *183, 184, 185, 188–189*

radar charts 172, *173,* 189, *189,* 248, *248*

rainbow gradients *108–109,* 107–108

rainbow ordinal palettes 124–127, *125–127*

ratio data 12

reddish light 149, *149*

red-green colorblindness 152–153, *152–153*

Rita (student) 7, 35, **36,** *36–41, 42, 43, 44,* 69, 86, 87, 88, 94, **94,** *94, 118,* **119,** *119,* 119, 120, *188–189,* 217, 218, 234, 235, *235*

rod cells 148, *148*
Rosie (student) 7, **13,** 54, *54,* 55, **55,** *56–58,* 91, 92, **92,** *92,* 93, 142, *142, 143, 153–155, 159,* 184, *184, 185, 228, 229,* 229

Sankey diagrams 190–192, *191, 192*
scatterplots 69–72, **70,** *70–72,* 88–91, **89,** *90*
  with a categorical axis 77–79, **78,** *78, 80*
Serena (student) 4, **12, 22,** 23, *23, 32, 34, 34,* **55,** *55–58, 56, 71, 72, 72, 228, 229,* 229
shapes
  categories 134–136, *135*
  and colors separately **137,** *37–138, 138*
  and colors together 136–137, *136*
  dotted lines *138,* 138–140, *140*
  exercises 144–145
  patterns and textures to fill *142, 142–143, 143*
short and flat graphs **208,** 208, *208*
size; *see also* area
  bubble charts 72–74, **73,** *73, 74, 248, 248*
  exercises 62–65
  legends 56–57, *57*
  packed circle charts 55–57, *55–57*
  problem with *60,* 60–62, *61*
  proportional area chart 54, *54*
  word clouds 58–60, **59,** *60*
sonification; *see* data sonification
Sophia (student) 6, 12, **12, 22,** 23, *23, 24, 32, 34, 34,* 46, **46,** *46, 47, 71–72*
spider charts 172; *see also* radar charts
spokes 173
stacked bar charts 35–37, **36,** *36, 37, 142, 143,* 211, *211*
star charts 172; *see also* radar charts
stoplight colors 114, *114*
strip plot *78, 79*
sunburst chart 188, *189*

table 11
tall or flat graphs **208,** 208, *208*
temperature *233,* 233–234
texture 231–232, *232*
3D 210–214, *211, 212, 214*
tick marks 41, *41, 43*
timbre *227–228,* 227
title 42–43, *43*
transparent/transparency 80
trees
  family trees 184, *184*
  icicle charts 186, *186*
  sunburst chart 188–189, *189*
  tree maps *187,* 187–188
triple-encoding 247
two-color gradients *102,* 102, *103,* **104**
two-color ordinal palettes *117,* 117–118, *118,* **119**
2D 210–211, *210*

undirected graphs 183, 185

value 10
variable 10
Veronica (student) 7, **12, 22,** 23, 24, *32, 34, 34, 71, 72,* 94, **94,** *94,* 118, *118,* 119, **119,** *119, 120, 234, 235*
visualize/visualizations 19; *see also specific terms*
visual literacy 2, 22
volume (of sound) 228–230, *229*

web charts 172; *see also* radar charts
Wei (student) 5, 89, **89,** *90, 90,* 94, *95, 116,* 134, *134, 135, 135, 136, 136,* 137, **137,** *138, 138, 149, 150, 150, 151, 183, 183,* 224, **225,** 226, *226,* 226, 227, 227, 228
weight 234–235, *235*
word clouds 58–60, **59,** *60*

x-axis 38–39, *39, 212*

y-axis 38–39, *39, 212*

z-axis 212–213, *212*